CREATING THE GOOD LIFE
APPLYING ARISTOTLE'S WISDOM
TO FIND MEANING AND HAPPINESS

JAMES O'TOOLE
FOREWORD BY WALTER ISAACSON

RODALE

MORTIMER J. ADLER
(1902-2001)

IN MEMORIAM

Printed in the United States of America
Rodale Inc. makes every effort to use acid-free ♾, recycled paper ♻.

Book design by Tara Long

Library of Congress Cataloging-in-Publication Data

O'Toole, James.
    Creating the good life : applying Aristotle's wisdom to find meaning and happiness / James
O'Toole ; foreword by Walter Isaacson.
        p.   cm.
    Includes bibliographical references and index.
    ISBN-13 978—1—59486—125—3 hardcover
    ISBN-10 1—59486—125—0 hardcover
        1. Aristotle.   2. Ethics.   3. Conduct of life.   4. Happiness.   I. Title.
    B491.E7O86   2005
    650.1'01—dc22   2004029661

Distributed to the trade by Holtzbrinck Publishers

2 4 6 8 10 9 7 5 3 1   hardcover

We inspire and enable people to improve their lives and the world around them
For more of our products visit **rodalestore.com** or call 800-848-4735

ACKNOWLEDGMENTS

We learn and grow through "reflection on experience," as my friend and mentor Warren Bennis teaches. This book is a summary of three years of reflections on my experiences and the experiences of the many friends whom I cite in its pages. I also wish to thank those men and women for providing sterling examples of lives well led. In particular I wish to thank Larry Fisher for his thoughtful, detailed, and immeasurably useful critique of an early draft of this book. I feel about his contribution to the book the way I imagine the prolix novelist Thomas Wolfe felt about the contribution of his editor, Maxwell Perkins—that is, one step above gratitude, one short of co-authorship.

My dear friends Keith and Sheena Berwick provided unflagging support throughout the whole authorship ordeal, Sheena teaching me useful lessons about Dante and writing, and Keith providing access to the marvelous Crown Fellows and keeping channels of communication open to the Aspen Institute. Along the way I subjected Erin, Kerry, and Marilyn O'Toole to too many versions of too many chapters, cruel tests of their love and patience, both of which I shall endeavor to reciprocate appropriately. Ed Lawler, my boss at the Center for Effective Organizations, also earned countless credits for patience and forbearance, for which I am deeply appreciative. My agent, Jim Levine, is both a prince and a rock, as everyone who knows him will attest. Zach Schisgal and the cast and crew at Rodale were a joy to work with; I thank them for their professionalism. Finally, I hope Douglas and Philip Adler will be pleased to find evidence of the lasting influence of their father in this highly personal reworking of the Aristotelian lessons he taught to me and to several generations of Aspen seminarians.

❧ CONTENTS ❧

ROOT OF ALL EVIL

CAN'T BUY HAPPINESS...

BLAH. BLAH. BLAH.

E-TRADE

—*BILLBOARD (2001)*

WHAT IF THE HOKEY-POKEY *IS* WHAT IT'S ALL ABOUT?

—*BUMPER STICKER (2004)*

 # FOREWORD

BY WALTER ISAACSON

At a certain point in our lives, many of us step back to reflect upon or perhaps even wrestle with what it takes to lead a life that is useful, moral, worthy, and spiritually meaningful. Maybe we have noticed ourselves trimming our principles and making too many compromises in our careers, and we want to reconnect with our values. Or we sense that we have pursued success without becoming more fulfilled. Or perhaps we yearn, in an era when both business and politics seem to have come unhinged from underlying values, to understand the great ideas and ideals that have shaped history.

For Benjamin Franklin, this moment came when he was 42, halfway through his remarkable life. After building the most successful publishing empire in colonial America, he scaled back his career in order to devote most of his time to learning, civic activities, public affairs, philanthropy, and, later, statecraft. When his mother expressed puzzlement, he explained to her: "I would rather have it said, 'He lived usefully,' than 'He died rich.'"

Franklin, whom I was writing a book about, inspired me, or at least emboldened me, when I decided that the time had come to make a transition in my own life at age 50. I had enjoyed a rather successful and stimulating career in journalism, and I had loved my work. But I realized that, as I rose in the ranks of corporate management, I had gotten further away from the endeavors that I found most rewarding, such as writing and the exploration of ideas. So I moved on to become president of the Aspen Institute, where, among other pleasures, I got the chance to know Jim O'Toole.

For 50 years, the Aspen Institute has been a place where successful executives and any other questing souls who choose to sign up for its seminars go to spend a week engaging with the values that are important to leadership, citizenship, and the good life. It has many programs, but at its core is a collection of weeklong retreats—restorative spas for the mind and body and soul—developed by Mortimer Adler and Robert Maynard Hutchins and then Jim O'Toole, which are based on readings and discussions about the great ideas and ideals that have informed the progress of civilization.

For more than a decade, Jim has served as a stimulating moderator, director, conceptualizer, and guiding force of these Aspen Institute seminars. The model he developed in his book *The Executive's Compass*, which shows the way we must balance values when making decisions, serves as a framework for many of our discussions. He is now the Mortimer Adler Senior Fellow of the Aspen Institute.

The starting point for most of these seminars is Aristotle's definition of "the good life." Aristotle provides the foundation, as Jim explains so well in that book, for such fundamental ideals as justice and fairness, which should guide our approach to business and everyday values. He likewise helps shape our notion of community, which is key to the moral quality of looking at the world from a perspective larger than the self. But he also provides a personal component: He explores how mature men and women may find the components of a good life if they embark on a diligent search, what Jim so aptly calls a *mid-course self-examination.*

When Jim was in his fifties, he undertook his own mid-course self-examination. He was inspired by Aristotle's understanding that most people can find happiness if they put aside their youthful fantasies about money and celebrity and seek instead to attain the awareness and knowledge, as well as the sense of companionship and community, that can lead to a complete life offering true fulfillment.

In this book, Jim not only explains the practical wisdom of Aristotle; he also shows how a variety of people, both famous and not, embarked on quests that led them closer to achieving a good life based on awareness and values rather than on riches and fame. These illustrative examples, some inspiring and others cautionary, make this book a practical self-help guide that is based on timeless wisdom rather than trite maxims. As Aristotle informs us, "Happiness is activity in accordance with virtue," and that requires engaging in contemplation. Aristotle speaks comfortably and clearly (in a manner that is sometimes missing these days) about ethics, about right and wrong, about virtue and vice. So, too, does Jim.

I think you will find Aristotle's wisdom and Jim's pragmatic application of it useful, provocative, and inspiring. And if you do, I hope that you will consider signing up for one of the seminars that Jim and his colleagues have created at Aspen over the years. You can do so at www.aspeninstitute.org.

Aristotle's core insight, which Jim explores in this book, is that the path to making virtue part of our character—acquiring a "general disposition to do what is best"—begins by critically examining the nature of our desires, understanding which of them is truly a component of the good life, and realizing how these fit into the concept of a good society. This is what the Aspen Institute seminars help participants to do.

The first step in pursuing the Aristotelian ideal of the good life is reflecting on what that concept means, both to you and to others. As Jim has shown, in his life and his seminars and now in this book, that step can be exciting and enriching.

ARISTOTLE'S INSIGHTS ON PLANNING A LIFE

Like many of my generation, men and women born in the years immediately after World War II, I found myself in my fifties full of questions and doubts. I didn't feel I had accomplished enough in my first five decades, and I wasn't sure how to make the best use of the time remaining to me. Conventional concepts of "the good life" seemed wanting in meaning, purpose, and practicality. I struggled to find an alternate definition of happiness that meant something to me personally and would give direction to the rest of my life. I found it in an unexpected source: Aristotle.

You may well ask what possible relevance the ideas of a Greek philosopher who lived more than 300 years before Christ have to the challenges facing modern men and women. It's a fair question, one I often have asked myself. The answer is that, in his career as a teacher and a consultant to leaders of ancient Athens, Aristotle thought long and hard about what it means to live a good life and how much it takes to finance it. His thoughts on this matter are particularly applicable today given the baby boom generation's anxiety over insufficient retirement savings and shaky investments: Aristotle shows how we can find happiness at almost any level of income. Moreover, he argues that the ability to find true contentment correlates only tangentially with the amount of money one has cached away. Unlike so many of today's "life advisors," Aristotle integrates financial planning with the broader task of life planning.

And, unlike pop psychologists, Aristotle does not offer a monolithic scheme whereby everyone can carve out a good life. He does not impart a magic, one-size-fits-all formula that pretends that all people are the same or

ix

that the conditions we face are givens, not variables. Instead, Aristotle offers practical and time-tested guidance to thoughtful people about how they can undertake their own life-planning exercises. In essence, he teaches us to fish rather than serving us a packaged fish stick TV dinner. His advice is essential because planning how to make the rest of our lives satisfying turns out to be an even harder task than financial planning. His ancient teachings remind boomers that we are not the first generation to have neglected the task of life planning. The accumulated lesson of history in this regard is clear and unequivocal: *Failure to engage in effective life planning is as risky in the long run as failure to engage in financial planning.* In fact, the two cannot be separated—trying to plan how much we need in the future, absent the context of what will provide us with meaning and happiness, is an exercise in fiction and futility.

QUESTIONS ARISTOTLE HELPS US ANSWER

What questions can Aristotle help us to answer? I can attest that Aristotle has helped me to think more clearly about the following:

- ❧ What does it mean to lead a good life?
- ❧ What is true happiness?
- ❧ How can I choose between (a) something pleasurable that I want now, and (b) something immediately less pleasant that I really need for long-term happiness?
- ❧ How much wealth do I need for leading a good life?
- ❧ What is personal excellence, and how do I achieve it?
- ❧ Is ambition necessary, or is it a trap?
- ❧ How can I be a success in my specialized career and, at the same time, a well-rounded person with a wide range of interests and knowledge?
- ❧ What is the relationship between virtue and happiness (do I have to be saintly to be happy)?

- How do love, friendship, luck, health, and religion contribute to the pursuit of happiness?
- To be happy, what should I be doing that I am not doing now? And what am I doing now that I should stop doing?
- What's next?

Aristotle helps us to work through such personal questions, but he doesn't stop there. To him, happiness isn't a selfish pursuit; rather, it occurs in a social context. That's why he also helps us to address the following questions about our roles in families, in communities, and, to use a modern concept, in workplaces, as well:

- To what extent does personal happiness entail a relationship with a community of others?
- How do I resolve the tensions between family and work?
- What can I pass on to the next generation? (To paraphrase Jonas Salk, "How can I be a good ancestor?")
- Will philanthropy make me virtuous and, perhaps, happy?
- How can I create the opportunity to be happy for the people who work for me?
- What is a fair distribution of financial and psychic rewards among those who participate with me in an enterprise?
- How can I create a successful business without harming others, or turning myself into a moral midget in the process?

These are questions many members of my generation have failed to answer—in some cases, have failed even to ask. For evidence, one need look no further than Enron's Jeff Skilling, Tyco's Dennis Kozlowski, and the heads of other scandal-plagued American corporations. In this regard, Aristotle is the ultimate realist. He understands that the greatest barrier to finding happiness is our unwillingness to ask ourselves tough moral questions, because honest answers to those questions would require us to change our behavior. He recognizes that almost all of us fervently seek happiness, yet we just as determinedly resist doing the things that would allow us to find it. Overcoming that paradoxical, self-defeating behavior is the challenge of midlife, and it is the central issue his moral exercises address.

If Aristotle doesn't provide answers to life's big questions, he at least shows why we need to ask them, and helps us to frame our personal inquiries in ways that increase the likelihood that we will find satisfying answers for our families, communities, organizations, and selves. Such answers, as subjective and diverse as they will be, are what amounts to wisdom in this life. And because our answers differ, there is no easy way to summarize here in a pithy phrase or even a paragraph what the good life ultimately entails. If wisdom were so quickly attained and compactable into nuggets of information, it would be available on the Internet. Aristotle shows us that it takes a bit of mental effort to find true happiness.

DOES HAPPINESS HINGE ON HAVING ENOUGH MONEY?

Because we boomers are by far the largest generation in history, commercial producers of goods and services cater to our wants and needs. Magazines like *Fortune, BusinessWeek,* and *U.S. News & World Report* annually devote entire issues to the subject of our retirement planning, focusing on how to calculate future income and expenditures, how to formulate prudent investment strategies, the prognosis for Medicare's coverage of health care costs, and where to find an affordable dream retirement home. This is practical stuff, particularly given the nasty stock market tumble in 2001 and with few experts predicting a return to the bullish heights of the late nineties.

Yet, though effective *financial planning* is obviously essential, many boomers are starting to realize that it's only part of the task we face. We have begun to notice that many people a decade or so older than us are not finding great satisfaction in their retirement, even when they have adequate incomes.

In private, these retirees admit they are unhappy, bored with watching television, and at a loss for how to fill their abundant free time in rewarding and useful ways. Worse, we note that many people who retire seem to age visibly almost from the moment they are no longer part of the action at work. In light of those object lessons, it is dawning on many of us that, in addition to financial planning, we need to engage in equally robust *life planning*. For, if truth be told, few of us have a clear or realistic view of how we intend to live good, meaningful lives in our remaining decades. *Money* magazine's 2002 special issue on retirement planning offers its readers "Thirty Questions That Can Change Your Life," 29 of which are financial in nature, with the remaining question addressing the short-term issue of "spending enough to make life enjoyable now." That ratio is probably indicative of the amount of effort we boomers devote to financial, as opposed to life, planning.

Sadly, experience demonstrates that those who misallocate their planning efforts in such a lopsided way end up with a lot of miserable, wasted time on their hands, no matter how well funded it is. This fate begins to feel worse than death the older we get and the less time we see remaining for us to find happiness. Psychologists say we live in fear of death, but Aristotle sees us fretting less about dying itself than worrying we will die or become incapacitated before we have had our innings. What most of us fear, in fact, is growing too old to do the things we have always wanted to do and to achieve the goals we long have wanted to achieve. Worse, some older men and women find themselves without goals, living lives that have lost their meaning. Owner of the L.A. Lakers, Jerry Buss, recently was quoted as saying, "I've accomplished all I've ever wanted to do." For his sake, let us hope he was either wrong or exaggerating, for this sounds too much like the suicide note of Kodak's founder, George Eastman: "My work is done, why wait?" Truly, was there no more for Eastman to do in life? Aristotle argues that no one has "done it all." And he finds it sad in the extreme that there are so many men and women quietly killing themselves by killing time. He wants us to live. And not just live, but live well.

Today, too many people who could be more fully engaged in life are settling for second best by killing time. To help us avoid that dreary prospect, this book offers Aristotelian advice about how to draw up an effective life plan for finding true and lasting happiness. I don't mean to suggest that Aristotle should be read as the last or only word on how to lead a good life. But the wisdom he offers is essential for navigating the moral thickets of adult life. Aristotle shows us that a robust life plan requires a clear view of our ultimate goal. He demonstrates that those who don't know what the good life entails are not likely to find it. This insight is critical for those of us in midlife because, although we may have abandoned the unrealistic financial expectations generated in the roaring nineties, there are distressing signs that we have not set aside the values that drove our behavior during that era of excess. Too many of us still cling to the belief that the good life depends on obtaining ever more material goods, prestige, power, career success, sensual pleasure, and social approval. Aristotle helps us to ask if, indeed, those conventional goals are consistent with leading the good life. And, if they are not, he helps us to identify goals more likely to bring us happiness.

A PHILOSOPHY FOR THE REST OF US

Aristotle knew his audience. He was writing neither for the nobility nor their hand servants, neither for the Fortunate Few (those who seemed perfectly content because they "had everything") nor the Unfortunate Many (those forced to be satisfied with what little they had). In Aristotle's day, most models for living the good life were derived from the experiences of the rich and famous of his time: kings, queens, conquerors, and Olympic laurelists. Today, our role models are updates of the same types: successful politicians, billionaires, movie stars, and sports figures. Call it Philosophy for the Few. Doubtless, the lifestyles of the rich and famous are glamorous, but Aristotle tells us we run a risk when we attempt to emulate them. When we establish the Fortunate Few as exemplars of the good life, we may doom ourselves to discontent if we don't make it in their terms. Aristotle also asks if the Fortunate Few are in fact happy, a question no less relevant today.

The postmodern antidote to Philosophy for the Few is Philosophy for the Many, as dispensed on afternoon television. This egalitarian approach is predicated on the assumption that the sources of happiness are relative and universal: in a word, "whatever." Aristotle's philosophy supports modern relativism to the extent that he believes in the right of the Many to live as they wish. But Aristotle says we should not emulate the Many if we have the opportunity and ability not to. His politically incorrect conclusion is that the Rest of Us should not seek contentment in what the unambitious or intellectually limited would find satisfying.

In fact, the ambitions and preferred lifestyles of most people are no closer to Joe Six-pack's than to Donald Trump's. That is why Aristotle does not address himself to either the Many or the Few. His is a Philosophy for the Rest of Us, people who want more but who are not wanting. His audience is mature, thoughtful people who have a healthy dissatisfaction with the way they are currently living. In a nutshell, he says that what is needed to find happiness is the enrichment of our lives. By enrichment, he means seriously endeavoring to develop our full and highest potential as human beings. Aristotle's central point is that life is about development. It is not just about growing up during adolescence at one end, then retiring comfortably at the other; instead, it is about growing and learning throughout the course of our lives. He shows us that happiness comes about as the continual growth of our minds, character, and humanity. Truly happy people are engaged in realizing the full diversity of their highest, most human capabilities.

Aristotle observes that all people are born with great potential for growth in many fields and endeavors, and that those who are happiest at the end are the ones who are able to look back on a full life of having exercised their many innate capacities. In contrast, the unhappiest men and women are those who, in old age, come to realize they will die without having sufficiently realized their potential. Although we understand this point intuitively, few of us know what we should do to realize our potential. Aristotle's contribution is to help us to overcome the convenient rationales we use to resist doing so.

The problem is that his philosophy flies in the face of what we "know" about the Fortunate Few, who, by all accounts, find success by narrowing the focus of their lives in order to develop a single talent or interest. Aristotle does not take issue with the fact that highly successful people develop their unique talents; he simply recognizes that the Rest of Us are neither superbly nor uniquely talented in one field. Instead, we often have many talents and diverse interests, and experience shows that those who develop that wide range of inherent potential are happiest in the end. Indeed, because even the most narrowly talented will become happier if they enrich their lives, he tells us there is no sound rationale for the Rest of Us to overly narrow our life experiences.

Aristotle's intent is, first, to help the Rest of Us break the unconscious habit of measuring our lives by the standards of the Fortunate Few, then to help us plan effectively to fulfill our potential in a way that will bring us true and lasting happiness. That first task turns out to be the hardest for people who have had a lifetime of conditioning in the Philosophy of the Few.

DISCIPLINE: THE ESSENCE OF CHARACTER

To Aristotle, the question of how we can most effectively realize the opportunity of our lives comes down to what might be called the ethical issue of character. He tells us we must be "virtuous" to be happy. But when he speaks of people with excellent character, he doesn't mean they necessarily follow the moral precepts of any religion or subscribe to a code of secular ethics. Rather, virtuous men and women have an overarching purpose in their lives—a rule or higher principle—which all their wealth, power, and actions serve or to which all are subordinated. The trick is to identify that good end, then to discipline ourselves to pursue it. The key is found in the word *disci-*

pline. People of excellent character are able to pursue happiness effectively because they discipline themselves to reject facile definitions of the end worthy of pursuit. Then, regardless of temptation, they focus their actions and behavior on achieving their self-defined good end.

Throughout this book, I offer examples of contemporary Americans who, consciously or not, are Aristotelian in the self-disciplined ways they pursue happiness. These ordinary, yet extraordinary, people demonstrate how each of us can apply Aristotle's lessons to our personal pursuit of the good life.

Consider William Mayer, a former bank executive, who felt he was ready to "retire" at age 50. At that point, he made an Aristotelian decision. He concluded he would be happiest in the long run if he divided his time into equal thirds: the first devoted to his personal development and to his family, the second to nonprofit institutions, and the third to his continuing business interests. A decade later, he has disciplined himself to stick with this life plan. He has engaged continually in formal and informal educational activities and is an avid skier, chef, and devoted family man. Among his many nonprofit activities, he serves as a trustee of the University of Maryland; significantly, he gives time and knowledge to such organizations as generously and thoughtfully as he gives money. In his remaining time, he runs a venture capital firm. From an Aristotelian perspective, Mayer is virtuous not so much because of what he does, but because he consciously planned how to live a good life, then dedicated himself to the hard work of following that plan in the face of distractions and temptations to do otherwise.

Similarly, Dr. Grace Gabe was enjoying a successful medical career in her early fifties, when she realized she had developed only a part of her potential. She found it rewarding, but not sufficient for happiness, to be a respected physician. So in the prime of her career and once her kids were out of the nest, she gave up the practice of medicine to devote herself to becoming a violinist. Her daily "practice" now is on her instrument, and she performs regularly with a chamber group. Dr. Gabe also has coauthored a book about families and is an avid devotee of the arts, constantly learning ever more about opera, drama, painting, and sculpture. A decade after she "retired," Dr. Gabe enrolled in a full load of undergraduate English courses at Harvard, studying poetry, early Shakespearean plays, Dante, and the Bible as literature—in effect, studying what she had missed years earlier in her technical, premed training. And, no, she isn't rich.

In his late fifties, attorney Norton Tennille set aside a successful D.C. law partnership to create an innovative educational enrichment program for disadvantaged students in Philippi, a tough suburb in Cape Town, South Africa. Prior to 1994, black South Africans were forced to live in such segregated shantytowns, often located on the fringes of all-white cities. Although free to live where they want to today, poor people raised in those ghettos lack the skills and job opportunities needed to move elsewhere. Visiting Cape Town in the mid-nineties, Tennille understood the sad reality that the end of apartheid was not leading to a great improvement in the standard of living for most African city dwellers. But how could one person, acting without significant resources, begin to make a dent in the vicious cycle that condemns so many to a life sentence of poverty? Tennille sensed that education was the key. He began by organizing an after-school debate program, encouraging high school students to learn more about the important policy issues facing their new democracy. Through debate, the students learned how to speak and write better English, to polish their study and research skills, and to develop the habits and discipline to help them get into universities and, ultimately, find good jobs.

Gradually the program has grown, and now Tennille and his wife, Jane, manage a variety of educational enrichment activities, ranging from supporting nine preschool crèches; to offering grade school and high school art, science, environmental, and cultural programs; to providing leadership and career development projects for high school graduates. Norton Tennille today has a lower standard of living and no longer gets the rush from being part of the "inside the beltway" action, but he has a higher quality of life, one in which he is using a fuller range of his many talents and helping hundreds of others to develop theirs.

One needn't leave one's country or give up one's career to find meaning and purpose in life. Buie Seawell, an ordained Presbyterian minister and practicing attorney who along the way has served as chief aide to a United States senator and later to a governor of Colorado, still has a hand in the political arena, performs the odd wedding, and keeps his legal credentials current. But in his fifties, he realized that the one activity he could continue to engage in successfully throughout his entire life is learning. And because the best way to keep learning is through teaching, he took a post on the faculty of the University of Denver's business school, where he teaches in a critically acclaimed ethics program designed to prevent future corporate scandals like the Enron/Arthur Andersen debacle. Significantly, in midlife, Seawell came to understand how to plan for and consciously pursue the good life as the result of reading Aristotle.

An obvious question: Why shouldn't readers simply pick up a volume of Aristotle's *Nicomachean Ethics* and read it on their own, without my filter and interpretation? Clearly that would be preferable if it weren't for the fact that his writings can be tough sledding for modern readers. Aristotle's language can seem arcane, but the real problem is that he didn't have a word processor! When he wanted to redraft a chapter, he had to hire a scribe, who would scratch the master's words on a scroll, a costly and time-consuming process. What has come down to us in the main, then, are probably Aristotle's first or second drafts, his notes, or possibly student transcriptions of his lectures. In short, Aristotle is hard to read, and his words require careful attention, analysis, and interpretation.

That kind of close reading is particularly difficult for those of us who attended college in the sixties and seventies. In general, we were the first university-educated generation who didn't study the classics of Western thought and literature. Early in the 20th century, Plato, Aristotle, and the other great thinkers of the Western tradition were at the core of higher education; but as the century progressed, their works were relegated to the periphery of the curriculum. By the 1960s, Plato had been replaced by

Herbert Marcusse, and Aristotle had been replaced by Norman O. Brown. I'm not sure our professors did us any favor by making such trendy trades.

So, for philosophical virgins who have never read classical philosophy and for those who don't have the patience to tackle Aristotle's *Ethics* on their own, these pages are my interpretation of what Aristotle says practical people need to ask themselves if they want to lead a good life. As an advisor to professionals and politicians, he took special care to describe how 4th-century B.C. Athenians might apply his philosophy to the conduct of their daily lives. In doing so, he anticipated many of the core findings of modern psychology and economics. But as practical as he was, he was not compelled to face such modern issues as dual-career families, the management of large business corporations, high technology, income tax, and IPOs. To bridge the millennia, I've attempted to show how his insights are applicable to the challenges faced by practical people in the 3rd millennium A.D. Consequently, this book is as much a transposition of Aristotle's thoughts to a modern context as it is a summary of what he said way back then. Think of it as "Variations on Themes by Aristotle."

ORGANIZATION OF THE BOOK

Aristotle offers a disciplined way to frame the question, How can I make the best use of the decades I have remaining? Because most people have little experience answering such questions, he encouraged his own students to begin their personal analyses with reference to the lives of the Fortunate Few, men and women of their era who had most successfully achieved wealth, fame, power, and pleasure. This initial test was designed to help them determine if such individuals were models worthy of emulation. Following that precedent, we, too, examine the lives of high-profile members of the boomer generation—politicians like Rudy Giuliani, Bill and Hillary Clinton, and George W. Bush, and business moguls like Carly Fiorina, Larry Ellison, and Jim Clark—

asking ourselves if we could become happy living as they have chosen to live. In doing so, we must keep in mind that our goal is not to emulate the lives of the rich and famous; instead, the purpose of the exercise is to help us clarify what paths to happiness we want to pursue. Aristotle asks the Rest of Us to test ourselves to see if we really believe that fame, wealth, power, or excessive sensual pleasure will make us truly happy.

In the early chapters of the book, we critically examine Aristotle's controversial conclusion that what is missing in the lives of most adults is the fulfillment of our potential—and what we must therefore do is to engage in developmental activities leading to that fulfillment. Because this conclusion is neither obvious nor what most people want to hear, we must examine his reasoning, seeking to answer as far as possible the thoughtful objections his critics offer to it. We analyze the pros and cons and costs and benefits of the many other, traditional ways in which people typically seek to be happy: accumulating and spending money, pursuing leisure-time physical pleasures, and persevering with unfinished quests for power, acclaim, and approval.

Having done that analysis, we then are able to ask the personal question, Would Aristotle's alternative path bring me happiness? Assuming the answer is yes, the last chapters deal with practical applications of Aristotle's philosophy to our own lives. It would be convenient if we could simply skip to these easier and more practical chapters; alas, they are useless without the benefit of the harder and more analytical chapters that precede them. Moreover, because his ideas have become an intrinsic part of Western thought, his conclusions may sound like platitudes if they are taken without a review of the logical process by which he arrives at them. Indeed, it is through the process of understanding how and why he reaches his conclusions that we develop the self-discipline to make the changes in our lives that may make us happy. As actor Will Smith wrote in 2002:

> Recently I read Aristotle's *Poetics*. It made me reevaluate all
> of the things I thought I knew, and it really sparked a fire in

me. . . . It made me realize that there's no reason to reinvent the wheel. Every emotion you'll ever feel, everything you're gonna do in your life has been done for thousands of years. . . . That book made me reevaluate every aspect of my life.

So if we struggle with Aristotle's exercises, we need only keep in mind that they are necessary to get us into shape for the big event of our lives: planning what we should do to find the fulfillment that thus far has eluded us.

One contemporary writer claims that the purpose of philosophy is "consolation." Aristotle disagrees: Consolation is the purpose of money; the purpose of philosophy is to serve as a practical guide to action. He called his action-oriented subject "ethics," but that term may be misleading to modern readers. Today we typically think of ethics in the context of making such decisions as when doctors should pull the plug on terminal patients or when it's okay for lawyers to double dip. Although the importance of such questions shouldn't be minimized, and Aristotle himself was concerned with their Classical Era equivalents, he meant something more by the term. Aristotelian ethics concern moral decisions related to how we should allocate the limited time of our lives. We each must plan how we will allocate our energies among such activities as earning, learning, playing, being with friends and family, and participating in our community. As we make these choices, Aristotle warns, we will fail to achieve "the chief good"—that is, we will fail to be happy—if we pursue the wrong ends.

To Aristotle, ethical thinking begins with a conscious identification of the long-term consequences of continuing along one's present course of action. If we believe those consequences will be negative, the task then is to apply our moral imaginations to creating better alternatives. But most of us don't create those alternatives, or if we do, we don't act on them. Though most of us wish to pursue the good life, we nonetheless say, "I'll wait until I'm rich," or "I'll wait 'til I retire." But that is almost always too late. Aristotle says that the time to begin leading the good life is *now*. One reason most people don't start while there is still ample time to complete the journey is because they don't know how to begin. That's because the common methods for choosing where to head in life—"going with your gut," reading signs from "On High," doing what "Mom" did—are too subjective and risky to give us the confidence needed to act. The value of Aristotle's ethical philosophy is that it provides a logical rationale and time-tested framework to get us going where we know we should be headed.

Aristotle also shows us that a reason we fail to find happiness is that we are looking in the wrong places. We commonly assume that happiness is a transient feeling, the presence of pleasure and the absence of pain, but he shows us that true happiness is, in fact, mental not physical, enduring not ephemeral, and rational not emotional. Happiness, Aristotle demonstrates, is what good people *do*, the sum of the best activities of which humans are capable. It is not, as commonly assumed, what we feel or what happens to us.

Aristotle concludes that if we don't know what happiness is we are destined not to find it. But if we have some understanding of "the chief good," he asks, "Will not that knowledge have some influence on our lives? Shall we not, like archers who have a mark to aim at, be more likely to hit on what is right?"

The exercises described in these pages are designed to help readers identify their own bull's-eyes of life—and to put to use Aristotle's insights on how they can improve their skill at hitting them.

GETTING STARTED

In helping adults develop life plans, mythologist David Oldfield begins by assigning a useful exercise that readers of this book might try as a "warmup" for the tougher Aristotelian exercises in the chapters to follow. Oldfield suggests that we each prepare a one-page "map" visually illustrating the course of our life. The intent of this symbolic map is to show graphically where we have been, where we are now, what roadblocks we have had to overcome, and what life-changing experiences we have had along life's journey. Importantly, the map should illustrate where we plan to go next and indicate our ultimate target (the destination where we believe we would find true happiness). Because this assignment is not as easy as it may seem, and we are unlikely to find the results fully satisfactory on the first try, it may be helpful to do this exercise with a friend or a group of friends at similar stages in life. In the course of the chapters that follow, the questions Aristotle raises should help us to develop robust action plans relating to the parts of our maps concerned with the future.

PART ONE

THE BASIC CONCEPTS UNDERLYING ARISTOTLE'S PHILOSOPHY

ARISTOTLE'S LIFE AND WAY OF THINKING

I THINK ACTUALLY THE MOST FUNDAMENTAL CHANGE OCCURRED WHEN I DEALT WITH THE PROSTATE CANCER [AT AGE 55]. THAT WAS THE FIRST TIME THAT REQUIRED ME TO SAY, "I AM GOING TO DIE. NOT NECESSARILY OF CANCER, BUT I AM GONNA DIE." SO YOU REALIZE YOU'D BETTER DO SOMETHING WITH YOUR LIFE THAT MAKES YOU HAPPY WITH YOURSELF. I DECIDED POLITICS WAS NOT MY ENTIRE LIFE.

—RUDOLPH GIULIANI

SOME PEOPLE BELIEVE THAT NATURE MAKES PEOPLE GOOD, OTHERS SAY THAT IT IS HABIT, AND STILL OTHERS SAY THAT IT IS TEACHING. EXPERIENCE SHOWS THAT LOGICAL ARGUMENTS AND TEACHING ARE NOT EFFECTIVE IN MOST CASES. THE SOUL OF THE STUDENT MUST FIRST HAVE BEEN CONDITIONED BY GOOD HABITS JUST AS LAND MUST BE CULTIVATED TO NURTURE SEED. FOR A PERSON WHOSE LIFE IS GUIDED BY EMOTION WILL NOT LISTEN TO A RATIONAL ARGUMENT, NOR WILL HE UNDERSTAND IT.

—ARISTOTLE

Aristotle says that mature men and women, if they search diligently, may find the opportunity of a lifetime awaiting them. Sometime around their fifties, thoughtful people may discover the perspective needed to make sense of their accumulated experience and the wisdom needed to identify what will bring them true happiness in their remaining years. And if they are more fortunate than Rudolph Giuliani, they will make this discovery without the trauma of a life-threatening disease, the disintegration of a marriage, or the tragic destruction of a great city.

Yet, in truth, embarking on a new life course requires hard work. Since the time of Aristotle, experience demonstrates that the only way mature people can become truly happy is to abandon their youthful fantasies and pursue more appropriate ends. This process of finally growing up is ultimately rewarding, but it is no easy task, as shown in the classic writings of great philosophers, poets, and playwrights, and buttressed by the modern writings of psychologists and social scientists. More viscerally, we can feel the pain of men and women we know personally when, at midlife, they realize they must finally start doing something to make themselves happy or risk failing to fulfill the promise of the one life they have.

Yet most of us equivocate, resist, and backtrack when it comes to actually changing the way we lead our lives. Giuliani, after overcoming a spate of self-defeating personal behavior in his early fifties to become our generation's leadership poster boy, continued to demonstrate recidivist adolescent tendencies. He may have declared, "Politics was not my entire life," but soon after his post–September 11 adrenaline rush wore off, he attempted to subvert the constitution of the state of New York by proposing to run for a third mayoral term. After all, what other high could fill the void of lost power and the limelight of worldwide publicity?

In more private and less flamboyant ways than Giuliani, most men and women in their fifties struggle with the question of what to do with the rest of their lives in order to find the fulfillment that has eluded them. I reluctantly joined their ranks when I was forced to recognize what should have been obvious to me for years: The Good Fairy was never going to grant my most fervent youthful wish.

Toward the end of the year 2000, I reluctantly admitted I wasn't finding happiness on the life path I had been following for three decades. I had begun the year, my fifty-fifth, filled with millennially grand expectations. A book I had written had just been published, and I was convinced that this one, my twelfth, would bring the recognition I desired, the acknowledgment that I felt my work had long deserved but, for this twist of fate and that stroke of bad timing, the earlier works had been denied. And it was definitely respect I was after. Sure, I wanted more money; but in my gut, I hungered for America's most sought-after prize: fame, renown, a name. I felt certain my new book was the vehicle aboard which I was bound for glory. In my considered opinion, it had all the requisites for success in the ultracompetitive business book market: I could visualize reviews praising the volume's "originality, wit, and practicality." Soon I would reap the long-desired ego boost associated with bestsellerdom, the miracle cure that would appease my pathetic craving for respect and approval.

Alas, as the year dwindled, I eventually had to accept that my precious volume had vanished into the black hole of obscurity that had devoured my previous literary efforts. In light of this, I needed to decide whether to continue my conventional pursuit of the goddess of success and, in the process, risk never finding happiness, or seek contentment chasing a different muse, one whose favor I was more likely to obtain. For the first time in my life, I found myself entertaining a troubling question: *Even if I were to obtain the one thing I wanted more than anything else, would I find happiness in its embrace?*

Turning to Aristotle's *Ethics* for guidance, I was encouraged by his belief that almost everyone can find happiness *if* they are willing to ask themselves tough questions, create a new life plan, and then have the discipline to carry it through. In particular, he believes that mature men and women find happiness when they abandon youthful fantasies about money, power, and fame and devote their time to realizing their untapped capacities to learn new things.

In our fifties, we are ready to take up the challenge of fulfilling our natural potential *if* we can accept that happiness means something other than being a movie star, president of the United States, founder of a successful software company, bestselling author, or whatever one's youthful fantasy still may be. Then we might actually realize the opportunity of a lifetime, the capacity to lead "the good life." If Aristotle is correct, the decades-long process of narrowing aspirations and trimming expectations is reversible. We probably won't achieve the Hollywood version of bliss that seemed so enticing in our youth; instead, we may find mature satisfaction in becoming a complete human being; we might achieve "excellence" in Aristotle's terms.

In light of the marketplace failure of my book, I began to understand the simple, practical, and personal significance of his philosophic message: I was unhappy because I was chasing the wrong ends and doing the wrong things. In particular, I was emulating the wrong role models: famous management gurus. In an Aristotelian view, those folks probably weren't any happier than I was, and even if they were, copying their behavior wouldn't work for me.

On gaining this insight, I was at first full of resolve to change my goals, role models, and how I spent the time of my life. But, damn it, over the next months, the process of taking Aristotle's message to heart and trying to put it into action did nothing so much as reveal my frailty, weakness, and vanity. I soon realized I wasn't ready to change course. I found I was comfortable with the conditions I had created for myself, even if they were less than satisfying. At my age, who wants to do the hard work involved in learning new behavior? Worse, I was afraid to change because the alternatives all seemed risky.

And on second thought, weren't those famous gurus the very people the world called successful? How the hell was I going to find happiness if I ended up being a nobody . . . and an impoverished one at that? Ergo, I concluded that Aristotle must have been wrong. And everything I read in magazines and watched on television argued against Aristotle's conclusions. According to conventional wisdom, happiness is found, variously, by way of

6

- a new job
- a new house
- a new city
- a new mate
- an adventure in faraway climes

The most attractive of these alternatives to me was the Geographic Solution. When a close friend limned his fantasy about circumnavigating Africa in a sailboat, visiting the exotic islands that float in the warm seas surrounding the continent, I could feel the ocean spray on my face and taste the promised spices (and vices) on my lips. (According to David Denby, the female version of this fantasy is Tuscany, "a primal paradise of sunshine, sex, love, terra-cotta tiles, and huge salads with real tomatoes.") In contrast, Aristotle said I needed to grow up and to use my time in more productive ways. He said it was virtue that would make me happy, and virtue started with disciplining myself to do things that contributed to my long-term development. Clearly, Aristotle must have been wrong! So I resisted. As Ogden Nash said, "You are only young once, but you can stay immature indefinitely."

I had prided myself on being flexible and open-minded, but in my fifties, I discovered I actually was a master of rigidity and resistant to unfamiliar ideas. When I looked at myself honestly, I saw a man capable of creating imaginative rationales for continuing his self-defeating behavior. My first line of defense was skepticism. I devised sound reasons to resist going where Aristotle's teaching ineluctably led. I concluded that his ideas were:

- badly dated
- elitist and politically incorrect
- prescriptive, naïve, and impractical
- hard to understand and translate into action

Who needs better reasons than those to reject the ideas of a defunct philosopher? Indeed, if you are as skeptical as I am, you, too, will want to examine Aristotle's credentials and check his character references before committing to a full course of study of his ideas. Before delving into his philosophy, it seems sensible to inquire about him personally, about the kinds of followers he attracted, and about his track record. Here's a brief summary of Aristotle's life, the foundations of his thought, and why his thinking has generated critics over the centuries. When I did this background check, it never occurred to me I was stalling!

THE SAGE'S C.V.

Although Aristotle lived two and a half millennia ago, I was able to discover a good deal about his career: In addition to his own writings, observations about him by contemporaries survive, and, miraculously, a copy of his will has come down through the ages. Nonetheless, I also found enormous gaps in knowledge about his personal life and motivations. After all, he lived in an era in which autobiography was self-indulgent. But from what we know as fact and what we can reasonably surmise, it would appear Aristotle was more like people today than one might expect, considering the enormous gulf in time separating antiquity from the 21st century. Of course, he wasn't exactly like us; he never heard of a PC, a BMW, a VCR, or an IRA, and he was definitely not P.C. But he was surprisingly like us in terms of his interpersonal relationships and the life and career challenges he faced. He wrote about the concerns of practical men and women as opposed to the more esoteric issues that preoccupy academics, and his political and ethical teachings were intended for the leadership class of his society. "The Ancient," as I think of him, was a teacher of bright, educated generalists in government and commerce as opposed to scholars and specialists.

Aristotle was born in 384 B.C. in a Greek colony in Macedonia. His father, Nicomachus, was court physician to the king of Macedonia, Alexander the Great's grandfather. Nicomachus died when Aristotle was 17, and he was then sent to the Athenian Academy, where he studied under Plato until he was 37. (He was either a slow learner or a precursor of the modern graduate student.) Like everyone, Aristotle had his shortcomings, weaknesses, and even vices. He was a bit of a dandy in his youth, sporting the latest designer fashions in cloaks and sandals, and was said to have worn ostentatious rings. He engaged in conspicuous consumption: He had the finest collection of books in Athens; his teacher, Plato, was said to be envious. As a student, he occasionally was arrogant: He would sit in Plato's class at the Academy and point out errors in his teacher's logic. Plato was not necessarily paying him a compliment in dubbing him "the mind." There is reason to believe he was smugly ambitious in midlife. When Plato died, Aristotle assumed he was the obvious candidate to succeed as head of the Academy. But it was not to be. Apparently, Aristotle's arrogance had alienated so many members of the faculty that he was passed over in favor of his best friend. He left Athens hurt, if not in a huff.

On the rebound from the disappointments of his academic career, Aristotle moved back to Macedonia, where he became tutor to Alexander from the time the prince was 13 until he was 16 years old. Significantly, Aristotle did not attempt to turn Alexander into an intellectual: "It is not merely unnecessary for a king to become a philosopher, it even may be a disadvantage," Aristotle wrote. "Instead, a king should take the advice of true philosophers. Then he would fill his reign with good deeds, not good words." Alas, it must have seemed to Aristotle that Alexander suffered from attention deficit disorder during his tutorials, because there is little evidence that the teacher had any more than a slight influence on his student's behavior then or later.

Nonetheless, we have reason to believe that Aristotle's home life in Macedonia was richer and emotionally more rewarding than his work life was with Alexander. After the career setback in Athens, Aristotle married an 18-year-old noblewoman, Pythias. They soon had a daughter, whom they also named Pythias. Based on what he wrote, Aristotle was deeply in love with his bride: "As for adultery, let it be held disgraceful for any man or woman to be found in any way unfaithful once they are married and call each other husband and wife." Sadly, the young wife died before the prime of her life. Aristotle never remarried but spent the rest of his days with a mistress, Herpyllis, who bore him a son, Nicomachus.

During the 13 years he was away from Athens, we may surmise that Aristotle gained wisdom and, perhaps, humility. Clearly, he sought to become self-aware. He worked to discover the unconscious appetites that had derailed his career. Abandoning those inappropriate desires, he disciplined himself to aim, instead, for "goods" that would make him truly virtuous and happy. To develop his potential, he read everything he could get his hands on and seriously studied all subjects imaginable. He made friends among others similarly inclined, and together they spent days and months discussing scientific and philosophical questions, challenging each other when one of them offered a facile answer to a complex question. In addition, Aristotle applied his growing store of learning, wisdom, and understanding to the practical problems that beset his community.

After years of such effort and around the beginning of that all-important sixth decade of life, he felt he understood, finally, what it meant to be happy. He concluded that true happiness results not from winning the admiration of others or from being appointed to a position of power (like deanship of the Academy); instead, happiness derives from dedication to the goal of living a good life, and that such a life entails a never-ending quest for knowledge and wisdom.

He returned to Athens at age 50, perhaps wishing to make amends and to convince his former colleagues to reform the Academy's idealistic and metaphysical curriculum by adopting a more realistic and scientific approach to learning and research. Again he was rebuffed (long memories among faculty sorts are as ingrained as their unwillingness to forgive). Unable to change the existing academic system, he acted like an entrepreneur today who finds himself frustrated inside established institutions: He started his own business, the Lyceum. Specializing in biological research and historical studies, the Lyceum ultimately became the model for formal higher education in the West. (The French still call their high schools *lycées*.) He led the institution for a dozen years, until anti-Macedonian agitation erupted in Athens and he was forced to retreat from the city.

Aristotle died in exile at about age 62 in 322 B.C. His friends remembered him for his loyalty, kindness, and generosity. What is striking about his life is that he appears to have practiced what he preached. He spent his last quarter century unswervingly dedicated to the pursuit of wisdom in exactly the way he recommended to others.

HIS PRIMARY CHARACTER REFERENCE

Aristotle is remembered today as a polymath and organizer of knowledge. A primary influence on medieval philosophy, he introduced a structure of logical thought that laid the groundwork for empirical science in the centuries to come. Although most of his scientific research had become embarrassingly dated by the time of the Renaissance, Aristotle's writings nonetheless gave scholars, inventors, and artists of that era license to explore previously off-limits secular and scientific worlds. Galileo himself noted that Aristotle would not have advanced his earth-centered model of the universe had the Ancient possessed a telescope. Be that as it may, his scientific works are seldom read today, but his books dealing with political and moral philosophy have stood the test of time.

It may seem as if Aristotle's ideas have been an integral part of the Western tradition uninterruptedly since the Classical age; in fact, from shortly after his death until the dawn of the Renaissance, his writings were little known in Christendom, and their very survival was in doubt. Scrolls containing Aristotle's writings disappeared in Europe during the Roman and early Christian eras. His thoughts were preserved thanks mainly to Syrian scholars who kept them in currency until they were propagated widely by the two greatest Islamic minds, Avicenna and Averroes.

The Ancient did not find a secure place in the literature of the West until the medieval scholar St. Thomas Aquinas became his advocate. While studying at the University of Paris in the mid-13th century, Aquinas chanced upon third-hand Latin translations of Aristotle's works based on Averroes' Arabic texts. Reading Aristotle even in such corrupted form, Aquinas was persuaded that the Ancient's philosophy was unusually timeless, logical, practical, moral, and, particularly important to a Benedictine monk, consistent with the teachings of Christ. Aquinas thus became the Christian Champion of the Pagan Aristotle. Now, how many résumés include a bona fide, Rome-certified saint as a reference?

Emerging from the cloistered, afterlife-obsessed Middle Ages, when learning had been focused on holy scriptures, Renaissance intellectuals rediscovered the great minds of antiquity and, in Aristotle, found a philosopher refreshingly practical and of this world. Unlike early Christian scholars, Aristotle had not cast his arguments in terms of either/or: sin or grace, angels or devils, heaven or hell. Instead, he argued that virtue lay in the middle ground between having too much and having too little of a good thing, whether money, fame, or power. So the goal in life was moderation, and the trick was knowing where to draw the line. This notion of a "golden mean" was quite alien to medieval Christian scholars, who typically had cast moral issues in all-or-nothing terms. They had accepted as gospel St. Paul's dictum "the love of money is the root of all evil," and then taken vows of poverty. But to Aristotle, wealth was intrinsically neither good nor bad; instead, he said the moral issue each person had to resolve was when he or she had enough. As capitalism evolved during the Renaissance, Aristotle's pagan take on wealth began to be viewed as more sensible than St. Paul's Christian construct.

Aquinas followed Aristotle's texts faithfully on the issue of moderation, teaching that virtue lay in "the just mean" and "sin lies in exceeding this mean." This formulation was adopted by the Church, and it became morally acceptable for Renaissance men to be rich even if, at the same time, it was sinful for them to pursue wealth as the sole object of life. The moral challenge was for each of them to answer the Aristotelian question, How much is enough?

Skeptics of the time found such moral questioning naïve, much as some today condemn as impractical the Aristotelian conclusion that a person totally absorbed in wealth creation is not leading a good life. After all, how can one say it is not virtuous for business people to devote their lives to wealth creation when society obviously benefits from their efforts? The issue is not easy to resolve, particularly if we believe it is imperative to act in a manner consistent with our beliefs. If Aristotle's concept of moderation is morally right, it calls into question the behavior of many of us, and it becomes incumbent on us to pursue different ends. But if he is wrong, and it is morally acceptable to maximize wealth at the expense of other activities and concerns, that conclusion, too, will influence the course of our life planning. But how do we decide what is right for us?

For most of us, of course, the issue isn't how excessive wealth accumulation gets in the way of our pursuit of happiness; we each have smaller and different fish to fry. Nonetheless, applying Aristotle's way of thinking is useful whatever our particular issue may be—pride, envy, anger—and however large or small it is. As I eventually learned in my efforts to overcome my own counterproductive desires for approval, the long-term payoff from Aristotle can be enormous. But I also learned we can't benefit from Aristotle's wisdom until we understand the analytical process he uses, then learn to apply it imaginatively to our own issues. The challenge is to overcome the decades of sloppy moral reasoning that inhibits our ability to do so.

THE FOUNDATIONS OF ARISTOTLE'S THOUGHT

Aristotle begins his own philosophical inquiries by taking the world as it is and humans as they are: in both cases, *imperfect*. He asks how these imperfect people can make their social and political institutions better and how they can individually lead better lives. He observes a rather nasty world in which men struggle for wealth and power, but he has no illusions that human nature can be changed or that it is desirable for government to try to enforce virtuous behavior. Aristotle is no utopian.

In this he differs greatly from his own esteemed teacher. In perhaps the most influential secular book ever written, *The Republic*, Plato imagines a brave new world led by a few virtuous "guardians" who create conditions under which the less-than-virtuous masses of humankind are made as happy as pigs in slop. Plato premises his utopia on the assumption that almost all humans are material boys and girls content only when their purses are filled with gold, their stomachs are stuffed with fattening goodies, and their possessions include the equivalent of a mortgage-free second house on Maui. To make such materialistic folk happy, Plato invents a class of paternalistic guardians who rule a well-ordered economic and political system. Because the guardians manage society so effectively, their followers are able to concentrate fully on trying to satiate their insatiable desires for wealth and sensual pleasure. In Plato's utopia, the masses are happy because they are not burdened by political, moral, and philosophical concerns that get in the way of enjoying gluttony, avarice, lust, and other sources of pleasure.

Were Plato alive today, it is clear what advice he would give us as we struggle with how to live a good life: "Kick back and relax," he would console us, "because only a few extremely smart and virtuous people can understand what the good life really entails. So have a glass of chardonnay, and leave philosophizing to your moral and intellectual betters." Over the millennia, Platonism has been extremely popular with people who measure their lives by the goods they possess and, even more, with those in power who believe the masses are incapable of governing their own animal impulses and, by logical extension, incapable of participating in government.

From his many frustrating and futile debates with Plato, Aristotle came to understand that how one thinks about happiness depends on the assumptions one makes about human nature. The more he thought about Plato's assumptions, the more he questioned whether it was true that people care only about satisfying their animal instincts. Further, he wondered if benevolent

14

dictators can, in fact, create utopia by satisfying their subjects' desires for bread and circuses. Ultimately, Aristotle came to reject both his mentor's premise and his conclusion. He then set out to refute Plato's views about human nature, the structure of a good society, and the wellsprings of individual happiness in his *Politics* and *Nicomachean Ethics*. Rejecting utopianism, he turned to empirical observation as his starting point.

HIERARCHIES AND MORE HIERARCHIES

Aristotle begins with the basics: Observing the human species in all its physical, intellectual, and moral variety, he concludes that its most salient characteristic is its diversity, the manifest and multifold differences found among its members. For example, there are tall people, short people, and lots of people in between. If all adults in the world stand in rank order according to height, the tallest at one end and the shortest at the other, the entire spectrum will be covered, ranging from some 8 feet to less than 4 feet, with the largest concentration around the middle. Most striking, there will be a *hierarchy* from shortest at the bottom to tallest at the top, covering in rank order humanity's incredible range of heights. Hence, Aristotle chooses hierarchy as his master organizing principle, except he doesn't use height to exemplify the main idea he is trying to convey. What he has to say is more controversial and more relevant to the issue of happiness.

15

To Aristotle, height matters only for giraffes. He believes that everything in nature has a purpose, and nothing is created in vain. The single purpose of any animal species is the thing that most distinguishes it from all other species, the thing it does "best." For example, more than any other mammal, the neck of a giraffe allows it to reach soft, nutritious shoots at the tops of tall trees. Ergo, giraffes are built for height. Although all giraffes are tall relative to other animals, there are marked differences among the heights of individual giraffes. So it is better to be a taller giraffe than a shorter one because the taller ones get the best shoots. As Darwin noted in *The Origin of Species,* Aristotle anticipated the theory of natural selection.

To the Ancient, the tallest giraffe is atop the hierarchy of giraffes because it has the salient characteristic of "giraffeness"—height—more fully developed than in any other giraffe. Similarly, he concludes that horses are created for speed because they run faster than other animals (Aristotle had never heard of cheetahs). Hence, the fastest horse is atop the hierarchy of horses because it has the most developed "horseness." Because oxen are the strongest bovines Aristotle knows about, he says strength is the salient characteristic of an ox; thus, the strongest ox is the "best" ox because it has the most fully developed "oxness."

Perhaps you have anticipated where Aristotle is headed: To him, the distinguishing characteristic of the human species is not height, speed, or strength. What most clearly distinguishes humans from other species, what we do best, is reasoning. Aristotle's precision of observation is strikingly scientific. He doesn't say that some humans aren't tall, fast, or strong, or that other animals can't think or don't have feelings. Instead, he says what truly distinguishes humans from other animals is the species' unique ability to engage in abstract thought and to put words to those thoughts. In sum, humanness is reasoning.

Yet, though all humans can reason, not all humans have the same capacity for reasoning. As there is a hierarchy among animal species and all things in nature, Aristotle argues that there is a natural hierarchy among humans, at the top of which are people with the greatest and most fully developed capacity to reason, that is, to engage in abstract thought. He believes that newborn humans are like empty vessels of various sizes, each with a different potential for reasoning. If we liken that capacity to empty milk cartons, some are born with a half-pint capacity and a few with half-gallon potential, but most are clustered around the quart mark. Moreover, the nature of individual capacities differs as well: John may have a large capacity for learning music but a small capacity for physics; Mary may have a large capacity for mathematics but a small capacity for the law. Nonetheless, all healthy humans possess at least some capacity for learning, reasoning, and speculative and moral thought.

Aristotle asks us to consider why we possess this higher-level human capacity. He concludes that there can be no other purpose in having it than to use it; therefore, we each fulfill our humanness by developing our naturally given potential. To him, it is a sign of wisdom to seek out the natural flow of things and then to go in that direction, as it is a sign of foolishness to fight Mother Nature. Hence, he says those who pursue "the good life" aim at fulfilling their highest-order human capabilities. The alternative, to choose to act like an animal, is absurd, irrational, and unhuman.

THE EQUALITY (AND INEQUALITY) OF THE SPECIES

17

Because Aristotle sees members of the human species as inherently unequal in their ability to engage in abstract reasoning, modern critics have been inclined to throw out his philosophy on the grounds of political incorrectness. Clearly, the major error in Aristotle's observations is his conclusion that observed differences among individuals are linked to the social class, caste, or gender to which they belong. Living in an age when slavery was rampant, Aristotle observed that slaves in Athens never engaged in higher-order intellectual activities; there were no slave politicians or philosophers. Instead, slaves behaved slavishly, engaging solely in repetitive toil, doing only what their masters bade them. Based on this observation, Aristotle concluded that there are "natural slaves" incapable of higher-order reasoning. His notion stood for some 2,000 years, until French philosopher Jean-Jacques Rousseau identified the logical error in the Ancient's thinking. "Aristotle was doubtless right" in terms of his observation, Rousseau wrote in 1740, that slaves do behave in a servile way. But they do so because they are beaten by their masters when they try to do otherwise. Hence, Rousseau explained, "Aristotle mistook the cause for the effect."

Because Aristotle's mistaken belief that caste differences are "natural" has been so thoroughly refuted, we may assume that Aristotle himself would have been convinced by Rousseau's logic and would have come to agree that his own philosophy is made more just, robust, and universal when applied equally to all humans. In fact, Aristotle's ideas are more logical if the observed differences among people are viewed as reflecting the variety of abilities and aptitudes found among individuals instead of as group traits. In the next chapter, we see how Harriet Taylor Mill "improved" Aristotle by expanding his conclusions to include women.

So it is safe for us to interpret Aristotle's notion of differences in a way to make it self-evidently true: People are as manifestly unequal in terms of their natural abilities as they are in terms of their height, but there is no reason to conclude that those differences demand differences in treatment. Quite the opposite, because on the issue mattering most to Aristotle, he himself recognizes that everyone is capable of learning and capable of development. While he believes individual potential is fixed at birth, he does not see this as an excuse for those with the smallest capacities not to try to develop their minds to the full. He argues that no one, regardless of the size of his or her potential, ever succeeds in fulfilling it. Therefore, the good life comes about from the process of *filling*, that is, learning, and not from the impossible end of a *filled* container, an idea as absurd as the Gary Larson cartoon depicting a grade school student with hand raised, asking: "Teacher, may I go home? My brain is full."

Proof we never fulfill our potential is found in the fact that all healthy people can continue to learn, even in extreme old age. Indeed, Aristotle says that developing our minds is the one activity everyone can engage in equally in old age. Because today's men and women in their fifties can expect to live at least another three decades, his insight is even more important now than in his time, when few people survived through their sixties.

Nonetheless, Aristotle is not saying Grandpa Bill ever will be as adept at learning French as Grandma Sue is or, conversely, that she can end up playing pinochle as well as he, no matter how hard he tries or how long she lives. One person simply has a greater capacity than another for learning one thing or another. In this way, Aristotle claims that people are different *and* unequal. He is fair and logical, but not relativistic, as we now shall see.

WHY POLITICS AND PHILOSOPHY TOP THE HIERARCHY OF HUMAN ENDEAVORS

He is particularly nonrelativistic when it comes to evaluating different types of activities. He would say the ability to ride a bike is not equal to the ability to perform heart surgery. Instead, there is a natural hierarchy of human activities (to Aristotle, there is a hierarchy of everything), and the measure of an activity is the degree to which it requires the highest-order, most abstract, mental capabilities. It is simply harder to learn calculus than arithmetic. Yet, as a believer in human development, he argues that a great many people who quit studying math after arithmetic would be surprised to learn that they are, in fact, capable of learning much more, up to and including calculus. He adds that if they make the effort to do so, they are likely to have the sense of fulfillment he calls happiness. (Of course, calculus wasn't invented until nearly 2,000 years after Aristotle's death. Here and throughout the book, I freely use anachronistic examples to illustrate Aristotle's timeless ideas.)

19

Aristotle concludes that the highest-order, most-human activities are "politics and philosophy" because these require the greatest deployment of abstract reasoning. This assertion is easily misinterpreted. Aristotle is not assuming that only people engaged in his kind of philosophy are using their full range of abilities. He is not so proscriptive. In the category of philosophy, he includes all of what we call the sciences, arts, and learned professions. Thus, engineers, lawyers, and doctors are "philosophers," as are journalists, teachers, playwrights, and so on through the professions. In the category of philosophers, he includes people who are merely studying those subjects, not just those who make their living practicing them. Likewise, he includes more than those serving in elected office when he talks about politics. To Aristotle, that category includes what we call community service, unpaid as well as paid. Later we see why he would include leadership of business organizations in his catchall category of politics.

The important thing to Aristotle is not a person's job, profession, or career; rather, it is the extent to which an individual is using his or her higher-order mental capabilities. Thus, his concepts of philosophy and politics should be thought of as inclusive: A factory worker who participates in decision making and problem solving is using those higher-level capabilities every bit as much as is the company's CEO.

Still, there is no denying that Aristotle is judgmental and elitist in a way that's unfashionable today. He not only believes there is a hierarchy of humans, he is willing to state who is at the top! Using the same principle of organization he applies to animals, he says individuals atop the human hierarchy are those who have both the greatest natural capacity for and, more important, the most fully developed potential in politics and philosophy. Granted, this is not the way we speak in an era in which the equality of our species is a given. Nonetheless, for good or ill, it is the way economists think and the way in which the hierarchical structure of organizations is justified, even if unconsciously.

ARISTOTELIAN MICROECONOMICS

Aristotle is an astute economist who understands markets and monopolies and whose writings about the division of labor anticipated the work of Adam Smith by over 2,000 years. In describing a proper and just division of labor, he links his observations about the hierarchy of human abilities to the broader social structure of society, arguing that people atop the natural hierarchy should be engaged in tasks where they can make the maximum contribution.

For example, it would do the people of Athens no good if those who possessed the greatest aptitude to design and build large structures, like the Parthenon, weren't doing so because they were denied the opportunity to develop their engineering capabilities. Justice would be lacking in a society where a person (say the brilliant mathematician Pythagoras) who had great technical potential ended up stuck for life in a cobbler's shop retreading soles on sandals. Indeed, Aristotle argues that the reason Athens is such a highly developed society in 400 B.C., and why most other places in the world are mired in the stage of subsistence agriculture, is exactly because the Athenians freed their most-talented individuals from the tyranny of toil and gave them the leisure to develop science, medicine, engineering, and the arts. Aristotle believes if Pythagoras had been born "barbarian" (non-Greek), he probably would have spent his life pushing a plow. No wonder barbarians didn't create acropolises: *They treated everyone as equals.*

To an Aristotelian, the great mathematician Euclid, another student of Plato, is not equal either to a person whose maximum capacity to contribute to society is pushing a plow, or to a high-capacity person who is satisfied with mere plow pushing. To deny one with Euclid's potential the opportunity to develop his skills in the name of equality is, in Aristotle's view, unjust. Worse, how can justice be served if those with limited capabilities are made leaders of society, or the bosses of enterprises, while those who have the greatest natural capacities are held down at the bottom carrying out orders?

Aristotle observes such injustice in the monarchies of his era, where princes impose their wills on people who are smarter, more productive, and more virtuous than they are. He thinks such systems are as unjust as ones in which less-capable people rule in the name of equality. Such was the case in Mao's China, where uneducated Communist cadres could veto managerial decisions made by engineers and other professionals. Equality may be served in such societies, but the collective good of the community is compromised. The Ancient concludes that meritocracy is the most just form of governance because everyone benefits from the rule of the most competent.

Paradoxically, for a philosopher concerned with personal happiness, Aristotle's ultimate point of reference is the overall good of the community and not the welfare of the individual. Although it may seem odd today, Aristotle believes that the natural hierarchy of humans should not serve as an excuse to reward those at the top for having been born with good genes, or to make the burden of life easier for those so privileged. He believes the opposite: *People at the top of a social or organizational hierarchy are responsible for making it possible for those lower down to lead good lives.* When they do, everyone benefits from inequalities based on real capabilities and economic contribution. Using a modern example, the reason Bill Gates and Steve Ballmer should make executive decisions at Microsoft is not because authority is their right, their due, their reward, or what satisfies their egos; instead, having the most qualified minds at the top of the company is in the best interest of all members of the organization, including those lower down. Who would want to work at Microsoft if equality were its main goal and the company's executive team had an average IQ of 100, while Gates, Ballmer, and the rest of the brain trust were assigned work as security guards?

To Aristotle, individuals capable of making greater contributions should be treated differently than those capable of only smaller ones. But differently in some respects only. In particular, those with the greatest capabilities should be freed from lower-level work so they can concentrate on activities making maximum use of their potential and social contribution. The question then becomes, *How large a share of the bounty produced by an organization are those at the top entitled to reap?* In a later chapter, we examine several Aristotelian tests of fairness of the distribution of rewards, but it is sufficient here to say corporate leaders like Gates and Ballmer are rewarded justly for their contributions if they have worked hard, if they have increased the wealth of society, and if they have made it possible for everyone in their organization to develop their full potential. It will require a greater understanding of Aristotle before we can see how to reckon who deserves how much.

ARISTOTLE'S CRITICS

There is a formidable list of critics who have supplied thoughtful arguments against Aristotle's way of thinking: Hobbes, Rousseau, the Mills (Harriet Taylor and John Stuart), and Bertrand Russell are some of the stars of philosophy who, over the centuries, offered refutations to the Ancient's ideas. Today, some modern conservatives argue he is "naïve," "impractical," and "anti-wealth creation" and, on the left, postmodernists claim he is "elitist" and "morally prescriptive." One thoughtful recent critic, David Denby, ends up rejecting the near entirety of Aristotle's philosophy because

> I could not dismiss politically correct objections; nor would I want to. No matter how you look at it—and no matter what qualifying historical context you place it in—Aristotle made a disastrous mistake.

Indeed, Aristotle's "disastrous mistake" of political incorrectness has led an entire generation of scholars to question his fitness to stand as a moral guide.

So, are Aristotle's ideas outmoded? Are they impractical, naïve, antibusiness, elitist, and politically incorrect, as his critics on the left and right claim in their briefs against him? In my reading, Aristotle turns out to be quite a modern fellow, particularly for one now 2,400 years old. Properly understood, the world according to Aristotle corresponds remarkably with contemporary thinking about human capabilities and meritocracy and about how organizations should be structured to maximize effectiveness. He was also deeply concerned with what we today call *social responsibility*. And if Aristotle wasn't exactly a capitalist, he was a protocapitalist to the extent that his ideas are consistent with modern economic concepts, particularly the linkage of rewards to contributions.

In the middle of a lecture at the Lyceum in 312 B.C. or thereabouts, we can imagine the gray-bearded Aristotle being interrupted by Simplicius, one of his students: "Tell us, Professor, why is it that philosophers are not rich if they know so much?" Aristotle takes no offense. In his mid-fifties, he has a secure sense of who he is and what he believes. If he winces, it is in recognition of how obnoxious he must have seemed years earlier when he had challenged his own teacher, Plato, at the Academy. So Aristotle restrains himself from giving the easy answer: an accounting of his landholdings and gold stashed away for his old age. Instead, he replies: "You raise an interesting question, one best answered by telling a true story about the great Milesian philosopher, Thales, whose work you doubtless recall we discussed last semester . . .

> Certain cynical people in Milesia reproached Thales for his poverty, saying it proved philosophy was of no use. So, to make a point, Thales decided to engage in a little demonstration. He was a skilled meteorologist and, from his analysis of the weather in the dead of winter, he concluded there was going to be a bumper crop of olives during the next year. So he leased all the olive presses in Miletus, which he got at a low price because no one bid against him. Then, when harvest time came and the presses were suddenly in great demand, he rented them out at exorbitant rates and made a windfall profit. Thus, he showed that philosophers can easily be rich, but their ambition is of another sort.

Aristotle pauses to decide how much he should explain to his students and how much he should leave them to discover for themselves. He then proceeds: "Doubtless you see the impoverished and 'impractical' Thales understood the workings of the most complicated of economic concepts: supply and demand, monopoly rents, and futures markets? So, then, would someone in the class explain the point of Thales' demonstration?"

"I get it, Prof," an eager pupil exclaims. "Thales is showing us that almost anyone can learn the ins and outs of finance, learn to play markets, and do economic calculations. In contrast, he wants us to see that few people are able to answer the questions occupying the minds of philosophers: *What is justice?*

What is a good life? What is a good society? What is happiness? He wants to show it is better to spend more time trying to answer such tough, important questions than working on easier, practical ones, right?"

And to be able to answer such profound questions, Aristotle tells his class, one must learn to think like a philosopher. "Of course," he admits, remembering his disagreements with Plato, "not all philosophers end up with the same conclusions because they start in different places and their arguments rest on different basic assumptions. That's why we spend so much class time testing the basic concepts underlying our arguments. If our foundation is rotten, our entire intellectual edifice crumbles when challenged."

So, as I read and thought more about Aristotle, I realized that the intellectual excuses I had used to keep him at bay were faulty. But I still wasn't ready to face the behavioral consequences of accepting his counsel. Intellectually, I grasped the undergirding of his thinking and was ready to see how he constructs the edifice of his moral philosophy on that foundation. But still I resisted. Emotionally, I wasn't ready to get out of the familiar rut I was in. It still didn't "feel right" that engaging in Aristotelian politics and philosophy would lead me to happiness.

25

AND YOU?

It's time for you to take your own temperature before moving on to practical applications of Aristotle's admittedly difficult and unusual way of thinking. Here are a few questions you might want to consider asking yourself: Where am I searching to find happiness? What are the main lines of resistance I habitually use when confronted with new ways of thinking that challenge my basic assumptions and upset my comfort level? Are those mechanisms in fact useful, or do they keep me from considering other, possibly more promising, ways of finding true happiness? Are those mechanisms the obstacles on my personal life map that prevent me from achieving the ends I desire?

2

WHAT IS HAPPINESS?

HAPPINESS, LIVING BLISSFULLY AND BEAUTIFULLY, IS SAID TO CONSIST
MAINLY OF THREE THINGS WHICH SEEM MOST DESIRABLE: SOME SAY
WISDOM IS THE GREATEST GOOD, SOME HONOR, AND SOME PLEASURE.
SOME ALSO DISPUTE THE MAGNITUDE OF THE CONTRIBUTION MADE BY
EACH OF THESE ELEMENTS, SOME DECLARING THE CONTRIBUTION OF
ONE TO BE GREATER, SOME SAYING WISDOM IS A GREATER GOOD THAN
HONOR, SOME THE OPPOSITE, WHILE OTHERS REGARD PLEASURE
AS A GREATER GOOD THAN EITHER. AND SOME CONSIDER HAPPINESS
TO BE A COMPOUND OF ALL, OR OF TWO, OF THESE, WHILE OTHERS
SAY IT CONSISTS OF ONE ALONE.

—ARISTOTLE

Is happiness success at work? Fame? Power? A few million in high-yield, safe investments? The respect of one's peers? Having more toys than everyone else in your yacht club? An afternoon in a secluded mountain glen smelling wildflowers with the one you love? Lusty sex? Good health? Or is happiness "all of the above," "none of the above," or "fill in the blank"? Of course, the practical answer is: "It all depends on whom you ask."

Aristotle acknowledges that happiness typically is defined in personal and relative terms: His fellow Athenians defined it as whatever made them feel "blissful." Today, thinking about happiness still brings out the relativist in nearly everyone. We each speak of happiness—more precisely, the source of happiness—as the ultimate among all forms of personal preference.

But Aristotle refused to accept the common wisdom and was convinced he could demonstrate that happiness has a definite meaning and definable source. His argument found favor 2,200 years later with Thomas Jefferson, whose famous Aristotelian phrase "the pursuit of happiness" is indelibly engraved in the memory of most every American. It's difficult to cite another historical figure more fully Aristotelian than the third president of the United States. Jefferson echoed nearly every aspect of Aristotle's views on ethics, politics, and the good life, even the few manifestly misguided ones. Because most of us believe that Jefferson's pursuit of happiness is a worthy endeavor, it is incumbent on us to learn what he and Aristotle meant by those words. In so doing, we discover the relevance of Aristotle's definition of happiness to the challenge of effective life planning.

"THE PURSUIT OF HAPPINESS"

In my own struggle to identify what would make me happy, I did what teachers often do when intellectually puzzled: I turned to my students for help. I asked several classes of MBA students to define what, in the final analysis, they wanted from their careers and lives. Most of these ambitious young people replied with variations on the old "I just wanna be happy" theme. In this regard, they were fervent Jeffersonians who revered the author of the Declaration of Independence because he said they had a right to pursue happiness. When I asked these young people what precisely they were pursuing, some of their lists featured *beaches, beer, Beemers,* and *blondes.*

But is it true that the Sage of Monticello had material and sensual pleasures in mind when he penned that lofty phrase about the right to pursue happiness? It turns out we know exactly what Jefferson meant because he was an Aristotelian through and through, so, as they say, "you could look it up." That's what I did with a perusal of passages Jefferson underscored in his copies of Aristotle's *Politics* and *Nicomachean Ethics,* which still grace the shelves of the Library of Congress. Because it is unlikely that readers of this book will have an opportunity to haunt the stacks in the Madison Building, here's a translation of what it says in Jefferson's leather-bound, Latin volume of the *Ethics*: Happiness is "an activity of the soul in accordance with virtue, and if there is more than one virtue, in accordance with the best and most complete . . . and in a complete life."

Even in translation, that's not very helpful. It's abstract, general, and certainly doesn't conform to the way moderns think. In fact, almost everyone associates happiness with the mental state of "feeling good." However, Aristotle says it is "an activity." He elaborates, explaining that happiness is the "highest of all goods achievable by actions." Apparently, happiness is something we do rather than something we feel. Then he says it is an activity "in accordance with virtue." Not even my students would talk about a day at the beach in terms of virtue.

Aristotle's happiness is something one accomplishes, more a product of our moral actions than a psychological condition. Moreover, it is neither fleeting nor a momentary thing; it is not measured by the hour, day, or week, nor is it a postponable gratification enjoyed at retirement. Instead, it is *a complete life led in accordance with virtue.* As I stood in the stacks on Capitol Hill reading Jefferson's book, happiness sounded more like a duty than an inalienable right.

What Aristotle and Jefferson mean by happiness turns out to be so counterintuitive that our initial reaction is to assume they must be wrong. Everybody knows happiness is about feeling good now, or as soon as possible.

To see how Aristotle arrives at his unconventional definition, we need to reflect on where he starts. He begins his analysis with one of his many hierarchies: Happiness is the highest good in the hierarchy of all the things that are good for us. How do we know happiness is the greatest of those many and various goods? Because it is the "only thing we seek for its own sake and never for the sake of something else." By this he means no one would ever say, "I want to be happy in order to be rich" or "I want happiness in order to be powerful, beautiful, or respected." Thus, happiness must be the highest end we seek.

In most cultures, we find the same common sense and practical idea of happiness: *It is the highest end being sought in this life.* When we were growing up, we read about a cowardly lion who said, "I want to be brave in order to be happy," about an airhead scarecrow who said, "I want to be smart to be happy," and about a rusty-hearted tin man who wanted friends (love) in order to be happy. Although stories in other times and cultures differ, the relationship of cause to effect is the same. In the myths of ancient Greece that Aristotle was taught in his youth, no one, neither mortals nor the gods, wanted happiness in order to get something else.

> If, then, there is some end of the things we do, which we desire for its own sake (everything else being desired for the sake of this), and if we do not choose everything for the sake of something else (for at that rate, the process would go on to infinity so that our desire would be empty and vain), clearly this must be the good and the chief good.

Translation: If happiness is not the "chief good," the alternative is, logically, absurd. Comedian Henry Youngman captured that absurdity when he asked, "What's the use of happiness? It can't buy you money." As the son of the cowardly lion, John Lahr says, "No one courts fame out of happiness." Therefore, happiness must be the supreme end to which we aspire, and every other good must be a means to that end.

My students are at least in line with Aristotle when they identify happiness as the goal of their careers and lives. But will the sensual and material goods they seek make them happy if they obtain them? Plato thought they would. He believed that material boys and girls were made perfectly content by an abundance of such goods as beer and Beemers. Aristotle grants that such goods may bring momentary pleasure, and that there is nothing wrong with a modicum of such pleasure. Nonetheless, he would argue that my students would not be truly happy if they had those goods because they still would need other goods, as well. If so, what other goods would my sensually satiated students be missing?

WHAT WE ALL NEED TO BE HAPPY

Here's the question Aristotle poses: What is the full complement of goods all people *need* to be happy? In answering, Aristotle begins with basics. He states a self-evident proposition: Though human desires differ, we all have the same needs for food, water, clothing, shelter, and good health. This is also a clue to what Jefferson meant by the phrase "all men are created equal." Because all humans are equally members of the same species, all have the same basic needs. For example, both Aristotle and Jefferson believe that everyone needs other people; we need others for love, family, friendship, and a sense of community.

Aristotle says normal people need not only the companionship of others, they need it more than just occasionally, much as having enough food for only one day is insufficient. In his most-quoted line from *Ethics*, Aristotle writes, "For one swallow does not make a summer, nor does one day; and so, too, one day, or a short time, does not make a man blessed and happy." Thus, to say particular people are happy, we have to be assured they have adequate food, clothing, and shelter throughout the course of their lives and some companionship from the time they are young until the end of their days. Can we call people happy who don't possess at least these few necessities for most of their lives?

Aristotle is aware of individuals who "stand alone," lone wolves who don't seem to want or need anybody else. But he tells us that such people must be "either gods or beasts" because their behavior is so contrary to the norm for our species. To him, the needs of a few social misfits who behave in nonhuman ways are not valid indicators of what people need in order to be happy. Exceptions don't invalidate the self-evident rule that the majority of the species has a small set of needs in common.

For the most part, what Aristotle says is common sense, but at the same time, it can be counterintuitive. He makes us want to argue with him: Wait a second, Aristotle. If the measure of happiness is a *complete* life well led, how come we so readily attribute happiness to children? We say children are happy, Aristotle explains, "by reason of the hope we have for them" and not by virtue of what they have accomplished, because "even the most prosperous may fall into great misfortune" as they grow older. He anticipates most of our objections. First, he grants the obvious: A complete life well led requires an element of good luck; the happiest of youngsters have a lot of time ahead of them to encounter sources of misery and woe. Even people who are happy in their mid-fifties aren't home safe: Aristotle describes Greeks in antiquity who were seemingly happy, but as they grew older, terrible luck befell them. They lost their money, their friends died, and, when they grew ill or prematurely feeble their children abandoned them. Aristotle asks, Could one say such once-fortunate people led happy lives? No, only if individuals have had (a) material basics, (b) good friends, and (c) good luck *throughout most of their lives* can we begin to say they are happy.

Still, Aristotle says such fortunate people are happy only in the way an elk might be said to have led a good life if it lived to old age, in good health, in a peaceable herd, in a vegetation-rich predator-free forest, having mated often, and never having wanted for food or drink. He concedes that humans share that kind of basic contentment with other animals. But he reminds us that humans aren't simply animals. We want more than basics. The long march of human civilization is about our species' collective desire to have more than bread on the table, animal skins on our backs, a lean-to shelter in winter, and sex on the hoof. Humans clearly won't be satisfied with a life in which only their animal needs are met. They want something more. Plato says they want more goodies. But is it really desire for material things that separates us from beasts, and if not, what does our species truly strive for?

Aristotle tells us "each thing is made for one purpose only," and as we have seen, that purpose for humans is the exercise of our capacity for higher-order reasoning. He says what we strive for is to develop that capacity. Happiness, he thus asserts, comes from trying to make ourselves the best humans we are capable of becoming. Because that conclusion isn't obvious, and to better understand Aristotle's reasoning, let's fast-forward a few millennia to examine briefly how modern psychologists define the source of human happiness. Their efforts may help clarify what seems obscure.

MODERN PSYCHOLOGICAL PERSPECTIVES ON HAPPINESS

Although many psychologists view happiness as a subjective feeling associated with hedonistic pleasures, a number who are Aristotelian in orientation argue, instead, that happiness is the objective result of how we live. One of the strongest Aristotelian definitions of happiness was offered by Erich Fromm, who employed the Greek word the Ancient used for happiness, *eudaimonia,* to make a distinction between

> those needs (desires) that are only subjectively felt and whose
> satisfaction leads to momentary pleasure, and those needs
> that are rooted in human nature and whose realization is con-

ducive to human growth and produces eudaimonia, or well-being. In other words . . . the distinction between purely subjectively felt needs and objectively valid needs—part of the former being harmful to human growth and the latter being in accordance with the requirements of human nature.

As Fromm explains, Aristotle's highest good, eudaimonia, has little to do with the feelings of pleasure and contentment typically implied in modern usage of the word *happiness*. In fact, what he means by happiness is something like *the deep sense of satisfaction one gets when one grows as a human being.* And that turns out to be approximately what many modern psychologists mean when they describe happiness. For example, although the psychologist Abraham Maslow was not as avowedly Aristotelian as Fromm was, his famous "hierarchy of needs" corresponds with Aristotle's hierarchy of goods. Maslow posited that humans progress up a ladder of needs, starting with the basics: food, water, and clothing. His hierarchy culminates with self-actualization, the state of fulfilling one's potential. Aristotle never uses the term *self-actualization,* but his highest good, the development of our uniquely human capabilities, amounts to roughly the same thing. Yet, Maslow and Aristotle aren't exactly on the same page. For example, Aristotle complicates matters when he elaborates on the nature of the good at the top of his hierarchy:

33

> If happiness is activity in accordance with *virtue*, it is reasonable that it should be in accordance with the highest virtue; and this will be *the best thing in us.* . . . That activity is *contemplation.*

The words I italicized—*virtue, the best thing in us*, and *contemplation*—require explanation. Although they seem dated and subjective, in fact these concepts are surprisingly consistent with the latest scientific research about the nature of happiness. In the 1990s, psychologist Martin Seligman initiated a research effort designed to discover how people can better move up Maslow's hierarchy.

Some 60 psychologists have taken part in this research, and they are learning that happiness isn't simply genetic or a matter of luck or circumstances. Contrary to conventional wisdom, it isn't caused by social standing, wealth, or even living in garden spots (so much for my African isles Geographic Solution).

Counterintuitively, the research indicates that happiness can be learned, and, therefore, there are things one can do to make oneself happier. Having good relationships with others helps, as does setting a progression of life and career goals. Another source of happiness is learning to do things that are good for you; for example, learning to enjoy healthy food in sensible quantities. Some of this research directly validates Aristotle's theory that happiness entails an entire lifespan and amounts to "the striving for perfection that represents the realization of one's true potential." In the end, the researchers find that people are made happy by pursuing "what is best in them." Seligman concludes that happiness is "the emotion that arises when we do something that stems from our strengths and virtues." In sum, Seligman and his colleagues have reinvented Aristotle's concept of happiness as a *virtue* that derives from developing *the best thing in us*.

Similarly, Aristotle's concept of *contemplation* has been dressed up in modern psychological lingo. Mihaly Csikszentmihalyi's notion that happiness equates with "flow" is one of the hottest ideas in psychology today. To him, flow is the ineffable feeling enjoyed by creative artists and writers when they are so absorbed in what they are doing that they lose track of time and place. In this blissful condition, one doesn't think about anything else, and all worries and concerns are set aside. Skilled athletes call this being "in the zone." Weekend warriors have enough of a taste of being in the zone to appreciate the blissful feeling Michael Jordan must have gotten when totally wrapped up in a game of basketball. Watching him in action, we saw the pleasure in his eyes. But one needn't be a sports star to get into the zone. My aunt Virginia tells me she gets the feeling while painting ceramics. I have experienced it writing these chapters. I know I have been in the zone when I look at the clock and discover I have been at work for many hours, though it felt like minutes.

In part, Csikszentmihalyi's "flow" comes from doing what we love to do. And the Aristotelian test of good work is that you would do it even if you weren't paid. Although this definition fits professional sports to a tee, the problem is that no one can play basketball 24/7 or engage in high-level competitive sports for all one's life. The recently retired Michael Jordan now must come to grips with what Aristotle understood long ago: Contemplation is the only activity that is absorbing "good work" for all one's life. Unfortunately, contemplation sounds like what former California governor Jerry Brown did when he meditated or what Einstein did while creating elegant equations. Though Aristotle's notion covers those activities, it also includes other forms of positively absorbing mental work: playing a piano, woodworking, solving a scientific problem in a laboratory, and hundreds more sources of bliss.

One might expect that economists would be among the least likely of professionals to find bliss at work, given the materialistic nature of the subject they contemplate. Yet history records no better example of being in the zone than the behavior of the author of *Wealth of Nations*. When Adam Smith was living in Scotland in the 18th century, he would lose track of time and wander for hours all over Glasgow and into the adjacent countryside. One day, while contemplating some peculiarly elusive economic concept, the absentminded Smith was observed to stumble headfirst into an especially noisome sewage ditch. When later asked about the golden years he had spent in solitary contemplation, Smith called them "by far the happiest and most-honorable part of my life."

There is, in fact, a new field called "happiness economics," which has demonstrated that people who become rich don't get any happier as a result, largely because they are on a "hedonic treadmill" which causes them continually to want more as they acquire more. Some of this is silly: *The Economist* cites one study concluding that the degree of marital happiness can be quantified by subtracting the number of spousal spats from the frequency of intercourse! Laugh we may, but the 2002 Nobel Prize in economics was shared by Daniel Kahneman, who, by way of an experiment in which students picked their favorite flavors of ice cream, demonstrated that most people cannot accurately predict what will make them happy.

If that is true, Michael Jordan may find an unexpected source of bliss now that he is retired from basketball and taking on mental work. Granted, when Jordan tried in his late thirties to change from the pursuit of physical pleasure to the pursuit of intellectual satisfaction, he failed. He discovered he couldn't get into the zone and went back to the hard courts in search of satisfaction, concluding he was "born to play basketball." But that doesn't mean he can't learn to find bliss in contemplation. If Aristotle is right, Jordan failed the first time because he had tried contemplation only once, and because he was too young when he did.

I speak with some confidence because I was once like Michael Jordan. I was never rich, handsome, talented, or famous, and although I am nearly 6'2", even in my prime I couldn't dunk a basketball. Yet I once shared a weakness in common with His Airness: *youth*. I discovered the importance of this passing similarity when, at age 50, I resolved to pick up a copy of Plato's *The Republic* and finally read what Aristotle's teacher had to say. To my surprise, the next day I found a dog-eared copy of the book in my study. When I began to leaf through it, I noticed that someone had underscored numerous passages in the text and written helpful comments in the margins. Most surprising, whoever had made those notes had done so in my hand!

After a long search of my memory, I recalled taking an introductory philosophy course in my junior year of college. In the end-of-course evaluation, I had dinged the professor because he hadn't been helpful in explaining the most difficult texts I had ever encountered. I had blamed him for my lack of understanding (and mediocre grade), but now, as I reread his lecture notes (dutifully transcribed by the young me), I discovered he had been an insightful commentator on Plato's classic. The real problem had been my immaturity. I didn't get it when I was 20—but, in hindsight, I now understand that the fault had been my own. Because I had so little life experience in 1965, there had been no context within which I could make sense of Plato. Not only that, I subsequently forgot having read *The Republic* and, thus, made no use of its wisdom over the next 3 decades. Now I found the book a relatively easy read, full of useful insights, and relevant to organizational and political issues I had struggled with over the years. At one moment, I caught myself thinking, "I wish I had read this earlier."

Most of us are not yet ready to pursue happiness à la Aristotle when we are young, and when we are ready to do so, we must discipline ourselves to try to find pleasure in activities we tasted but found unpalatable in our youth. The work of psychologist Erik Erikson and others supports Aristotle's conclusion that contemplation is the one blissful activity we all can engage in for all of our lives and the one we appreciate and benefit most from as we grow older. In sum, modern psychologists have validated much of what Aristotle intuited. But unlike modern researchers, he reached his conclusions by way of reasoning, observation, and a touch of religious faith.

THE BEASTLY AND THE DIVINE

Aristotle observes a duality in the "souls" of humans. He calls the best in us "divine," or most like "the gods," and the worst "beastly," or animal-like. In some ways, his "divine" and "beastly" categories of souls correspond with Freud's "ego" and "id" aspects of our psyches. And to become happy (Aristotle) and healthy (Freud), both believe we should try "to accentuate the positive and eliminate the negative." But what exactly must we do to be more divine and less beastly, to develop a healthy ego strong enough to keep our id in check? Here the psychiatrist and the philosopher differ: The former prescribes analysis, the latter contemplation.

Aristotle again starts with the fact that humans are animals, but, he optimistically observes, we are "the best of the animals." Setting us apart and above the others is our ability to engage in abstract thought. But that isn't of much practical use. How should we spend our time if we want to be less beastly and more divine? Aristotle's answer, "in contemplation," is not helpful, particularly when he says that activity has "no direct use." Ethereal contemplation seems a bit like the subject of the famous Cambridge University toast to the study of higher mathematics: "May it never be of any use to anyone." Indeed, because mathematics is the most abstract form of reasoning, Aristotle cites it as the prime example of contemplation.

So is that it? To get more human and less beastly, we should study Boolean algebra? A fuller reading of the Ancient leads to a broader definition of the concept he uses to distinguish us from beasts. For starters, humans differ from animals in the way we perceive time. Beasts are ahistorical: They know nothing of the generations preceding them and think nothing about the future facing their kind. Only humans understand that they had grandparents and know they may have grandchildren who will live on after them. And we are never more uniquely human than when, living in the present, we are conscious of both the past and the future. Indeed, when we are fully conscious in this way, we are most godlike in Aristotle's view. Hence, studying history, and planning to create a better future, are preeminently human and virtuous forms of contemplation.

Although Aristotle was the first scholar to engage consciously in empirical research, he also speculated on the activities of the gods. He wonders what daily activity they engage in: Are the gods like animals, struggling over territory and mating rights, devoting their every effort to satisfying basic instincts? Or, are they like us? Do they have bad habits? Do they imbibe too much, or are they greedy? Aristotle answers "No" to all of the above. Because humans worship the gods, he assumes that the gods must be worthy of our respect. Hence, they can't be like us, struggling with urges to overindulge in fish cakes (the Athenian equivalent of ice cream), and trying to stay on the wagon and out of the way of temptation with our neighbor's spouse. So are the gods then engaged in practical matters, as in business and finance? He answers: "Will not the gods seem absurd if they make contracts and return deposits?" Please, the gods do not concern themselves with matters of profit and loss!

But they must be doing *something*. They are, Aristotle supposes, engaged in deep contemplation about the most theoretical, abstract, and, therefore, most difficult and important moral issues: *What is right and wrong? What is justice? How should the universe be ordered?* Aristotle concludes that the gods spend their leisure time in such contemplation and, if we wish to be more than animals, that we should follow their example.

In sum, we are least beastly when we engage in moral deliberations and when we use our uniquely human ability to make distinctions based on abstract reasoning. Thus, contemplative activity is "the best thing in us," and we act the most godlike when we seek to understand the great ideas that have troubled the minds of humans in all cultures and eras. Moreover, we are free to act godlike if we so choose, because the divine capacity for contemplation is present in all our souls.

THE HIGHEST GOOD

Aristotle also says we are virtuous when we engage in contemplation. Virtuous people partake in theoretical and abstract reasoning not simply to find answers to great questions, but to find real pleasure in the asking. "All men by nature want to know," he tells us. Because the ability to know is the best thing about humans, he concludes that reasoning well should be our highest goal. Additionally, trying to reason well brings us virtue because, in doing so, we pursue excellence, which Aristotle equated with "the highest good."

In practical terms, Aristotle was teaching Athenian leaders the importance of excellence. To achieve excellence, they needed to develop the capacity to engage in disciplined explorations of profound questions—ones that illuminate basic truths and examine fundamental questions about the human condition. He observed that business and political leaders of his era spent too little time on, and attached too little importance to, such issues. Those leaders lacked virtue because they neither saw the need to build their own capacity to contemplate nor believed it important for their followers to do so.

The leadership practices of Theodore Roosevelt provide a useful illustration of Aristotelian excellence. Throughout his life, T.R. invariably made full use of his inherited wealth and social standing as the means to living a full and good life, developing his talents, and serving society. Before he was 40, Roosevelt made his mark as an author, cowboy, civil servant, and soldier. He never met a subject he wasn't curious to learn more about. He made serious study of paleontology, ornithology, mammalogy, criminology, technology, geography, and history, in addition to his major field of geopolitics. Over his life, he read some 20,000 books, ranging from Aristotle to Tolstoy and, in his spare time, wrote 15 of his own, not to mention all his own public speeches and scores of long and loving letters to his children. But the youngest president depicted on Mount Rushmore was far from bookish. He was an avid horseman, tennis player, boxer, mountain climber, and bodybuilder who never walked anywhere he could run.

Roosevelt's goal was to leave the world a better place, and to that end, he tirelessly advanced the causes of conservation, democracy, and political reform. He was a work-in-progress until the day he died, constantly seeking new knowledge and experience and using it to test and refine his ideas. Although he was principled—some said opinionated—when presented with facts and sound analysis to the contrary, he was willing to admit he was wrong and to change course accordingly. When faced with the challenge of creating national policy to control monopolies, T.R. threw himself into the study of antitrust, working long hours to master a field about which he had little previous knowledge. As the result of applying his reason to the subject, he arrived at a position different from his party's. More concerned with doing the virtuous thing than satisfying campaign contributors, T.R. was Aristotelian to the extreme.

Aristotle warns that leaders cannot achieve excellence unless they pursue "noble and divine" objectives. But what is a "noble" objective? Because humans have the unique ability to ask "what is justice," leadership excellence entails trying to create a society or organization aimed at justice. To attempt less is to be less than human, less than excellent, less than virtuous, and less than noble. Put positively, leaders who try to create a good life for others exercise the noble human capacities that lead to a good life and happiness for themselves.

Aristotle doesn't propose that leaders should abandon practical matters and just think great thoughts. Instead, they should make the link between their practical actions and the consequences of those actions on others—in particular, the extent to which such actions allow their followers to pursue happiness. An Aristotelian assessment that certain leaders lack virtue is not based on disagreement with their policies; instead, it is reserved for those who make policy mindlessly, without the full application of moral reasoning. The issue isn't right or wrong; instead, it is thoughtful or thoughtless. Aristotle appeals to disciplined minds of all ideological persuasions.

AMUSEMENT AND OTHER LEISURE-TIME PURSUITS

At a minimum, Aristotle counsels leaders to devote their leisure time to the pursuit of excellence rather than amusement. When their workday was done, influential Greeks typically headed to places of entertainment where they would unwind with food, wine, sex, and a board game akin to checkers. People then, like now, believed they worked in order to play. They equated happiness with fun and games, with going to the equivalent of a bar after work to hang out with their buddies.

Aristotle tried to teach Athenian leaders that happiness couldn't be separated from the rest of their lives. They wouldn't be made happy by what they did after work or on vacation. By extension, modern businesspeople who slave all day in order to come home at night and console themselves with gin are not happy, even if the gin gives them momentary pleasure. And people who lead unfulfilling lives throughout their working years will not make themselves happy or their lives full by retiring to a country club, even if their passion is playing golf. Aristotle has a different view of the relationship between amusement and happiness:

> Happiness does not lie in amusement; it would, indeed, be strange if the end were amusement, and one were to take trouble and suffer hardship all one's life in order to amuse oneself. Remember, everything we choose we choose for the sake of something else—except happiness, which is an end. So to exert oneself and work for the sake of amusement seems silly and utterly childish. But to amuse oneself in order that one may exert oneself, as Anacharsis puts it, seems right; for amusement is a sort of relaxation, and we need relaxation because we cannot work continuously. Relaxation, then, is not an end; for it is taken for the sake of another activity.

42   Here Aristotle endorses the conclusion that *we should amuse ourselves in order to refresh ourselves in order that we may exert ourselves again.* In his view, amusement and relaxation are means, unlike happiness, which is an end in itself. Thus, Aristotle has no problem with fun and games when those are used briefly to restore us for more virtuous pursuits. However, when amusement is viewed as an end, it leads us off the virtuous path. "I live in order to go to the beach and have a good time" is quite different morally than "I go to the beach when I am mentally exhausted, and a good swim helps to restore my energy." Aristotle rejects the former as vice but includes the latter expression of pleasure as a legitimate part of happiness. He specifically rejects sensual pleasure for its own sake, concluding that hedonists are no better than animals. He tells us we can't achieve the good by following animal impulses, for if we could, drunks, satyrs, and gluttons would be excellent and happy.

Aristotle asks: *To what end can we best put our leisure time?* He grants the common wisdom that we work hard to buy leisure time in which to pursue happiness. But then he challenges us to consider the following: If we waste our precious leisure time on amusement, are we not wasting our best opportunity to find happiness? Don't we need that free time for study, for contemplation, to reflect—in sum, to seek excellence?

This argument is hard for moderns to follow because Aristotle draws distinctions we don't usually make between amusement, leisure, and work. To Aristotle, the most valuable time of our lives is leisure time because that's when we can be most truly human. If our work is dull, routine, repetitive, or physically arduous, Aristotle calls it beastly. In an ideal society, he says that all such work will be done by animals or machines and, with remarkable prescience, predicts that bad work in the future will be automated. He says a goal of a good society should be to maximize work fit for humans, work that intrinsically allows those who do it to grow, learn, develop, and become more "divine through contemplation." Here, again, modern psychology has reinvented Aristotle. In the 1950s, industrial psychologist Frederick Herzberg posited, "Man has two sets of needs . . . his need as an animal to avoid pain and his need as a human to grow psychologically." Consequently, he argued that jobs should be "enriched" to minimize animal elements and maximize human ones.

Aristotle says that when we are engaged in good work—studying, learning, creating, analyzing, inventing, teaching, solving problems, researching, discussing great ideas and moral questions—we are not engaged in work at all. These activities are, in fact, leisure. Here's a way to test the quality of your own work: If you can't get into "the zone" while doing it, it is *work/work*. When engaged in drudgery, the hands on a clock seem to stand still, but time flies when engaged in *leisure/work*.

This is the crux of Aristotelian ethics, so we should make clear what he is saying: Since we want to be as much like the gods as possible, we should engage in "noble and divine" activities as much as we can. If we have to do work/work—if we can't avoid it, and he recognizes that most of us can't— we should reduce to a minimum the amount of time we must spend at activities that machines and animals should be doing.

My father, a teamster warehouseman, understood this. His role model was a fellow San Francisco laborer, longshoreman Eric Hoffer, who, at the end of his workday, headed directly to the library. Hoffer heeded Aristotle's dictum that one should maximize leisure/work by exerting oneself as much as practically possible in efforts to develop intellectual capabilities. This is not to say there is no dignity in working with one's hands, but as my father explained, "Most manual laborers work with their backs, not their hands."

GOLF AND HAPPINESS

The difficult decisions we make every day about how we will use our limited time are the stuff of Aristotelian ethical exercises. He says virtuous people choose to use their scarce free time on activities that lead to their development as complete humans. For many of us, this comes down to a tougher choice than Eric Hoffer faced: the question of how much golf we should play. Doubtless, most of us have a long way to go to fulfill our golf potential; however, in an Aristotelian reckoning, that capacity is both limited by our natural abilities and diminishes as we grow older. In contrast, Aristotle says our most important and rewarding human capacity is to learn new ideas and, especially, to apply that learning to helping and teaching others. That capability is not only far less tapped than our golf capacity, it actually increases as we accumulate life experience.

Aristotle doesn't say we shouldn't play golf or that golf is bad. Instead, he would ask, does golf equal happiness? He would answer that golf may be a contributing factor to one's happiness, but that if you treat it as the highest good, you may be in great trouble—for example, if you develop an illness that prevents you from playing. Moreover, even if you are lucky enough to play until you are in your nineties, the question is, *Will that alone cause you to consider your life meaningful?* A great number of people who lead full lives play

44

golf and play often (novelist John Updike, for example), but golf isn't what gives purpose and meaning to their existence. The question then is, How much golf? And Aristotle would answer: As much as you need in order to refresh yourself, but not so much as to prevent you from doing the developmental things that will bring true happiness in the long term.

CONTEMPORARY ARISTOTELIANS

If mere amusement isn't the best use of our time, shouldn't we then spend it developing our greatest talent? Aristotle answers yes and no. Yes, men and women who are born with a high aptitude for science, mathematics, and spatial thinking obviously should study to become the best engineers they are capable of becoming and never be satisfied with the depth of engineering knowledge they possess. But no, such people still will be unidimensional, having failed to develop all their potential in the arts and social sciences, for instance. While their potential may not be as deep in those fields, they nonetheless have almost unlimited potential in terms of breadth. They can study Chinese, history, ecology, psychology, anthropology, and learn to play the piano. Likewise, an artist will find a lifetime of learning about science, engineering, business, and technology in any good library. And for both the engineer and the artist, there is no limit to the contemplative challenges awaiting them if they choose to grapple with such profound questions as, Am I leading a good life? and Am I doing the right thing? To Aristotle, men and women who devote as much of their lives as possible to fulfilling their potential in such ways are engaged in true leisure, which he calls philosophy, and are on their way to being happy.

Alas, the world isn't organized to facilitate our personal pursuits of happiness, and workplaces aren't the only institutions structured in ways that mitigate against the fullest development of individuals. Ironically, the policies of universities also are narrowing and limiting. As management guru Tom Peters points out, not only is this bad for individuals, it undermines the practical purposes the educational system is designed to serve:

> I'm angry that I attended Cornell as an undergraduate for five and a half years and basically never made it out of the engineering quad into the liberal arts part of the school. I spent the ages of 18 to 23 there and literally came out a functional illiterate. I think I've talked to every engineering dean in the 37 years since I graduated and told them all, "You didn't educate me, and I'm pissed off."

The 60-year-old Peters stands as a contemporary Aristotelian, thanks to his high-energy, midlife pursuit of the broad education he missed in his youth. He did the virtuous thing by organizing his own adult life to realize his full potential. Significantly, his self-taught knowledge not only broadens his personal perspectives, it adds a deeper dimension to his writings on management.

Catherine Dain is another contemporary Aristotelian who, in her fifties, disciplined herself to pursue the highest good. In her twenties, she began a typical business career as a stockbroker; then, in her thirties, she obtained an MBA for reasons of career advancement. But in her early forties, she discovered that learning more was more fulfilling than earning more, so she started teaching in the California State University system, which gave her a built-in excuse to study a variety of new subjects. Along the way, she discovered she had an untapped talent for writing, which she then developed to the point where, beginning in her late forties, she produced the series of highly entertaining Freddie O'Neal detective novels.

Not ready to quit growing, in her late fifties Dain took a plunge that few women her age dare to take: She decided to scratch an old itch and become a stage actress. Admitting that the roles open to her now are not as glamorous as they would have been in her twenties ("Actually, I end up playing someone's mother"), she finds this far more satisfying than not being on the stage at all. What allows Dain to have the courage and discipline to continually try new things? "People say 'life is short,'" she explains, "but they're wrong: Life is long. It is too long, in fact, to get trapped doing something you hate and too long to not fill it doing things you love."

The danger in citing such examples is that Aristotle might appear antibusiness or, heaven forfend, anti-academic. He is neither. In fact, he is simply pro-stretching ourselves. Instead of doing what we have always done, instead of making an extra buck, writing yet another academic article, playing another round of golf, he encourages us to try new things, learn new skills, and learn about new places and new people. Here are some examples of midlife stretching he might applaud:

- A corporate executive who quit business to devote his energies to creating sculpture
- A respected professor who embarked on serious study of the jazz harmonica and now plays regularly with a professional blues band
- Eight business and professional women who started a formal study group, initially focusing on an area they knew little about: the Middle East
- A humanities professor who became an entrepreneur

Each of those individuals made a conscious choice to develop an untapped capacity; in each case, a *different* capacity. Because growth for a professor may entail starting a business, and growth for a business executive may entail becoming an artist, each of us must pursue happiness in our own way. Yet, Aristotle says, even such adventurous personal choices are not enough to constitute a good life. In addition, virtuous men and women pursue what he calls "the complete good."

THE COMPLETE GOOD

Aristotle calls *Homo sapiens* the "reasoning animal." Then, somewhat confusingly, he says "the highest good" of reasoning is not "the complete good."

He argues that it is not enough merely to possess the capacity to reason, and not even enough to develop it. In addition, to be virtuous, we humans must *use* our reasoning capacity. That is because we are also "political animals" who must apply our continually developing talents and abilities to meeting the needs of our communities. In Aristotelian language, *In addition to philosophy, virtuous men and women also engage in the practical world of politics.*

With that two-pronged requirement in mind, we may summarize Aristotle's overarching philosophy of virtue, excellence, and happiness: There is a moral difference between just living, on the one hand, and living well, on the other. Virtue enters the equation when we make the conscious choice to strive for excellence. Individuals become virtuous to the extent that they choose to develop their many talents and capacities, particularly their highest-order reasoning abilities. And, in their public personas as leaders of communities and organizations, they "complete their virtue" to the extent that they provide conditions under which others can pursue happiness and achieve excellence, as well. Hence, a woman with a high aptitude for accountancy should work not only to become the best accountant she is capable of becoming, she must also work to become the best human being, in toto. She must develop all facets of her talents and abilities to the full extent throughout her entire life, and then apply them for the good of her fellow workers and community. That stretching is "the complete good."

SO WHAT IS HAPPINESS?

When Jefferson declared "the pursuit of happiness" to be "a natural right" for "all men," he was citing contemporary notions recently advanced by Enlightenment figures Locke, Rousseau, and Kant. Those great thinkers argued that the majority of commoners in Europe at the time were denied the opportunity to realize what was best in them because the resources needed for that pursuit were reserved for the privileged few. Any aristocrat, no matter how thick-skulled, could attend Oxford, but only rarely were middle-class youth admitted, and the university's hallowed halls were completely off-limits to the working class. In the Declaration, Jefferson proclaimed that a new social contract was being drawn up in America, a major tenet of which was that every young man, regardless of station, would be free to make of himself all he was capable of becoming. Almost from the moment Jefferson penned those words, critics noted that his category of "all men" did not include slaves of African descent; indeed, it did not include the wives and daughters of the European men who signed the Declaration.

In this, Jefferson was a perfect Aristotelian, because the Ancient, too, had not extended the promise of happiness to Athens's slaves (who were ethnic Europeans and Middle Easterners) or to the city-state's free Greek women. Aristotle believed that entire castes were inherently incapable of the reasoning needed to engage in contemplation; and though he acknowledged that his own wife and daughter had the latent capacity, he thought it proper that they lack the "authority" to engage in philosophy and politics.

49

In refuting Aristotle's inaccurate assessment of the capabilities of women, Harriet Taylor Mill found that the most powerful argument she could muster against the Ancient was his own philosophy of happiness. In 1873, Mill argued that the greatest tragedy resulting from the inferior social status of women was the unrealized potential of half of humanity. For all of history, women had been denied the opportunity to participate in politics and philosophy, the very activities Aristotle called "most human." Hence, to allow women to contribute their higher-order reasoning skills to society, and to allow them the same opportunity for happiness as men, Mill advocated that women be allowed to vote, hold office, and serve in the learned professions. Mill cited the Declaration, explaining what America's founders had in mind when they used the famous words "all men are created equal":

We do not imagine that any American democrat will evade the force of these expressions by the dishonest and ignorant subterfuge that "men" in this historical document does not stand for human beings but for one sex only; that "life, liberty, and the pursuit of happiness" are "inalienable rights" of only one moiety of the human species . . .

In clear Aristotelian terms, she explained that the pursuit of happiness was shorthand for the process by which individuals develop their God-given capacities. Hence, societies in which women and members of denigrated castes, classes, and races were denied the right to realize their potential were inherently unjust. In effect, members of those groups were denied their humanity.

Mill thus simultaneously offered an elegant explication, and refutation, of Aristotle. She was able to do so because she understood that happiness was not a relativistic concept. In the Declaration, Jefferson used the term exactly the way Aristotle had 2 millennia earlier: as shorthand for the fulfillment of the highest-order human capacities. Nonetheless, Jefferson and Mill changed Aristotle's intent in one significant regard. To Aristotle, the pursuit of happiness is a duty, and the crime is to be born with the greatest of all natural capacities and not to use it. Hence, he believes we each have a responsibility to develop our innate capabilities, for who could be called happy who had failed to become as truly human as he was capable? To Mill, in contrast and distinction, the real crime is denying anyone the opportunity or right to become as fully human as possible. One must add that it was a shortcoming on Aristotle's part not to see happiness also as a right, as it was a shortcoming of Mill not to see it also as a duty. And, finally, Aristotle and Jefferson both were wrong to exclude any human from the right or duty to pursue happiness.

Unless one wishes to ignore Aristotle and Mill, there is but one way to understand "the pursuit of happiness" in the Declaration: *It refers to the process of realizing one's full potential.* Though relativistic readings might serve to justify other, preconceived notions of happiness, they simply don't work in light of Jefferson's acknowledged debt to Aristotle and Mill's debt to them both.

Hence, happiness is not about pleasure, feeling good, or anything else on the list of possibilities with which we began the present inquiry. And, thanks to Mill's clarification, the duty and right to pursue happiness applies to every human being. Understanding her emendation thus removes the political correctness objections to Aristotle, voiced by David Denby and others, and allows all men and women to benefit from the Ancient's philosophy.

TIME FOR A TEST

In light of what we now understand about Aristotle's view of happiness, we have sufficient information to decide for ourselves if we agree with him. We can flip back to the list of alternative sources of happiness found at the beginning of this chapter and ask about each if we believe it would bring us happiness. For example, can we expect to find happiness through the possession of expensive toys? We know that many people claim to be perfectly happy leading a materialistic life, but the question for each of us to ask ourselves is: *Will I find happiness that way?*

The answer isn't simple or obvious. In fact, I have a friend—I'll call him Bill—who says he will be "perfectly happy" when he owns a Mercedes convertible. I would say he was joking if his actions weren't consistent with his words. And when Michael Jordan "unretired," he seemed to believe that the only source of happiness for him is found on a basketball court. And neither Bill nor Jordan seems to believe it possible to "get into the zone" by developing their interests more fully and broadly, by asking profound questions, by seeking to lead a full life as Aristotle defines it. But we must ask if they are right in general and, in particular, if their conclusion is accurate as far as we are personally concerned. We each need to ask ourselves, *When am I truly in the zone? How can I get there more often? How can I organize my life so I can be in the zone as I grow older?* These questions are not easy, but they are important. Particularly in our fifties, we need to know if Aristotle is correct that the true source of happiness is the development of what is best in us. For if he is wrong, we need to identify the actual source before it is too late.

The burden of proof is on Aristotle because most of our experience tells us he is wrong. We remember what a drag it was trying to learn calculus in high school, so how can any sound-minded person conclude that using our brains is the source of happiness? Aristotle does not dismiss such doubts, nor does he discount the powerful sources of resistance to his notion of happiness. He will grant that contemplation doesn't sound like much fun and will concede that we do find pleasure playing golf, and do find it easier to coast in idle than to engage our minds. And he acknowledges that we have the right to say, "Leave me alone. I know what makes me happy (and it's not heavy lifting in the library)." But, as the bumper sticker says, we shouldn't believe everything we think. Aristotle says we will no longer be satisfied with frivolous activities once we fully understand how true happiness derives from serious contemplation.

That's what I learned about the pursuit of happiness from rereading Aristotle. But, of course, that isn't what most of us believe, and it isn't the way most of us live.

MODELS OF THE GOOD LIFE: THE VOLUPTUARY, THE SULTAN, AND THE SAGE

WHY DO MY DREAMS, MY WANTS, CONSTANTLY HUMILIATE ME?

—*JOHN GUARE*, THE HOUSE OF BLUE LEAVES

According to Aristotle, happiness derives from choosing "the good life" dedicated to politics and philosophy but, in the modern world, the behavior of most people doesn't square with his construct. Even in antiquity, Aristotle admits that few Greeks he observes believe happiness is derived from the sage's pursuit of "understanding and wisdom." Instead, most people opt for one of two other paths to happiness, either:

- ❧ The voluptuary's life of pleasure, in which the end sought is the enjoyment of sensual and material goods. In modern terms, that's a second house in Aspen, a Ferrari in the garage, steamy sex, gourmet food, and vintage wine.

or,

- ❧ The sultan's life of honor, in which the objective is fame, status, power, admiration, the respect of one's underlings, and the ego-satisfying envy of one's peers.

Clearly, Aristotle's life of the sage is not the majority's preference. In fact, the number of people who attempt to combine the life of the voluptuary with the life of the sultan far outnumber those who choose the life of the sage! Moreover, he knows it is futile to preach to the majority that their behavior is wrong and unjust to try to force them to do what he thinks is right. Nonetheless, he believes that people are more likely to achieve satisfying ends if they make those explicit, as opposed to being driven by social pressures or subconscious forces. Hence, the intent of his philosophy is to convince thoughtful people of the value of a disciplined examination of their life goals. If they do that, he feels they have a running start at planning a good life.

To that end, he asks his students to consider the following question: *Who is most likely to be happy at life's endgame, the voluptuary who pursues pleasure, the sultan who pursues honor, or the sage who pursues understanding?* Many people today will answer, "Depending on what turns you on, any of those alternatives might make you happy." Aristotle concedes that the relativist's "whatever" is partially right. Some people can find happiness in almost anything, even in an animal (or vegetable) kind of existence. To those who are satisfied with idle bliss, and to those who can honestly say, "I am happy as things stand," Aristotle says, "Good-bye and good luck." Philosophical inquiry is not for them.

But Aristotle observes that few thoughtful people find lasting contentment on permanent vacation. Most people are appropriately ambitious and eventually get bored sitting on the beach drinking Mai Tais. Although everyone enjoys a few weeks of sweet idleness now and then, most want to accomplish something, not just sit on their duffs in warm sand.

Vacations aside, Aristotle observes that thoughtful people find it particularly hard to attain and sustain a state of satisfaction. Worse, the more ambitious people are, the more imperative they feel the need to achieve real, lasting happiness, but at the same time, the more elusive that state seems. When Aristotle made his way through the beggars, lepers, and slaves who inhabited the alleyways of ancient Athens, he seldom heard them talk of happiness. That condition was so beyond their ken and resources that it was futile to pine for it. In contrast, he heard constant complaints from educated and affluent Athenians about their discontent because happiness seems more attainable as one's basic needs become satisfied. As people start to check off the items on their personal lists of wants, they assume they will become happy when they have the last remaining item in hand. That's where a lot of us are today. We have most of what we thought we wanted.

If, indeed, getting "whatever turns you on" makes people happy, then lucky folks who have reeled in the goodies they desire ought to be content. Aristotle the empiricist observes otherwise. When people get what they want, when they become rich, powerful, or "whatever," they almost always are disappointed when they don't then get the expected happiness payoff. That ages-old paradox continues to puzzle mature, thoughtful people today: *If getting what we want doesn't make us happy, what will?*

Why do people compete so determinedly for fortune, fame, and power if those things are not worth fighting for? If the things most commonly desired will not bring happiness, why do we continue the futile chase to obtain them?

Why, no matter what the great religious figures have preached, philosophers have argued, and experience has shown, do most people continue to believe that lives led in the pursuit of pleasure and honor are happy lives? Aristotle's answer: *because the lifestyles of the rich and powerful are more compelling—more exciting, more enticing, and sexier—than the counterexamples of sages.*

In Aristotle's society, the accepted models of success included generals, Olympic champions, plutocrats, potentates, and powerful politicians as, today, modern media spotlight sports and entertainment figures, business moguls, and powerful politicians. And in both societies, the Rest of Us have tended to measure ourselves by the standards of those who are rich, famous, and powerful. Aristotle doesn't say it is wrong to admire or emulate the Fabulous Few; but, because society doesn't offer success metrics for the Rest of Us, he asks us to consider if there might be more appropriate measures of our own lives. To help us find those for ourselves, he implicitly suggests we administer two personal self-examinations:

- ❧ the *threshold test,* in which we explore whether the rich, famous, and powerful are truly happy; and, if so, would the sources of that happiness bring us similar contentment
- ❧ the *deathbed test,* in which we imagine our last day on this earth, then ask ourselves by what measure we would look back and evaluate our lives

THE THRESHOLD TEST

Aristotle knows what he is up against: The strongest counterarguments to his advocacy of the life of the sage aren't contained in the writings of other philosophers. To the contrary, the most powerful case against his argument is the manifest attractiveness of the lives of voluptuaries and sultans. So Aristotle's main concern is not answering his academic critics. Instead, he addresses practical men and women, asking them to apply their reasoning powers to test the validity of what "everyone knows" to see if, indeed, those who "have it all" are happy. Aristotle asks us to closely examine the experiences of those who are clearly anti-Aristotelian in the conduct of their lives. He challenges us to reflect on the lives and careers of such people, then to ask ourselves some simple questions: *Have those who have succeeded in attaining fortune, fame, and power also found happiness? If so, have they found it in a way that would satisfy me? If not, what would really make me happy in the end?*

There is a time-tested reason for using bigger-than-life examples in such moral exercises. In Aristotle's *Poetics*, he explains why we learn valuable lessons by observing the lives of powerful individuals. He concludes that those more notable than ourselves are no more or less human; however, because their lives are projected on a larger screen, the moral dilemmas they face are clearer to see. As a theatergoer attending the tragedies of Sophocles, Aristotle asks why it is that men in the audience identify with the character of Oedipus to the point of crying in empathy with the monarch's travails even though they aren't kings themselves, and why it is that women who aren't princesses have no trouble seeing themselves in the character of Antigone? When we see the tragic flaws of such great people dramatized, he posits, we empathize more easily than if the characters on stage are equally flawed but ordinary folk like us. Ordinary men and women were never protagonists in Greek tragedies because audiences were too willing to make excuses for the flaws of commoners and to see them, like themselves, as victims. Not only are the virtues and vices of the powerful clearer to see, the consequences of their moral choices are more pronounced. When the powerful fall, there is collateral damage, and innocent bystanders are hurt in the process. If nothing else, that gets our attention.

Because the point of moral inquiry is to get people to examine their own lives and own up to their responsibilities, the ancient tragedians couldn't afford to use examples that allowed the audience to wiggle off the moral hook. Instead, powerful characters with unambiguously obsessive behavior forced people to examine their own assumptions about what they should and should not do, just as 2,000 years later, reports of Bill Clinton's tawdry philandering caused countless Americans to examine their own character and behavior in ways they would not have done had it been the local postmaster caught dallying with a clerk in his employ.

In early 2001, I decided to try Aristotle's exercise for myself. I chose high-tech heroes Jim Clark and Larry Ellison as my designated anti-Aristotelians. For a year, I collected everything I could that was written about them and talked with people in nearby Silicon Valley who knew them. I was drawn to them because they are about my age and, like me, weren't born with silver spoons in their mouths. They are just a couple of West Coast guys from down the peninsula who, almost by accident, have garnered the attention of the media and the envy of all. Moreover, I admired their candor about their ambitions, which they have come as close to realizing as anyone in our generation. The main difference between us was that they are rich, famous, and powerful, but my failure to match their record in those regards hadn't been for want of desire or trying!

The first question I set out to answer was, *Could I reasonably expect to find happiness living the way they have chosen to live?* That is the question Aristotle suggests his students should ask about their chosen exemplars of conventionally defined happiness, and it's what I trust readers will ask about their own designated anti-Aristotelians. This is a "threshold test" because, if we conclude that people who choose the paths of voluptuaries and sultans do find happiness, then we don't have to make the effort to understand Aristotle! If we can convince ourselves that pursuing wealth, power, sensual pleasure, and fame will make us happy, then we need not trouble ourselves with a lengthy and perhaps painful exploration of alternatives. However, if we conclude that such goals are dead ends, at least for us personally, we owe it to ourselves to give the Aristotelian alternative a try. Because that necessitates some difficult thinking and painful changes in the conduct of our lives, why go there if we don't have to? Here's how I did the exercise.

ANTI-ARISTOTELIAN I: THE VOLUPTUARY

Jim Clark is a Silicon Valley legend, a former Stanford engineering professor often credited as the only person ever to have created three separate billion-dollar start-up companies. It is a bit surprising that Clark became a Digital Age role model because he was relatively unknown outside of Silicon Valley until he spilled his guts to writer Michael Lewis in his bestselling book *The New New Thing*. As a result, readers of business books know the story of Clark's dirt-poor Texas childhood and abandonment by his father. Early on, Clark decided that making money was the best way to compensate for the weak hand he was dealt at birth. According to his mother, "When Jim came home from the navy, he told his uncle that someday he was going to make fifty thousand dollars a year." That was circa 1965, when fifty grand was real money, particularly in hardscrabble Texas.

Clark launched his career in a way contraindicated for those seeking great wealth: He earned a Ph.D. A math near-genius, he found university work as easy as calculating pi. Engineering was his natural academic home because Clark loved machines, and he soon discovered the glamour machine of the age, the computer. From there, it was a mere hop, skip, and jump from the Stanford campus to the start-up gold mines of Silicon Valley. Clark's first "machine" allowed engineers to design cars and planes on a computer. Silicon Graphics, the company he started in order to build the device, was soon to be a billion-dollar firm. But Clark did not share fully in the financial success of the company and was convinced he was taken by the venture capitalists who underwrote the start-up. So he bailed out of the company and, according to Lewis, shortly thereafter ran into Rocky Rhodes, also a Silicon Graphics (SGI) pioneer:

> Jim said right out, "I'm going to make $100 million." And I said, "That's great, Jim," and also something about how pleased I was with the way SGI had worked out. And then I said, "But even if it hadn't worked out, I've had a great time, met great people, learned a lot." And Jim got mad. He said, "NO! If I go and do this next thing and don't make $100 million, it'll be a failure."

That next thing was Netscape, creator of the browser, the ingenious application that turned the World Wide Web into a mass market. However, for a computer scientist, Clark seemed oddly uninterested in Netscape's technology. Nor was he drawn to the challenge of managing the company. So with nothing to hold him, he made his exit from Netscape, too, without ever actually having run a company that made a sustained success. If his motivation isn't technological or managerial, what is it? David Kaplan, author of *The Silicon Boys*, writes:

> Clark is more honest than the I'm-not-in-it-for-the-money crowd. Indeed, Clark has acknowledged countless times that he brought Netscape to market five years ago not because he wanted to change the world but because he wanted a boat, he wanted a plane, he wanted not to have to think about whether he could buy the next thing he wanted.

60 The next "next thing" was Healtheon, an idea for a company that would revolutionize the provision of health care through Internet applications. It was just an idea, and Clark seemed no more interested in the intricacies of health care policy than he was in figuring out what it meant to apply computers to solving the problems plaguing America's health care system. Nor was he interested in managing Healtheon. Instead, the purpose of the exercise was to make money and lots of it: "He had just himself reached the point where he associated the word *dollars* not with 'millions' but with 'billions,'" Lewis reports. Then he quotes Clark: "I could always make fifty million dollars. But who needs that?" In 1965, his goal had been fifty *thousand*.

For the record, in 2000, Clark was number 334 on the *Forbes* list of wealthiest Americans, with a fortune of $875 million. That buys a lot of stuff. His particular passion is a 155-foot sloop carrying a price tag of $37 million. It has the world's largest sail on the world's largest mast (he worried that the 17-story pole wouldn't fit under the Golden Gate Bridge). As a fillip, he covered the cabin walls with $30 million worth of French impressionist paintings. But even that big boat wasn't big enough. Kaplan wrote in 2002 that "Clark's now building a 292-foot, three-masted schooner—a football field that floats—which will be one of the world's largest yachts not owned by a navy."

Well, I wasn't quite into money to the extent Clark was, but I had to admit to certain materialistic urges—to be exact, excessive passion for a 1937 Cord 812 Phaeton auto. This art deco gem, a cream-colored convertible with cherry red upholstery, is so classically beautiful that you could park it in your living room. But I'd want to drive it around town. I could picture myself at the wheel, the envy of all. I imagined I could pick one up for a few hundred thousand, more or less. I calculated that if I spent more time consulting, got my speaking career in order, sold stocks socked away for retirement, and re-mortgaged the house, I might be able to pull it off in a couple of years. Fantasy? Foolish? You bet. But that car was damnably difficult to get out of my mind. I knew how Clark felt about the yacht.

ANTI-ARISTOTELIAN II: THE SULTAN

Arguably, Larry Ellison is America's most powerful and successful high-tech entrepreneur. He hails from a middle-class Chicago family in which he felt unappreciated by the stepfather who had adopted him. His ascendancy in the high-tech world was achieved, remarkably, without benefit of an advanced technical education. Ellison is a classic entrepreneur. Founder of the Oracle Corporation, he was (in late 1999) briefly the $50 billion man. His wealth comes entirely from Oracle's success, which is largely due to the strategy he created for the company in the late 1990s. At the end of the millennium, Ellison spectacularly reinvented Oracle as an e-business software provider whose databases allow corporations to manage vast amounts of information and on-line transactions with other companies.

Larry Ellison deserves the ample credit he gets for making Oracle into Silicon Valley's most successful software business, and he has reaped material rewards for doing so. Like Clark, he is a conspicuous consumer. He owns an 80-foot yacht, a Marchetti jet fighter, a Ferrari, a Bentley, and three Acura NSX sports cars. He has a 23-acre estate in pricey Woodside, California, on which sits a new $40 million Japanese-style house. His second home, located less than 30 miles away in San Francisco, is legendary for "the best view money can buy" of the Golden Gate. The picture windows are said to be 44 feet wide and 13 feet high. Like Clark, Ellison spends much of his spare time at sea, spending millions in an effort to win the America's Cup yacht race.

Yet Ellison differs from Clark in that he appears to have many and diverse business and intellectual interests. He is now investing heavily in biotechnology. He has thought and perhaps read widely about medical research, religion, poetry, architecture, medical science, and Japan. In particular, he seems to have knowledge of and good taste in Japanese art, architecture, and artifacts. Unlike Clark, it appears that Ellison's highest motivation is not the accumulation of wealth. In all that is said about him, *respect* and *power* are the operative words. In his personal life, he has been surrounded by a bevy of glamorous and adoring women, and he presents himself to the public in the guise of a rock star. His view of the corporation is simple: win. Oracle is an extension of his competitive impulses and desire for power. To succeed in the marketplace, he has bent the truth about the quality of Oracle products and engaged in dirty tactics against competitors. To show who's boss, he has fired long-term employees only hours before their stock options vested. As a *Business Week* cover story reports, "To get staffers to bend to his will, Ellison uses the carrot first—and then the stick." Most articles about Ellison use the words *power* and *control:* "It's all about centralized control—with Ellison in charge." But more than power and control, he admits that his greatest motivation is public admiration. His metric of success is to be widely acknowledged as America's premier chief executive. What a complex man. He seems almost Aristotelian in the way he pursues so many interests, yet at the same time, he seems to lack an ethical core.

In sum, Ellison is the model of the modern megamogul: smart, charismatic, hip, powerful, rich as Croesus, and living a fast-paced life in which he is able to satisfy his voracious sensual and material appetites. He is, in short, the man many American men want to be. In the words of his biographer, Karen Southwick, "By turns brilliant and intolerant, inspiring and chilling, energetic and disinterested, Ellison is one of the most intriguing, dominant, and misguided leaders of a major twenty-first-century corporation." He is, in fact, much like the legendary Dr. Faust, who made a pact with the devil to live life more fully than other mortals, to outstrip all in terms of knowledge, power, appetite, and experience. In both Marlowe's Elizabethan play and Goethe's Enlightenment-era poem, Faust is proud and complex, a brilliant and dissatisfied idealist overfilled with ambitions and hungers he is determined to realize rather than repress. Faust brazenly rejects virtue and embraces vice and is prepared to pay the price. He's an unfettered egotist unwilling to accept the limits of a moral life, a truly brave man who risks all in order to grasp the power and pleasure about which others are willing only to fantasize. Though most people would be insulted or shocked to be likened to Faust, one has the feeling that Larry Ellison might be flattered.

APPLYING THE THRESHOLD TEST

As I reviewed what the larger-than-life Clark and Ellison had accomplished and accumulated, I felt more than a twinge of personal inadequacy and, yes, envy. Here were two men who had realized the great boomer dream of the roaring nineties. Unlike me, they appeared to have realized their potential, achieved their goals, and reaped their just rewards. Then I started to think about the Aristotelian questions, the first of which is, *Are they really happy?* But who could ever know that about another individual? All I could do is look at the evidence I had accumulated in order to see what they said about themselves on that score.

The first thing I discovered is that they didn't share my view of their successes. By all reports, they were dissatisfied with what they had achieved and wanted more. Indeed, everything I heard about Jim Clark indicated he was chronically unhappy with the amount of money he possessed: "He was the least happy optimist there ever was," Lewis writes. Clark told Lewis he wouldn't die happy until he was as rich as Larry Ellison, who had four times more wealth than Clark at the time. Ironically, Ellison seemed to be in the same boat. He has said he will not be satisfied until all modifiers are deleted from stories written about him, and he becomes *the* most powerful and respected business leader in America. He wants us to forget Jack Welch, and, in particular, he wants us to forget Bill Gates. As Clark measures himself in dollar terms against Ellison, Ellison's metric of success is Bill Gates's standing in the high-tech world. He suffers from Gates Envy.

There is, of course, a positive way of looking at this: Ellison and Clark simply exhibit classic and necessary entrepreneurial attitudes and behavior. It is often said that if people like them were content, they would lack the motivation to create and excel. The belief that unhappiness is a spur to productivity is advanced in Dinesh D'Souza's *The Virtue of Prosperity*, where he argues that creators of new technology contribute the wealth necessary for the rest of us to lead happy, virtuous lives. D'Souza approvingly quotes Adam Smith on entrepreneurs' mistaken belief that ceaseless accumulation of wealth will bring them happiness: "It is this deception which rouses and keeps in continual motion the industry of mankind." D'Souza "translates" Smith's comment in this fashion:

> Let these pathetic bastards keep at it! Who knows if they are really adding to their happiness? What we do know is that they are producing things that make society better off. Far from exploiting us, we are, admittedly with their full consent, exploiting them.

D'Souza is right to remind us that the world needs entrepreneurs and wealth creators. But the issue before us isn't the manifold benefits we receive

64

from "exploiting" those poor souls. The issue is whether we, like Smith, should disdain their goals. After all, we don't just get a free ride on the technology that entrepreneurs create. We also partake of the value system driving their efforts. In this regard, Aristotle's threshold test raised questions I was unprepared to answer: Can we succeed in our chosen, specialized professions and still be complete human beings? Is unhappiness an inevitable by-product of the conventional model of success? Is it possible for someone like Clark or Ellison to make entrepreneurial contributions and also be happy?

I suppose it shouldn't matter to us whether Clark and Ellison are happy or not. And it wouldn't matter if people like them weren't heroes to so many men and women my age in the high-tech and financial worlds, if so many younger men and women weren't modeling their lives on sultans and voluptuaries like them, if so many people didn't measure their self-worth by their metrics, and if so many of those people weren't also unhappy. So I concluded that it mattered. At least, it mattered to me to the extent I shared their goals.

Yet, I feared I had loaded the dice and, thus, invalidated Aristotle's test. Perhaps the examples of Clark and Ellison weren't instructive because they were such extreme cases, almost caricatures of high-tech moguls. After all, who among us can identify with individuals who go so far overboard in pursuit of pleasure and honor? Don't most people just want a "normal" amount of money and respect? Here I caught myself resisting the personal conclusions to which the analysis was leading: *That's them; I'm different.* To avoid such rationalization, I forced myself to consider what the implications would be for normal people—say ones like me—who pursue the same goals as Clark and Ellison but with less success. The test then became, *Could I reasonably expect poorer, less-powerful, less-famous, and less-envied individuals to be happier than those who pursue those same goals more successfully?* The question may sound silly, but the answer helps to clarify whether the moral repulsion many people feel about the behavior of moguls arises from their possession of wealth and power or, instead, from their choice of those goods as the ultimate ends to be pursued.

Aristotle says this distinction is important because, although we identify with the fabulously rich, the Rest of Us feel that our own pursuit of wealth is morally different than theirs. The difference, we assume, is that we are merely trying to make enough to satisfy our needs. Hence, we will know when we have earned enough, whereas the multimillionaire doesn't know when to stop. But are we right? How do we know when we have enough? That's no easy question, and even moderately well-off people are faced with the need to answer it. With an income that is magnitudes smaller than Jim Clark's, I knew I couldn't say with certainty how much is enough for me. And without that knowledge, I ended up acting like Clark, always wanting more, never having enough, and never finding happiness. Perhaps that luscious 1937 Cord was the missing ingredient?

Applying Aristotle's threshold test, I began to wonder whether I would be any happier than Clark if I were as wealthy as he is. Even as it stood, it occurred to me that I was worse off than he was: I was on the same treadmill in terms of making myself unhappy, but I am not getting rich! And I doubt that I was alone in this regard. Though Clark's vast wealth does make him an extreme example, unhappiness became epidemic in the corporate world a few years back as the value of shares plummeted and tens of thousands of people who had evaluated their lives in terms of stock options were forced to reassess their self-worth—not just their net worth—downward. Today, as nest eggs have morphed into goose eggs, and dark jokes are made about "201K plans," countless fifty-somethings are being forced to rethink the degree to which wealth is an appropriate measure of a good life.

THE DEATHBED TEST

Because a formidable initial obstacle to living a good life is the inability to assess if we are doing so, Aristotle provides a yardstick by which his students can take the measure of their lives, a tool to use from time to time to check if the road they are on leads to happiness. Metrics are important. We can't tell how a business is doing without a clear measure of success, usually profitability, and the same is true of a person's life and career.

Recently, the importance of life metrics was brought home to me when a former college classmate of my wife's and mine informed us she was facing a difficult life choice. Mary is a successful professional who has never married because she "has been too busy managing the life and career" of the powerful executive for whom she had worked for over 2 decades. Now she had an offer to be chief of staff for an even bigger corporate chieftain, a CEO with a household name. "He's offered me an incredible salary and a retirement package that will allow me, in a decade or so, to buy that little Sonoma winery I've always dreamed about. But . . ." Mary then told us she also had been offered the directorship of a small foundation at a third the salary offered by the CEO. "But I'd be my own boss," she said. "I could really run the organization and have the satisfaction of making it into something important and meaningful. Of course, when I reach 65, I might not be able to afford to buy even a bottle of good wine, let alone a winery."

Mary surprised us when she then explained that, in struggling with her difficult choice, her metric was not how much money she needed, but how she thought she would evaluate it from the perspective of her old age:

> Regardless of how you feel about Hillary Rodham Clinton's politics or her marriage, professional women our age identify with her, at least in terms of the choices she recently faced. The issue for many fifty-something women is how they want to be remembered in the end: either "She helped powerful, successful men become more powerful and more successful" or "She realized her own full potential." When I'm old and gray and look back on what I've done, I hope to find I made the right choice.

Aristotle, too, concludes that the acid test of whether a person has led a good life can be applied only at the end. From this Aristotelian perspective,

Catholics have it right with the last sacrament of extreme unction: The time to assess the state of one's soul is at the end of the game, not at halftime. So Aristotle suggests we ask ourselves the following: *Imagine you are on your deathbed. Now, as you review the final draft of your curriculum vitae, what in your record will cause you to look back on your life with a sense of satisfaction?* In other words, how do you really want to measure the worth of your life?

Let's apply Aristotle's test to what we know about Jim Clark. Trying to find an accurate measure of the value of his life, Jim Clark tells Lewis he won't die happy until he is as rich as Larry Ellison, who is "worth" four times more than Clark at the time. Assuming his wish comes true and one day he ends up with more money than Ellison, let's flash forward a few more years to find Clark on his deathbed rehearsing what he is going to say to St. Peter. Because heaven's chief concierge asks everyone the same question, *"Did you lead a good life?"* Clark is prepared with his answer: "Hell, yes!" St. Peter then hits him with the predictable follow-up: *"By what measure did you lead a good life?"* Clark is ready for this one, too: "It's simple: I made $4.1 billion to that loser Ellison's miserable $4 billion and no change!"

That's one measure of a life. But in contrast to Clark's monetary metric, Aristotle's test of whether a person has led a good life—the measure of whether a man or woman is truly happy—is *the degree to which one is free of deathbed regrets about his or her unfulfilled potential.* According to Aristotle, there is nothing sadder than people who, at the end of life, are filled with disappointment about what they might have done, might have been, might have become. That condition is the opposite of happiness.

Here's how Aristotle's metric can be used as a practical tool: He advises thoughtful, younger people to extrapolate forward to the end of their lives in order to assess the degree to which now, at mid-course, they are effectively pursuing happiness. Unlike Clark's dollar-denominated metric, Aristotle's deathbed test is valid for everyone, everywhere, and in all cultures. It's the test Mohandas K. Gandhi applied to himself in his forties, and the results of that personal assessment caused him to alter radically the course of his life.

Gandhi was enjoying the material fruits of a successful legal career in South Africa when he came to feel terror at the prospect of living to old age in conventional comfort. He trembled when he imagined himself on his deathbed uttering the most tragic of all last words: "I could have done more with my life." Gandhi recoiled at the sorry mantra of "could have," "should have," and "might have." He decided then and there that he was not going to die knowing he could have brought independence to India but, instead, had chosen a life of material pleasure. At that point, he understood that he would not find happiness in the wealth he was accumulating and would have to change the direction of his life. To oversimplify, he quit chasing ambulances and began to work on his previously undeveloped capabilities as a leader, statesman, and creator of a just society.

Most of us are not and cannot become heroic figures who change the world. Nonetheless, we can ask what capabilities, talents, and interests we have that would give us a true sense of fulfillment if we were to develop them. We know instinctively that we should try to fulfill the natural promise with which we are born. This seems like common sense because we've heard others say something like, "Poor John wasted his life; he could have been a great scientist but frittered away his potential." We don't want to be thought of as "poor John" or "poor Mary" and don't want to end up thinking of ourselves in terms of our wasted potential. Instead, Aristotle says we want to become all we are capable of becoming. I suspect early recognition of that fact is why the young Jim Clark was able to break out of Nowhere, Texas, and make something of himself.

However, by his own metric, Clark was in trouble in early 2000. Thanks to a bull market in Oracle stock, Larry Ellison was worth somewhere between $40 billion and a gazillion dollars. Meanwhile, Clark's stock in Healtheon (later WebMD) was headed south. If we accept Clark's measure of his own life, those events raise interesting questions: Can Clark ever look forward to being happy? Is Ellison truly "worth" 40 times more than Clark? If Clark were to die tomorrow, should he assess his life a failure because he has failed to reach his goal? Or should the man who made the Internet a reality measure the contribution of his life in ways other than dollars? And should he start asking what he might do now, besides pursue wealth, which will allow him eventually to die happy?

Wait, there's a postscript: In 2001, an article under Jim Clark's name appeared on the *New York Times* op-ed page. It contained the startling news that Clark had decided to hold back a substantial portion of the $150 million he had pledged to Stanford to create a bioengineering center. In thoughtful, well-reasoned prose, Clark explained he was protesting President George W. Bush's decision to limit federal funding for stem cell research, which was to have been a major activity of the center. People who knew Clark were stunned. Had he found something besides money he cared enough about to engage him intellectually and emotionally? Had he done the homework on stem cell research that George W. Bush should have done but didn't? Had Clark, in his late fifties, chosen to do the leisure work that would finally make him happy? If he is ever to do so, Aristotle says the time is now.

LARRY ELLISON'S
TOXIC DESIRE (AND MINE)

Clark's goal of fabulous wealth appears relatively commonplace and straight-forward compared with Ellison's seemingly more complex and unusual desires for honor and respect. Yet Ellison's success metric, the approval of others, may be even more universal than the desire for excessive wealth. David McCullough's treatment of Adams and Jefferson in *John Adams* is instructive because the common failing of both presidents was their excessive desire for admiration and renown. Adams called this "passion for distinction" *vanity* and believed it rested in the hearts of everyone:

> Whether they be old or young, rich or poor, high or low, wise or foolish, ignorant or learned, every individual is seen to be strongly activated by a desire to be seen, heard, talked of, approved and respected.

Adams concluded, "To be wholly overlooked, and to know it, are intolerable." When he felt he was "overlooked," his vanity was crushed and he succumbed to depression. His rival, Jefferson, was capable of making questionable political compromises in order to be viewed with public honor. In their forties and fifties, both great men behaved immaturely, Adams exposing his vanity by constantly needing to be the center of attention and Jefferson by blatantly dissembling, all to the end of public approval. Thus, the human desire for honor that Adams found "natural" turns poisonous in large quantities. The question for me was, *At what level did my own, albeit smaller, needs become toxic?*

As we have seen, excessive need for public approval was also Aristotle's personal shortcoming when he had felt entitled to lead the Academy by virtue of his manifest brilliance. The Ancient was perhaps thinking about his own vanity when he observed that politicians in his day sought the respect and recognition of the cognoscenti: "They seem to pursue this honor in order to persuade themselves that they are good." Aristotle thus concludes that the insatiable craving for respect is actually desire to have significant others validate one's worth. He believes that kind of honor is not a true measure of virtue, because it is something bestowed by others and not an intrinsic quality of an individual. Real honor, he says, comes in recognition of good works to those who don't seek it. Good people thus break themselves of the habit of seeking the approval of others and focus, instead, on living a good life.

Thanks to the threshold test, I was relieved to find that my own chronic need for approval put me in good company. However, on reflection, I could draw little lasting comfort from the fact; it merely demonstrated how hard the failing is to overcome. And Aristotle warns that the obstacles we unwittingly erect in the path of happiness don't just wither away with time. If our own behavior is the cause of our discontent, we need to devise a plan to change it. Particularly if we are chasing the wrong ends, it does us no good to pick up the pace of our pursuit. Again, *if we aim for the wrong thing, we are likely to hit it.*

That's what the threshold test taught me. The eye opener came when I realized I shared Clark's and Ellison's moral shortcomings. We desired the same nonvirtuous things. Because I was simply far less skillful than they in obtaining what we wanted, our moral differences were matters of degree, not kind. And I could expect to be even less happy than Clark and Ellison so long as my models were voluptuaries and sultans, because there would always be someone with more goodies and public recognition than I had.

And the deathbed test demonstrated that I was flailing around in the dark like Clark and Ellison with no clear idea of what moral end I was pursuing. Self-administering the two simple tests convinced me that, if they had not found happiness pursuing wealth and honor, I was unlikely to find it digging where they had dug, in the same empty hole I'd been mining for over 3 decades. I saw that I needed a plan aimed at finding more promising ground.

Aristotle believes the first sign of wisdom is when we are able to learn from the experiences of others. The utility of the threshold test was that it forced me to draw moral lessons from analyzing the lives of two contemporary heroes. Aristotle was right: I could see my own flaws more clearly reflected in the harsh light of bigger-than-life characters than I could when I looked in a mirror. But he also taught that having such insight isn't enough; we must then act on our knowledge. That seemed a tougher row to hoe. I was a lot less sure that Aristotle was right in claiming we can rationally choose to change our behavior and that, without experiencing some sort of personal trauma, we can discipline ourselves to live in the way experience shows us is obviously right. In fact, don't we all act like fools, doing exactly what we know will make us unhappy in the long run?

ANTI-ARISTOTELIAN III:
THE WANNABE (AND ME)

Ellison and Clark may have situated themselves at the extreme end on a continuum of human behavior, but I now saw they are not of a different species. If not to the same degree as business tycoons, even sensible, middle-class professionals are susceptible to the sirens of money, fame, approval, and sensual pleasure, much as we might deny it. In *American Sucker,* David Denby chronicles how he, the *New Yorker*'s mild-mannered movie reviewer, blew a fair chunk of his life savings speculating in high-tech stock. I almost wrote *pointy-headed* movie reviewer because it is hard to imagine how so intelligent a man also could be so gullible, so naïve, and, most unattractive, so drawn to unworthy pursuits. So like the rest of us, in fact. Reading the account of his misadventures, our hearts immediately go out to this poor soul whose beloved wife of 18 years walks out on him, suddenly discovering she has other needs. But sympathy turns to surprise when the heretofore sensible Denby decides *his* other needs include making a million and a half dollars, and quick, in order to buy out her share of their Upper Westside apartment.

The apparently solid, sober, 56-year-old intellectual suddenly turns himself into an adolescent monster, a material boy hooked not only on maintaining his lifestyle but augmenting it with a flashy sport cars and tall blondes. He turns commonplace anxiety about money into obsessional materialism. Throwing caution to the wind, he follows the investment advice of newfound friends and role models—the soon-to-be indicted Sam Waksal, and business gurus Henry Blodget and George "Telecosm" Gilder—sinking his life savings into risky stocks which that trio self-servingly recommend. These three sophisticated, articulate, and cultured men turn out to be Denby's East Coast equivalents of what the cruder Ellison and Clark represented for me in California: They embodied what he thought he wanted.

Despite sound warnings, which he ignores, Denby gleefully hops on the hedonic treadmill. He understands money can't buy happiness "but it could certainly buy pleasure." It ends up buying neither, and Denby is left at the end of his tale even more miserable psychologically, spiritually, and financially than when we met him. But not necessarily wiser. We are left shaking our heads about our own behavior: Why are we so blind to what is obvious?

Denby defines his vice as greed, a superficially true but simplistic diagnosis. In the course of the book, he unconsciously refers to his many "appetites," his insatiable hunger for this and that accoutrement of the lives of sultans and voluptuaries. Denby confesses that Waksal is attractive as a role model because "his appetite was irresistible" and muses that Waksal may be "the kind of man I would have been if I had my choice." But it really isn't Waksal's fortune that generates Denby's envy; what actually turns him on is that the socially connected doctor is a player in the Manhattan power game. Denby longs to be part of the action, to run in the fast company of our sprinting techno-age, to have his worth validated by people who count. Ironically, in a *60 Minutes* television interview after he was sentenced to federal prison, Waksal revealed that his own Achilles' heel was the pathetic need for approval by Manhattan's high society! So, on both the right coast and the left, vanity, vanity, all is vanity among the rich, powerful, and famous, all the way down the line to Denby and me.

Denby's story reads like *The New New Thing, East.* Where Gandhi had concluded, "There is more to life than increasing its speed," Denby takes the opposite tack. He loves the speed of the market, "the thrilling oxygen-rich happiness of wealth being created overnight." He is addicted to news in real time. For him, what counts is the now, the moment, the ephemeral, "life as ceaseless change." Looking for an adrenaline rush, he briefly gets into Internet pornography, then becomes addicted to watching talking heads on CNBC pontificate on breaking news. He admires their instant analysis and is seduced by their vacuous technobabble. He says their artifice seems more real to him than boring books and works of art, more real than boring engagement with family, friends, and perplexing ideas. Indeed, Denby's operative pejorative is *boring.* To him, the good life becomes excitement and the ceaseless pursuit of more; virtue and the contemplation of enduring art and nature are, well, boring: "Finding the winner was the great excitement of American life." He becomes an apologist for greed, envy, and lust, helpfully reminding readers that the seven deadly sins have their positive sides! Only one condition is unmitigatedly vile: boredom.

Through it all, Denby comes across as a likable enough fellow. In the mode of Ellison and Clark, he is a communicant in the faith of candid self-revelation. There is nothing too embarrassing about his life to proclaim in public. Though he makes no attempt to mislead others about his vices, I believe he nonetheless fools himself. Even after his painful comeuppance, he still doesn't get it. He thinks his troubles started in early 2000 with the breakup of his marriage, believing that is what led to his sudden metamorphosis from sober citizen into deranged Waksal wannabe. In fact, Denby had been struggling for some time with the vices that eventually bring him down. A look back at his 1996 bestseller, *Great Books,* reveals how, at that earlier date, Denby has rejected Artistotelian notions of virtue:

> So even as I sat reading the *Ethics* and *Poetics*, and enjoying Aristotle's plainness and efficiency, and the well-tended-garden of pleasure that he gave, I sensed that order was something imposed by power—genuine enough, but not intrinsic, not natural. I wanted to unseat Aristotle, or at least confront him. I was bored by his shrewd, very sane advice in the *Nicomachean Ethics* that we avoid the extremes of behavior and choose the "golden mean" or middle way, a mode of existence practiced by the virtuous man as a way of taming the excesses of appetite. True enough, but so what? All this platitudinous harping on virtue was perhaps the preoccupation of the ancients that was least invigorating to modern taste.

Hence, though he may not have remembered it in 2004, Denby had dismissed as "platitudinous" the need to tame excesses of appetite four years before he took his high dive into the fast life. Even back then, greed "was neither good nor bad" to his "modern mind." He specifically had rejected Aristotle's view that greed is by definition excessive, always a vice because it knows no end. And where Aristotle advocates consciously finding the right balance between time spent with family, friends, nature, art, work, and contemplation, Denby's focus is on satisfying his appetites for money, speed, excitement, and being part of the action. The consequences of holding such values escaped Denby in 1996, as they did 4 and 8 years later. One is reminded of the words of Edna St. Vincent Millay, "Pity me that the heart is slow to learn / What the swift mind beholds at every turn."

There is, in the end, something comical about Denby's pathetic fall. As Samuel Beckett wrote, "Nothing is funnier than unhappiness." Denby ultimately comes across as Faust *manqué*, Larry Ellison without the brio, brilliance, and big bucks. Worse, for unlike Ellison, Denby knows better. He even tells us he twice read Goethe's *Faust* and

> I hated it, even though I obviously shared—with all due proportions kept—Faust's ambitions, dissatisfactions, and hungers, and immediately would have made a deal had any Satan been around to propose one.

What is both troubling and instructive about Denby is that he is a thoughtful man who refuses to learn from either the experiences of contemporaries or the more recondite wisdom of the ages in which he is so well versed: "The boredom of the classics! Noisy, redundant, crass, overbearing, dislikable." So, unlike the unlettered fly-by-the-gut entrepreneurs Ellison and Clark, the well-educated Denby knew better, or should have. This is not what Aristotle would have predicted.

For me, this was scary stuff because I was far closer to Denby than to my West Coast moguls in terms of profession, educational background, life experience, interests, income level, and, alas, appetites. Could it be that one can't learn from the experience of others that vanity is followed by a painful fall, that one can't draw the lesson from the world's great religions that selling one's soul for immediate pleasure is a bad bargain? It worried me that I might have to fall even farther before I would be ready to pursue true happiness.

Making matters worse, I attended playwright David Mamet's new take on *Dr. Faust,* in which the protagonist's ultimate failing is that he diddles far too long before finally deciding to put his life in order. Only when it is too late, when he has lost his wife and son, missed his deathbed chance to embrace the good, and finds himself eternally damned, does Faust seem ready to confront who he is and how he has lived his life. But, good Lord, by then he is dead! Many of us can identify with that kind of indecision and procrastination. When heroes finally acquire self-knowledge in the Greek tragedies Aristotle admired so greatly, it is too late. Scary, but my own powers of resistance and denial seemed Classically heroic.

A CONTEMPORARY ARISTOTELIAN?

As I was wrestling with these issues, I chanced upon a loving remembrance of a man who appeared to be the quintessential Aristotelian. John Jerome was the author of 11 books; however, when he died in early 2002, his passing went largely unnoticed even in literary and publishing circles. His work had never received much public recognition during his life despite the fact that his med- itations on such topics as swimming, mountains, the weather, and building a stone wall were thoughtful and well crafted. According to his brother-in-law, *New Yorker* writer Bruce McCall, Jerome once had been bothered by his lack of financial and critical success, until he realized that the purpose of his writing was the pleasure he derived from the act itself:

> Writing his books indeed seemed almost to become John's compensation for not selling books, until one had almost no relation to the other and he was free to turn his writing to the purest purpose of all: to explain the world he lived in to himself.

According to McCall, Jerome was up at dawn and at his keyboard nearly every day of the year, challenging himself to get his words right, working as carefully "as if he were being paid a thousand bucks an hour." McCall concludes, "John Jerome, hands down, was the most successful writer I've ever known" because he wrote "exactly what he wanted to write about so diligently and uncompromisingly that as the end approached, he seemed . . . at peace in the knowledge that he'd given it his best." From this account, it appears Jerome was "in the zone" nearly every working day of his life. Moreover, he doubtless passed Aristotle's deathbed test with flying colors. *Wow*, I said to myself, *if John Jerome could do it, so can I.* And I could identify readily with Jerome not only to the extent that we both had produced roughly the same number of worst-sellers, but also because I once had even outlined a book on the pleasures of swimming!

Yet, when I reflected further, hadn't I also identified with Clark and Ellison, and for almost the opposite reasons? How could that be? As I thought about it, I realized that I envied Ellison's and Clark's public contributions, and on reflection, those seemed as rewarding to me as the private pleasures Jerome derived from his solitary labors. Indeed, when I applied the threshold test to what I knew about John Jerome's life, I concluded that I could never be happy pursuing his ascetic lifestyle. Maybe I didn't need the 1937 Cord, but I wouldn't mind a new PT Cruiser. And reapplying the deathbed test led to an important insight: I would have to find something between the life of the sultan and the life of the sage. I didn't need to be famous and rich, but couldn't I have a couple of good reviews and an occasional modest-seller? Now the question became, How could I reconcile my seemingly contradictory desires? Getting it right in life, identifying goals that would be satisfying and meaningful in the end, was turning out to be the job of a lifetime. Could Aristotle help?

4

HOW MUCH IS ENOUGH?

A HARVARD MBA TOOK A VACATION TO A SUNNY CLIME,
WHERE HE HIRED A FISHING GUIDE NAMED JOE TO HELP HIM
LAND A MARLIN. JOE WAS IN HIS FORTIES AND LIVED IN
A MODEST HOUSE BY THE SEASHORE WITH HIS WIFE AND TWO
CHILDREN. EVERY DAY, JOE ROSE WHEN THE SUN WAS
WARM AND TOOK A SWIM IN THE OCEAN WITH HIS FAMILY.
THREE DAYS A WEEK, HE ESCORTED CLIENTS OUT TO SEA
IN HIS BOAT, AND THEY WOULD FISH UNTIL THEY HOOKED
A BIG ONE. THE FOUR MORNINGS WHEN HE CHOSE NOT
TO WORK, JOE WOULD SIT IN HIS HAMMOCK AND READ
FROM BREAKFAST UNTIL IT WAS TIME FOR MIDDAY LUNCH
WITH HIS WIFE. ALMOST EVERY AFTERNOON,
HE PICKED HIS KIDS UP AFTER SCHOOL AND TOOK THEM
ON "AN ADVENTURE" OR TO HIS WORKSHOP
FOR HANDICRAFTS. AFTER A LONG DINNER, EN FAMILLE,
JOE AND HIS WIFE WOULD WALK TO A NEARBY CAFÉ
WHERE THE LOCALS GATHERED
TO DISCUSS ISSUES FACING THEIR COMMUNITY.

As the vacationing MBA immediately appreciated, Joe's fishing expeditions were first rate: Joe was a skilled guide, knowledgeable not only about anglers' tackle but also marine biology, oceanography, meteorology, and other subjects about which vacationers were curious. The MBA saw the potential for a big, profitable enterprise. He explained to Joe that it would be easy to put together a group of venture capitalists to "build your underperforming business." Instead of inefficiently taking one client out at a time, Joe could have a fleet of high-tech fishing boats, each accommodating a dozen or more clients. With a little strategic advice, he could branch out into related businesses, perhaps build a high-rise hotel on the beach. Most important, Joe could go on TV and become the marketing face for his business, creating a brand that could be franchised at other sleepy fishing communities: "A guy like you could become a celebrity." The MBA then delivered the clincher: "When that happens, we have an IPO and you get rich!"

After listening patiently, Joe asked, "And what then?"

The MBA quickly answered: "Well, you retire to some nice place on the beach, do a little fishing and reading, and get to spend some time with your wife and kids . . ."

—Story circulating on the Internet

The pursuit of happiness is hard work. If my own experience is a reliable guide, only those well disciplined should attempt the feat, and even they should be prepared to face setbacks in the process. Halfway through writing this book, it became clear that I kept defeating my own efforts to achieve happiness. I had been writing primarily because it made me happy to do so. I was regularly getting into "the zone," spending blissful days pounding the keyboard while hours passed unnoticed and unlamented. I was engaged fully in reading Aristotle, thinking about what I was learning, and seeking ways to convey in simple words the complex things the Ancient had to say about planning the good life. By making a conscious effort to describe behavior that would make me happy, I was convinced I was internalizing the pattern. Virtue, I assumed, was starting to come naturally.

Then the market collapse of 2001 hit me with a vengeance. Caught flat-footed as my retirement account lost much of its value, I realized I would not be able to retire as comfortably or as soon as planned unless I earned more money and invested it more wisely than in the past. So I went into heavy production mode: consulting here, writing a commissioned article there, and picking up the odd honorarium speaking at the Elks' Club. I became so caught up in those labors that it was some time before it dawned on me that I hadn't added a word to this book in months. When I examined my calendar for the coming year, I saw that I had committed almost all my time to work for hire, leaving only a few scattered days for "leisure work" on the book. I had the discipline of a recidivist: I kept postponing the pursuit of happiness.

I told myself I was sensibly investing a little now to enjoy more later, as any practical person would do. But growing unease caused me to question that conventional wisdom. I found myself wondering how much I really needed to retire comfortably, and how anyone ever knew how much money he truly required. As I went back over the process by which I had done my retirement planning, I realized I had not asked those questions in a serious way. Instead, I had accepted the general guidelines in Charles Schwab's retirement manual,

You're Fifty—Now What? Given the amount an individual desires in the future, Schwab offers advice about what investments to make in order to achieve one's goal. In hindsight, I saw that Schwab dealt only with the easy, financial part of retirement planning. The harder part, I now realized, was philosophical: figuring out how much I really needed to support the contemplative activities that put me in the zone. Without such a clear reckoning, I would end up spending the rest of my life making money and never get around to writing the book!

THE PARADOX OF WORKING
IN ORDER TO NOT WORK

Aristotle observes that most people postpone happiness, often until it is too late, because they become caught up in the never-ending pursuit of more. Many feel they have no choice. Although the gods can devote all their time to contemplation, there is no way on earth that humans can do so because, unlike gods, we have to eat. And in order to eat, we have to work. Hence, in this world of scarcity, the pursuit of happiness requires resources.

Aristotle, always practical, addresses our need for resources. He offers a list of necessary ones, including wealth, health, position, friends, children, luck, honor, and good looks, which he says are instrumental to happiness. Though not themselves constituent parts of happiness, these goods may be prerequisites. Having them won't make you happy, but not having them may prevent you from becoming so. For example, good looks are not integral to happiness; if so, Marilyn Monroe would have been happy. Yet a truly ugly person might find it difficult to find friends or a partner to love and be loved by in return, which would limit his or her opportunity to be happy. Thus, Aristotle says good looks may be instrumental to happiness, although characteristically, he doesn't tell us how good-looking we need to be. One of the clearest anti-Aristotelians in all of literature, Oscar Wilde's voluptuary, Dorian Gray, thinks he not only needs to be the most handsome man in the world, he needs to remain handsome even in old age. The extremely handsome Gray dies unhappy.

Among the panoply of instrumental goods needed to pursue happiness, the foremost and most morally complex is money. As a species, we are sometimes called *Homo economicus* because, without wealth creation, we cannot have food, clothing, shelter, and other necessities. And because humans are not beasts, we want to be comfortable, to enjoy good food, nice clothes, and a safe and secure home, not to mention a little decent wine and an occasional trip to Paris. Maybe even a nice vintage Cord auto. So work is a natural activity and, like the wealth it produces, is instrumental to a higher end: We work to live; we don't live to work.

After confirming that there is no avoiding necessity and that we all want a few luxuries, Aristotle then asks, But is it enough merely to live, or even to live comfortably? He answers his own question: What we really want is *to live well*. And living well must mean doing things so blissful that we do them for their own sake, not for the sake of any extrinsic compensation. By definition, such activity is leisure, not work. This is tricky: Recall that Aristotle doesn't categorize professional activities as *work*. Computer nerds are not working when they are hacking, scientists are not working when they are doing research, and professors are not working when they are writing because they all would do those activities even if they weren't paid to do them. To Aristotle, such contemplative activities are *leisure*.

If we are not fortunate enough to have intrinsically leisurelike professions, Aristotle says we have to find a way to free ourselves from work/work in order to make time to contemplate. Ergo, we need money to afford the leisure time required to pursue happiness. To Aristotle, money isn't the root of evil; instead, it is actually a good when it is instrumental to the higher end of creating the opportunity for leisure.

How much leisure time do we need? Obviously, the more the better. The trick is to free ourselves from as much work/work as practical to have as much leisure time for contemplation as possible. Here's the rub: If more leisure

83

requires more money to free up time away from work, only the relatively wealthy can be happy. Indeed, Aristotle says it is easier to pursue excellence if you are affluent, because you have less need to toil and more time for leisure.

Yet few rich people whom Aristotle knew took full advantage of the leisure time their wealth afforded them. Paradoxically, they wasted the opportunity to live well on acquiring yet more money, more than they needed to free themselves to contemplate. It's like that today: A character in the Dilbert comic strip asks, "Can I trade my happiness for more money?"

However, Aristotle observes that some people who are not fabulously rich utilize their money well: They use their limited wealth to maximize their productive leisure time. Although Aristotle was denied the true happiness derived from attending a baseball game on a perfect summer's day at Boston's Fenway Park, I am confident that former Red Sox slugger Ted Williams personified what the Ancient had in mind when he spoke of using one's money well. (At least during Williams's lifetime. Aristotle was silent on the subject of the happiness of freeze-dried corpses!) At the time of Williams's death in July 2002, his biographer, John Underwood, penned these Aristotelian words about the Splendid Splinter:

> He was sensitive about his education (he barely made it through high school), but he could tell you in scientific terms how jet engines worked in the fighter planes he flew in combat in Korea, and exactly why the baseballs he hit with such frequency curved when pitched properly. He was always hammering (his word) at himself to improve: reading, inquiring, listening. Once when we were fishing off Islamorada in the Florida Keys, he announced he had just bought a set of the World Book Encyclopedia. He said: "I know I'm going to be in those books all the time. Every night I'll be in those books." He was fifty years old.

When Williams was a player, baseball stars didn't earn the megabucks they do today, but Underwood says he made enough to "carve out for himself the idyllic, responsibility-free outdoorsman's life." A lifestyle much like the one enjoyed by the Internet's fictional "fisherman Joe." Because Aristotle had known people who behaved like Williams, he concluded that almost everyone is free and able to choose to live a good life, even if they do not have formal educations or oodles of money. Yet everyone needs at least some money.

SO HOW MUCH?

Today we are faced with the same ethical question people have been asking themselves since the glory days of ancient Greece: *How much is enough for me?* Aristotle says this is the right question and offers the barest outline of an answer: We each need enough wealth not to worry where the next drachma is coming from. We need enough to free us from basic concerns about putting bread on our tables, clothes on our backs, and roofs over our heads. Further, we need enough to be comfortable and to have adequate savings, for without a sense of security, we won't have the peace of mind needed to concentrate on higher pursuits.

85

Aristotle likens the pursuit of happiness to training for the Olympics. To get to the starting line, you need resources: a coach, income to support you while you train, good nutrition, and a well-equipped place to work out. But you don't need an infinite amount of such resources. To decide which resources are most important, how much of each you need, and how you are going to obtain them, you must engage in a little analysis. To do that analysis thoughtfully requires a modicum of economic common sense and practical skills. Lacking those, some people who start off with the goal of making the Olympics never get past the stage of garnering the resources needed to support their training. They have to work so hard at fund-raising, they never find time to work out.

Aristotle views people with so little practical sense as unworthy of the big event. Still others raise the necessary funds but then get hooked on the money and lose sight of their original goal. That's a prescription for unhappiness, even for those who appear to realize their dreams. When 1988 Olympic bronze medalist Kim Gallagher died of a stroke at age 38, her obituary did not read like an ode to a happy hero. Here's how she had summed up her "successful" track career in her own words:

> I needed to run for all the wrong reasons. I needed to run to keep my shoe contract. I needed to run to pay my bills. I learned a huge lesson. When I ran in the 1984 Olympics, I was going to be a star. I was going to make so much money, and I did. But it doesn't last if you're not devoted to what you are doing. I was not devoted to my running, and it showed. I don't get a great joy from running or training or going out and doing all the work. Running is not something I love . . .

In Aristotelian terms, Kim Gallagher's unhappiness stemmed from pursuing the wrong ends. Unlike Ted Williams, Gallagher never loved her sport. However, as her obituary writer, Frank Litsky, reported, "She liked what it bought, especially a Mercedes-Benz and a Malibu Home."

In Aristotle's day, the only material reward an Olympian could hope for was an olive wreath. Nonetheless, he warns that financial windfalls, in general, distract from virtuous activity because the responsibility of managing great wealth detracts from the time needed for contemplation and self-development. In sum: Too little money, and one is unable to train effectively; too much money, and one may become lost in materialism. Aristotle explains:

> It seems to some people that good fortune is the same as happiness. But it isn't. It is actually an impediment when it is excessive and, in that case, perhaps it is no longer right to call it good fortune. For wealth has a limit in its relationship to happiness.

In other words, wealth in the right amount supports the pursuit of higher ends, but more is too much. For example, large inheritances often discourage heirs from activities of self-improvement. Larry Ellison might take note of this. Because he will never spend all his billions, he says he plans to leave a fortune to his son, hoping to create a career in philanthropy for him. But would Ellison be doing his son a favor by leaving him filthy rich? Aristotle asks if children from wealthy families wouldn't be better off in the long run if their parents nurtured them and encouraged them to get a good education, to develop their own talents, and, especially, to figure out for themselves what a good life means for them. Warren Buffet makes the same point, asking if it isn't wisest to leave children "enough money so they would feel they could do anything, but not so much that they could do nothing."

To Aristotle, a virtuous person recognizes the point at which he or she has too much of a good thing, whether money, power, or chocolate cake. That's why Imelda Marcos's insatiable love of shoes made her a poster girl of vice and self-delusion. Virtuous common folk know when they don't need a new suit of clothes or an extra glass of beer, as virtuous business leaders know when they don't need another company-sponsored celebration honoring their genius, don't need a new corporate jet, and don't need an extra million in order to be happy. The issue is the same for everyone; just the stakes differ.

87

In Aristotle's view, "Happiness stands on its own without need of any other goods" and is "self-sufficient." A truly happy person won't say, "I'd be happier if I were richer (more powerful) (better looking)." In contrast, people who are hooked on wealth, power, or good looks are prone to unhappiness because there is always something missing in their lives. They always want more. And if their luck turns bad, they sorely miss the money, power, or beauty they once had. But when self-sufficient people run into a spell of misfortune, they are not as badly hurt because they do not value material things so highly, and they have a store of nonmaterial goods to fall back on, which fickle fortune can never take away. The once-rich Mohandas Gandhi and Leo Tolstoy found themselves without appreciable wealth in the waning years of their lives, but they didn't miss the material things they once had in abundance. And when Galileo was imprisoned in Rome for the heresy of saying the earth revolves around the sun, he was not nearly as miserable as the powerless Napoleon was when exiled on St. Helena. Galileo, Gandhi, and Tolstoy were *self-sufficient* because they had contemplative resources to draw on in the absence of material goods. In contrast, when Dorian Gray lost his beauty, he felt the pain as Napoleon did when deprived of his power. Even though Gray and Napoleon had sufficient financial resources to live comfortably, they could not live well because they were not morally self-sufficient.

THE GOLDEN MEAN

In answering the question, *How much is enough?* Aristotle warns us not to expect precise answers from philosophical inquiry. Ethical analysis is not scientific; it does not produce clear and quantifiable results.

> Our discussion will be adequate if it has as much clearness as the subject-matter admits of, for precision is not to be sought for alike in all discussions. . . . It is the mark of an educated man to look for precision in each class of things just so far as the nature of the subject admits; it is evidently foolish to accept probable reasoning from a mathematician and to demand demonstrative proofs from a rhetorician.

Aristotle tells us not to expect to find rules of right and wrong or definitive prescriptions in ethical analysis. Nonetheless, he believes that reasoning men and women can come to rough agreement on most broad ethical issues. But more important than the conclusions we reach is how we construct and think through such problems. When we answer the question, *How much is enough?* Aristotle doesn't care what dollar amount we arrive at; what matters is that we engage in a disciplined moral analysis. To begin that process, he believes we must pose our question in an appropriate context. We should start with a definition of the good life and then ask how much leisure time we will need in order to achieve it. He says we always must keep the highest end in view in order to plan effectively.

Indeed, that concern distinguishes his ethical position from others with which it might be easily confused. For example, an ecologist or person dedicated to a life of material simplicity might mistakenly believe her philosophy is the same as Aristotle's. In fact, Aristotle's ethics of enough is not directly concerned with limiting wealth, production, consumption, or economic growth, per se. To make one's life simpler by consuming less may be of ecological value, but that is not Aristotle's aim (although in some instances, it may be a by-product). Instead, he says we should either increase or decrease our economic activity in light of what we need for living well. Sometimes we must earn more money to have enough to live well; in other circumstances, we need to earn less to achieve the same end. Hence, a good ecologist, who consumes little but spends all her free time channel surfing, surfing the net, or surfing the Pacific, is no more virtuous in Aristotle's eyes than a millionaire who spends his free time making big-ticket purchases. It is what you do with the time not devoted to earning that counts.

Keeping the end in mind, Aristotle counsels us to employ a disciplined process in our individual analysis of what is enough. He suggests we objectively look at all sides of the question, trying to answer the logical objections of those who would disagree with our conclusions. In this way, we will be forced to be honest with ourselves. Aristotle believes that the one person we typically fool in moral analysis is ourself.

To help us decide how much is enough, Aristotle offers the general principle, *We should all strive to live temperate lives.* He proposes that moderation is good and that excess ought to be avoided in passions and actions. This ethical principle should not be thought of as a law. It is not applicable to the sins enumerated in the Ten Commandments because there is no virtue in moderate amounts of killing or stealing. His principle relates more precisely to the Seven Deadly Sins: gluttony, lust, envy, avarice, and so forth. In such arenas where the principle is appropriately applied, Aristotle suggests that there is a golden mean between an excess of a certain behavior on the one hand, and a defect, or shortage, on the other.

Fear and confidence and appetite and anger and pity and in general pleasure and pain may be felt both too much and too little, and in both cases not well; but to feel them at the right times, with reference to the right objects, towards the right people, with the right motive, and in the right way, is what is both intermediate and best, and this is characteristic of virtue. Similarly, with regards to actions there is also excess, defect, and the intermediate.

Thus, to fear everything is cowardly, and to fear nothing is foolhardy and rash. At the golden mean between the two extremes lies the virtue of courage. Another example: At one extreme, abstaining from drinking wine is insensible or unfeeling; at the other, not to limit one's imbibing is self-indulgent. Temperance is intermediate, the virtue found between the defect and the excess. But because the measure of such things is imprecise, no one can say exactly where virtue lies on a continuum. Even brave men feel fear in a battle; and if you are at a party, you ought to have a good time! But too much fear or too much partying is never virtuous.

So where do we find virtue—the golden mean—on a continuum? The mean *in a mathematical sense* is a definable spot, computable by all who seek it. In distinction, Aristotle says that the intermediate *in an ethical sense* is "relative to us." Two glasses of wine might be excessive for me, but you can handle four. (For an alcoholic, virtue is found in abstinence, not temperance. Again, Aristotle's point of reference is the "normal" individual.)

Aristotle uses Olympic training to illustrate his point: If eating $4\frac{1}{2}$ pounds of food a day is excessive and $\frac{1}{2}$ pound is too little, an Olympic coach shouldn't necessarily order $2\frac{1}{2}$ pounds, the arithmetic mean, for all athletes at the training table. Although $4\frac{1}{2}$ pounds would be too much for almost anyone, Aristotle notes that it isn't too much for everyone. He recalls the case of a heavyweight Olympic wrestler named Milo, who once ate an entire ox at one sitting! But there is a point of excess even for the likes of Milo (two oxen?). Aristotle says that the location of the ethical mean, virtue, depends on circumstances we must reckon for ourselves.

TAKING THE MEASURE OF OUR VIRTUE: AN ETHICAL RULE OF THUMB

Aristotle uses art to illustrate why the golden mean isn't found by precisely splitting the difference between extremes. A great work of art, he says, is one that cannot be improved by either adding or subtracting any element from it. But who is the final judge of that? *The artist,* Aristotle answers. He doesn't say others can't judge later; in fact, the definitive judgment of their works is usually rendered after artists have died. Similarly, Aristotle says others should not and probably cannot judge accurately the degree of our own virtue, a judgment of history best levied after we are dead. For the time being, the call is ours.

In assessing our own behavior, the golden mean is a useful, albeit imprecise, metric. For example, in various degrees, the character trait of ambition is either a virtue or a vice. If we lack all ambition, we will never accomplish anything; if we have too much, we may use, perhaps abuse, people and behave immorally to achieve our ends. Too much ambition is excess; too little is defect. So we must ask ourselves, *How much ambition is virtuous?*

Aristotle says we must each determine the proper amount and form of our behavior by conscious moral deliberation in the context of our own particular circumstances and, then, discipline our actions with reference to the golden mean. For example, how temperate a wine drinker should be is a matter of moral deliberation in which the person, time, place, and circumstances are variables to be reckoned with, but excess is obeisance to animal appetite, and defect is ascetic denial of sensual pleasure. Similarly, when political leaders wonder how gutsy a stand they should take on an important issue, the moral question they are asking is, *How much courage is virtuous?* In general, the answer will be that the defect is cowardliness (and inaction) and the excess

91

is foolhardiness (and rashness). But the exact amount depends on the leader and the situation. To Aristotle, we start our individual moral analysis with the general knowledge that virtue almost always lies between two faults along a continuum:

DEFECT (VICE)	MEAN (VIRTUE)	EXCESS (VICE)
COWARDICE	COURAGE	RASHNESS
INSENSIBILITY	TEMPERANCE	INTEMPERANCE
CHURLISHNESS	FRIENDLINESS	OBSEQUIOUSNESS
HUMORLESSNESS	WIT	BUFFOONERY
MISERLINESS	GENEROSITY	VULGARITY
SLOTHFULNESS	PHYSICAL FITNESS	FANATICISM
TIMIDITY	CONFIDENCE	ARROGANCE

A self-confident person is virtuous. She neither thinks too highly of herself nor lacks appreciation of her own capabilities; her virtue of confidence lies between the defect of timidity and the excess of arrogance. And so it is with other virtues and activities.

> Both excessive and defective exercise destroy strength, and similarly drink or food which is above or below a certain amount destroys health, while that which is proportionate produces, increases, and preserves both. So, too, in the case of temperance, courage, and other excellences. For the individual who flies from and fears everything, and does not stand his ground against anything, becomes a coward, and the individual who fears nothing at all but goes to meet every danger becomes rash; similarly, the man who indulges in every pleasure and abstains from none becomes self-indulgent, while the one who shuns every pleasure, as boors do, becomes insensible; temperance and courage, then, are destroyed by excess and defect, and preserved by the mean.

While reminding us that virtue is not exactly in the middle of two extremes, Aristotle nonetheless says we should keep in mind the principle of moderation: Do nothing to excess. To modern sensibilities, this may seem a bit quirky. Too much exercise? We ask how that can be. When he talked about athletic fanaticism, Aristotle had in mind a person like the one I recently read about who took early retirement to devote his life to training for Ironman triathlons. At last count, he was competing in his umpteenth such event (swim 2.4 miles, bike 112 miles, run 26.2 miles). He obviously has remarkable self-discipline to maintain himself at 6 percent body fat, but he has accomplished this at the expense of developing other, higher aspects of his being. When one is working out 4 or 5 hours a day and then recovering, one doesn't have much time for serving on a school board. Indeed, a recent study by medical researchers confirms Aristotle's suspicion, identifying excessive exercise as an addictive vice among 2 percent of college-age males. Those who were exercise-dependent, "put their obsessions first, often ignoring family, work, and their own health."

So how much time should one spend on a lower-level, pleasurable activity? Again, Aristotle offers only general guidelines. The moral task for each of us is to define for ourselves how we should behave between a set of extremes. The process by which we arrive at our definition of virtue is through the application of humankind's unique and most godlike faculty. The exact location of the moral mean must be determined by *reason*.

Here it may seem that Aristotle is all left-brained and rational, ignoring feelings and, thus, being out of step with modern psychology. In fact, his thinking about the mean anticipates the 20th-century work of psychologist Erik Erikson, who places behavior on a continuum with "maladaptive tendencies" at one extreme and "malignant tendencies" at the other. What Erickson calls "healthy" behavior is somewhere in between:

EXTREME	HEALTHY	EXTREME
ISOLATION	LOVE	PROMISCUITY

Erikson concludes that people need to make their behavior conscious, and in so doing, they can help themselves to become healthy. Aristotle's language is different, but his intent is similar. To become fully human ("healthy"), he says we need to overcome our animal impulses ("malignant tendencies"). Building on this, Aristotle says the human virtues of courage, temperance, and generosity can be developed to overcome the "animal instincts" of cowardice, intemperance, and greed. Thus, each of the qualities we call virtues represents mastery over a particular vice or animal-like emotion. To become more virtuous, more fully human, "healthier," we need consciously to discipline our animal impulses based on the guiding principle of the golden mean.

> Since one must choose the mean and not excess or deficiency, and the mean is what right reason says it is, we need to define this. In all the states mentioned, as well as others, there is a certain target to which a person who has reason looks as he tightens or relaxes; and there is a certain place that we say lies between excess and deficiency, being in accordance with right reason. To say this is true but not precise.

Nor is it particularly helpful, unless we apply reasoning to understand it. Aristotle says we set our aim correctly by keeping in mind our ultimate end: a good life. That end should be the "target to which the person who has reason looks as he tightens or relaxes" while searching for the behavioral mean. Thus, there is a sweet spot between excess and deficiency, a place that practically wise people recognize as appropriate for them when they apply reason to the question, *How should I behave if I want to lead a good life?* You want greater precision? Sorry, you have to work it out for yourself! Just remember that Aristotle's general rule is moderation: not too much food, wine, sex, power, money, chocolate, or exercise; but keep in mind that we can never have too much of intrinsic goods like virtue, wisdom, knowledge, integrity, and understanding. The rest, the details, are up to you.

APPLICATIONS (THE HARD PART)

A primary use of the golden mean is to help us answer the question at hand: *How much money do I need to live a good life?* To get us started, Aristotle offers a few general observations:

> Solon, too, was perhaps sketching the happy man when he described him as moderately furnished with externals, but having done the noblest acts and lived temperately; for with only moderate possessions we can do what we ought to do. Anaxagoras also seemed to say that the happy man should not be rich nor a despot when he said that he would not be surprised if the happy man were to seem to most people a strange person; for they judge by externals, since those are all they perceive. The opinions of the wise thus seem to harmonize with our arguments.

95

When wise men and women ask how much it takes in order to be happy, Aristotle says they invariably answer, Not all that much. In the 18th century, John Adams came to a similar conclusion about the virtue of moderation in a letter he wrote to his daughter, Nabby, concerning what she should value in a potential mate.

> No matter whether he is rich, provided he be independent . . . think of no other greatness but that of the soul, no other riches but those of the heart. An honest, sensible, humane man, above all with the littleness of vanity and extravagancies of imagination, laboring to do good rather than be rich, to be useful rather than make a show, living in modest simplicity clearly within his means and free from debts and obligations, is really the most respectable man in society, [and] makes himself and all about him most happy.

The notion that virtue—and, by extension, happiness—is found in moderation is still the dominant belief in America, even after the 1990s' decade-long celebration of excess. Most people today are Aristotelians when it comes to answering the question, *How much money do I need to be happy?*

In 2001, the AARP commissioned a national survey to determine how mature Americans think about wealth and happiness. In the survey, the vast majority of respondents say they need money to provide for their families (74 percent), obtain good medical care (68 percent), and stay healthy (64 percent). But only 18 percent say they need money "to buy more stuff." In proper Aristotelian fashion, most people make the distinction between what they need on the one hand, and what they want—more unnecessary stuff—on the other. At one level, the survey simply confirms what everyone knows: We all must work to earn and save enough so we and our families can lead long and healthy lives without undue concern about future rainy days.

The AARP survey also shows that a shortage of money can make us unhappy, because insufficient wealth prevents us from satisfying our basic needs. Not surprising, a lack of money has negative effects on family life, health, and education. According to the survey, too little money was cited as causing respondents to "delay or skip college" and to "limit school options." To realize our potential, to develop our most human capacities, we need sufficient funds to free us of the necessity to work, exactly as Aristotle said 2,400 years ago.

Although too little money can make us unhappy, the survey revealed that a lot of money doesn't necessarily make us content: Only 18 percent of those surveyed believe "money can buy happiness," and only 23 percent think money leads to "self-esteem." On the other hand, 71 percent of those polled believe money buys "freedom to choose," and 68 percent say it brings "excitement" to the lives of those who have it.

But excitement isn't what most mature Americans have in mind when they pursue happiness. Few people over 50 are observed riding roller coasters at amusement parks, and few put their life savings on the line with a thrilling roll of the dice in Vegas.

Moreover, most Americans see a downside to being too rich. Four-fifths of those polled say excessive wealth makes people greedy and leads to a false sense of superiority, and three out of four believe "insensitivity" is a by-product of great wealth. We might interpret such findings with a touch of skepticism. Many of the people who say they don't want to be rich are older folks who clearly missed their chance, who have realistically downsized their expectations, and who are engaging in ego-saving rationalization about both the root of all evil and the porcine character of those who root for it.

In sum, most people today share certain commonsense, Aristotelian concepts about wealth: Almost all make distinctions between wants and needs; most say happiness is more a product of who you are than of what you have; and nearly everyone views money as a necessary instrument to free up time from work in order to learn and to grow. And there is general agreement that money equates with having the freedom to choose how we will live.

Moreover, there is some consensus about how much wealth is necessary: More than half of those polled define sufficient wealth as about $500,000 in total assets (only 8 percent say they require a million dollars). As a professor of business, I find these numbers quite low, until I remind myself that the average annual income in the United States is about $35,000. For people at or around that level, a half million in assets represents a sum considerably beyond what they realistically can expect to accumulate in their lives. So their calculations are probably right. If people with average incomes were to accumulate that much wealth, they probably would be free to choose. They could get the education they desire and pursue opportunities to develop their potential.

In a casual way, we all make rough calculations of how much is enough. Recently, Ray Lane, Oracle's *numero dos,* decided to leave the company. With some $850 million in the bank, the 53-year-old Lane opted for a more balanced lifestyle: "If I could simply eliminate travel and unproductive meetings, I'd get half of my life back," he told the *New York Times.* He says he now wants to focus on his family and can do so because his new job "is ten minutes from my house. . . . I have no desire to get to the office before 9 A.M., and I won't be taking any business dinners after 7 P.M." Because Lane says he doesn't want to be as rich as Larry Ellison, he has turned down lucrative offers to run big companies: "[But] if I had just a few hundred thousand dollars in the bank, then I'd probably take a CEO job."

So how much is enough for Lane? All we know is that it's more than "just a few hundred thousand dollars" but less than $850 million! How would he know where to draw the line? He doesn't tell us, and it is unlikely he knows. Few people do. That is why we need Aristotle.

Aristotle is in the business of philosophy and not the issuing of moral commandments, so he doesn't tell us exactly how much we need. Instead, he offers a framework by which we each can decide for ourselves. First, he says we must distinguish between needs and wants. He tells us we need a certain amount of money to pay bills and provide comfort for our families. But we do not need unlimited amounts of money to be free from worries about such necessities. Second, in deciding how much we need in order to live comfortably, we must avoid the defect of want and the excess of conspicuous consumption. We need incomes that cover the costs of necessities (food, clothes, rent or mortgage, utilities, insurance), of raising and educating our children, of leisure activities like travel that help us to grow throughout our lives, and of investments sufficient to provide income for our retirement. But we don't need Brioni suits and original Picassos.

The precise amount one needs depends on such factors as age, interests, family situation, and place of residence. Older, single people who live in rural areas do not need as much as younger couples raising kids in Manhattan. Those who enjoy attending opera and those who engage in ecotourism need more than those who contentedly stay at home with a stack of library books. This is one ethical arena where relativism is appropriate. Personal situations and preferences are not only relevant, they are germane to the analysis. In doing our personal calculations, we must be realistic. Though "enough" for Aristotle was tasty food, a comfortable couch on which to recline, and a fashionable toga, even that minimum requires a few more drachmae today than in classical Athens. Let's face it, a million dollars ain't what it used to be; in the posh parts on the San Francisco peninsula, it barely buys a teardown. With such caveats and considerations in mind, we are ready to make our own calculations.

DOING THE NUMBERS

By coincidence, as I was writing this chapter, I received a phone call from an old friend who is a successful businessman living in Marin County. After inquiring about my health and my daughters' latest adventures, he quickly got to what I assumed was the real reason for the call.

> I've been offered the position of principal at _____ [a well-known prep school]. They are honest about why they want me: They think I'll be an effective fundraiser. But that's okay, since I'll also work with the faculty to establish a new curriculum, and I'll be a teacher myself in the math department. That'll be easy for me, but, eventually, I have this passion to teach history. Sure, that'll take several years of preparation and maybe a few college courses, but that's okay, too.

So what isn't okay? I asked.

He answered: "I don't think I can afford to make the change."

As my friend explained, the principal's job paid less than a fifth of what he had been earning as an executive: "I've done the calculations, and I don't see how I could afford to pay the mortgage and other expenses on such a low salary." Because I was "in the teaching racket" myself, he asked if I had any advice to offer.

Had he ever come to the right place! In my wildest dreams, I couldn't have imagined a more sterling opportunity to put Aristotle's ideas to a practical test. Not wanting to frighten him off—and wanting to appear tough-minded and modern—I concealed the ancient source of the advice I proffered. I suggested that he and his wife should draw up three lists:

* One, things they truly need (as opposed to want)
* Two, little luxuries they truly would feel deprived of not having
* Three, things they now have that, in fact, they really wouldn't miss

Once they were confident they could defend the placing of each item on each list, I suggested they make a dollar estimate of the annual costs of each. "Before or after retirement?" my friend asked. I hadn't thought about that, so I winged it. "Well, make up two lists and see if they're different." He agreed to try the exercise and call me back to tell me if it was useful.

A week, then two, passed and my friend didn't call. After I had pretty well forgotten our conversation, he phoned to say he was now principal of the school. He was clearly excited about the prospects. But he didn't mention the exercise I had given him. After a while, I couldn't stand not knowing if he had tried it, so I stealthily asked how he had come to be able to afford to take the job. He answered, "As we started thinking about it, we realized we didn't need a four-bedroom house now that our kid is grown and off on her own. And, as I thought about it, my buying a new car every other year seemed a bit excessive; you know, I don't really like cars all that much. Finally, my wife looked at what she spent every year on clothes and jewels and decided she'd be overdressed at faculty parties. So, all and all, there are going to be fewer pricey presents at Christmas, fewer trips to Europe—and by coach, not business class—and a general downsizing. But it'll be okay; we'll manage."

But how did he finally decide? What tipped the scales in favor of taking the new job? "Well, after 30 years in business, I saw that I was bored, burnt out, and not growing. I decided that I couldn't afford *not* to make the change, no matter how much it cost!" After he hung up, I found myself wishing he had said something more profoundly Aristotelian, perhaps along the order of "We saw that we had become full-time materialists devoting our lives to consumption. Through careful analysis of our needs, we realized that possessors ultimately become prisoners of their possessions. So we decided to free our-selves to find happiness." I would have settled for some acknowledgment that my exercise had been useful! Still, I was proud of my friend.

And what about me? I ran the numbers for myself and discovered that the amount I thought I needed for my retirement was, in fact, excessive. Because I had never enjoyed anywhere near the income to which my friend had be-come accustomed, the exercise was less painful and the sacrifices less dramatic for me than it had been for him. Over my life, I had bought a new car, on av-erage, once every decade. Though the magnitudes differed, the effect was nonetheless the same. When I drew up a list of things I really needed, it dawned on me that my assumptions of future requirements had been based on current levels of expenditures. Because I recently had enjoyed a nice in-come, I had gotten into the habit of buying CDs I seldom, if ever, listened to and videos I could have rented. My wine expenditures bordered on the em-barrassing; the golden mean was a useful guide in right-sizing my consump-tion. I put my contributions to the opera association on the list of "nice but not necessary" expenditures. The "generous" charitable contributions I had been making were really bribes to get better seats, and the money went to subsidize an activity that, on the whole, benefited people more affluent than me. In distinction, I kept my annual donations to the local food kitchen and homeless shelter on the "needs list" (more on this in chapter 10). Finally, some expenditures that I could do without ended up on my list of wants. For example, my wife and I had been going to a lot of restaurants; when I thought about it, most of the time I actually preferred to eat at home. We concluded that we would enjoy dining out more if we did it less. All the above were, per-haps, little things; but when I added them up, the exercise had the same ef-fect on me that it had had on my friend the principal. I hemmed, hawed, resisted, backslid, and, when I finally ran out of excuses, decided there was no alternative but to pursue happiness. So I bowed out of a consulting gig and went back to writing this book.

OBJECTIONS, REASONABLE
AND OTHERWISE

What lessons should others draw from these experiences? Implicit is the conclusion that a great many more people can afford to start pursuing happiness now than are currently doing so. But does that mean everyone should spend less time earning and more time learning? In general, should members of the baby boom generation—at least those who have invested wisely—now say that they have accumulated "enough" and devote the rest of their lives to Aristotlean philosophy and politics?

It seems to me that there are two reasonable objections to moving from the particular (what is good for my friends and me) to the general (what is good for everybody). We have touched on the first, but it bears repeating: Some, perhaps many, people are perfectly happy pursuing more and prefer their material goodies to the (nonexistent for them) benefits of contemplation. In this vein, author James B. Twitchell caused a stir in 2002, when he offered this contrarian view: "Let's give happiness a rest. Consumption of the new luxury is about far more interesting sensations."

I don't know if he has his tongue in cheek, but Twitchell offers an interesting twist on the old idea that the things money buys compensate for the emptiness in our lives. He says going shopping is as therapeutic as psychoanalysis: "The solution to modern angst, to filling up the self, happens both at the psychologist's office and down at the mall." In *Living It Up: Our Love Affair with Luxury,* Twitchell claims, "In the psychiatrist's office you are offered a choice of therapeutic personalities, and at the store you are offered an equally varied choice of adaptable lifestyles." *Choice* is Twitchell's operative word. It is also central to Aristotle's ethics, but the Ancient feels that not all choices are equal. For example, he says that a luxury is of less moral value than a necessity is. But to Twitchell, those who advance such value-laden judgments are, in fact, offering expressions of preferences for "those things that you have that I think you shouldn't have."

Twitchell thus applauds expenditures that an Aristotelian would label as excessive consumption. He believes that America's democratic consumerism, in which even the poor participate, is the prime indicator of the success of our system. He believes it's a sign of social progress that members of today's middle class enjoy consumption the way only the wealthy could a few generations ago: "The act of wanting what we don't need is indeed doing the work of a generation of idealists." Finally, he accuses those with Aristotelian leanings of hypocrisy:

> You are thinking that this may be an interesting subject but that it really doesn't pertain to you. You are certainly not buying all this stuff. You don't like luxury, let alone *love* it. You are not duped by advertising. You can be perfectly happy without most things. In fact, all you need is a few good books, a few interesting ideas, a few friends, a few good conversations, a few sunsets, and you are content.

103

To those who think such Aristotelian thoughts, Twitchell says, *Horse-feathers, you are in denial. That is how you want to think about yourself but, in fact, it is what money buys that makes you and everyone else happy.*

About the time Twitchell's book was published, the *New Yorker* ran a cartoon that summed up his anti-Aristotelian argument: An old man on his deathbed confides to his grandson, "I should have bought more crap." In his day, Aristotle met people with views similar to Twitchell's, and he agreed with them on the point that everyone should be free to pursue happiness as he or she defines it. Nonetheless, he felt a moral obligation to warn them that they wouldn't find it where they were looking. He concluded that all one can do with people like Twitchell is to try to reason with them.

The second objection to Aristotle's views is more substantive and complex. This is the macro version of Adam Smith's micro belief that individual unhappiness breeds productivity. Realists, cynics, and economists say Aristotle is naïve to assume there is a limit to the amount of wealth people should accumulate. They ask, What would happen to the economy if everyone reached a certain dollar amount and said, "That's enough"? Wouldn't growth and innovation stop, jobs cease to be created, and the economy collapse?

A June 2004 *Wall Street Journal* op-ed piece by Daniel Akst takes this position. Akst advises young people to reject the calls to "do good" that they hear at graduation ceremonies. Instead, he argues that new grads should dedicate their lives to "doing well," specifically to making as much money as they can. Because "capital is the life blood of the economy," he says it is the "moral obligation" of everyone to create as much of it as possible. In so doing, he says society prospers and civilization progresses. He even claims that moneymaking is far more "socially responsible" than such "selfish" or self-indulgent activities as teaching, social work, and art, all of which are economically less productive than business and, ergo, less useful. Much as Machiavelli advised leaders that they "must learn how not to be good," Akst counsels young Americans to reject the high-minded advice they hear at graduation time about "public service" and "following their dreams" and, instead, simply "create and amass" wealth.

Four days later, on the *New York Times* op-ed page, David Brooks took the argument a step further, writing that people who devote themselves to making money are most in touch with the masses of Americans and, therefore, possess the essential virtues most needed for leadership. In contrast, people who are "overly intellectual or narcissistically self-reflective" are "decadent elitists" in the eyes of practical men and women and, hence, unfit to govern them. In essence, Brooks and Akst divide the world neatly between, on the one hand, a class of hardworking people who are moneymaking machines (if a bit mindless) and, on the other, the ilk of unproductive pointy-heads who disdain the very system that allows them the luxury of intellectualization and self-reflection.

Aristotle is not interested in class warfare. Like Brooks and Akst, he is firmly on the side of the establishment. He doesn't disdain wealth and doesn't condescendingly argue that the rich should be social workers instead of entrepreneurs. But Aristotle is not interested in ingratiating himself with the rich by endorsing their life choices; instead, he wants to help those who are well off also to live well. He sees no reason that a practical-minded businessperson can't live a full life, indeed every bit as full as the intellectual's. To that end, he argues that it is a mistake for people who have the option to do otherwise to unnecessarily foreshorten their horizons, limit their activities, narrow their experiences, and use only a part of the potential they were born with. In this construct, the professor who churns out narrow technical articles year after year is no more leading the good life than is the businessperson who spends an entire career focused on the pursuit of wealth.

It might be argued that people who dedicate their lives to making money already are leading full lives, and, thus, Aristotle is a condescending elitist to say otherwise. Though it is true that Aristotle has a clear set of values, and he thinks those values are superior to others, he is not trying to impose them on anyone. Instead, he is responding to what he heard from wealthy and powerful people in his era who asked, Is this all there is?

Of course, not all of them asked that question, but a significantly large number did to warrant his trying to help them find a disciplined way to answer it for themselves. In response, he suggests to all those capable of doing so to consider what it would mean for them to live a fuller, more interesting life. That is, what it would be like to be more interested in science, art, politics, history, and economics and what it would mean to spend more time with family and friends and enjoying nature and exploring the great world around them. He thinks it would be useful if everyone were to consider the potential joys of curiosity and learning, activities they can fully engage in throughout their lives. He asks everyone who has the means to do so to take time to consider those possibilities, because he worries that too many bright, hardworking people will miss out on the greatest joys in life because they get caught up in the pursuit of the material goods that Twitchell, Akst, and Brooks say we should desire.

Let's be clear: Aristotle says the issue isn't material goods versus the free "best things in life," and the struggles that matter aren't those between those who are rich and those who are not, or between practical people and intellectuals. Instead, *the real struggle is within each of us about how we will live.* Aristotle might ask which of two wealthy businessmen, both founders of Sun Microsystems, is living the good life: the hard-driving Scott McNealy, who, in his sixties, remains as narrowly focused on accumulating power and wealth as he was in his twenties, or Bill Joy, who, once having made a fortune, stepped out of the daily grind at Sun at age 49 in order to pursue various and multiple interests, often for the sake of merely exploring, and to spend time with family and interesting people who have nothing to do with his work. In Aristotle's eyes, what separates these two similar men is not their wealth or profession but their curiosity. McNealy's interests extend to the world he already knows: the computer business. Joy's expansive horizons include serious study of a gamut of subjects ranging from government regulation to the risks of biotechnology. Joy, who has been called "the Edison of Silicon Valley," is constantly engaged in a multifaceted process of self-development. Significantly, he renews and revitalizes his primary technology skills in the process.

Some will argue that McNealy, the "businessperson" at Sun, doesn't have the same freedom as does Joy, the "creative guy." Though true in the extreme, Aristotle says there is no end to the rationales that people can offer for postponing living a full life. There are always reasons for needing to make that million more. But in midlife, Lalita Tademy, a former VP at Sun, chose to forgo her years of highest income to develop her research and writing skills. Upon discovering papers relating to an ancestor who had been a slave in the 18th-century South, she spent fruitful years uncovering and re-creating her family's past, the story of which was eventually published as the critically acclaimed *Cane River*.

Aristotle assumes all humans are like Bill Joy and Lalita Tademy in that they "desire understanding." Obviously he is wrong. What he probably means to say is that all people *ought* to desire understanding. Indeed, he recognizes that some people do not because they cannot. But others, like McNealy, who are obviously capable of living a fuller life, nonetheless choose not to do so. Brooks and Akst argue such people are doing the morally right thing to focus on wealth accumulation. That is their free choice and their contribution to society. Aristotle agrees it is up to the likes of McNealy to choose to live as they wish; however, *because he respects their intelligence,* he feels an obligation to show them they have other alternatives and to make the case that they at least should reflect on where they are and where they are going.

In so doing, Aristotle does not propose that entrepreneurs and corporate executives should sacrifice their own good for the good of others. In Aristotle's realistic philosophy, selflessness is not a virtue. Instead, the sign of virtue is to act consciously, choosing one's ends rationally and from the "proper disposition" of seeking excellence. The key to virtue is "to deliberate well." Virtuous people are introspective, self-critical, rational, and curious—the acquired characteristics Brooks and Akst call decadent and unproductive. But Aristotle thinks practical people also possess and benefit from those traits; he even doubts they can prosper in their business affairs without them. He says virtuous, practical people ask tough questions about what is right for themselves and for others. When they do so habitually, he believes that not only do they come to understand what is right for themselves, they also do what is right.

Aristotle doesn't say what that right thing is for everybody; he says only that habitually deliberative people are more likely to hit on what is right for themselves, their families, and their communities. Here is his point: If you assume that garnering socially prized goods is what leads to happiness, then it is socially prized goods that you will pursue. But he asks us to consider if the highest goods in life are, in fact, those things that are fashionable. He asks us to at least consider if the biggest social prizes—second homes in Aspen, expensive cars, the power to make decisions that affect other people's lives, attending social events with the beautiful people—are, in fact, the things that would truly make us happy. If we answer yes, he pities us but defends our right to pursue the goods we choose. If we answer no, he asks, "What, then, is the good?" He offers some guidance as we attempt to answer that question, by suggesting that we may be more likely to find what we are looking for if we learn to distinguish between those goods that are socially prized—wealth, fame, sensual pleasure—and those goods that are universally praised— honesty, justice, moral courage, and integrity. Although he tells us what he thinks the good is not, he never defines what it is. That is for us to discover.

Aristotle believes that the process of deliberation will cause more people to act like Bill Joy than like Scott McNealy, but he is not an extremist, and he is more than realistic. When he concludes that deliberate men and women will choose to limit their wealth production, he does not mean that entrepreneurial activity should cease or that millionaires should give up their fortunes and join ashrams. His point is not that wealth creation is bad, but, instead, that moderation is good.

It is simply unrealistic to assume a doomsday scenario in which all people quit producing and head to the library. Here's an example of how Aristotelian virtue manifests itself in the real world: Dan Lynch, a noted venture capitalist, told a friend how he once bet an entrepreneur which of them would become a billionaire first. They were neck and neck for a while, but, thanks to Lynch's investments in CyberCash and InfoSeek, it appeared he would be the first to make the grade. Then, as Lynch tells the story, "One day I called my friend up and said, 'I'm out. I don't want to play any longer.'" What made him come to this? "I saw myself cramming people for a point or two, but what did a point or two mean to me at that stage?" Translation: He was squeezing the percentage of the action that founders of businesses got as their share of an IPO he was financing. He realized he had enough when he saw that he was making money solely for its own sake and was willing to hurt others in the process. He then moderated his behavior accordingly. And Lynch's contribution to the economy wasn't missed when he later pursued other, less-macho investments.

Will the economy collapse if more mature business leaders behave like Dan Lynch and Bill Joy, choosing to spend more time with their children, more time working on the problems of their communities and society, and more time becoming fully aware and multidimensional human beings . . . and, of course, less time trying to be the richest, most powerful men in the world? Only if one believes that there aren't plenty of other ambitious young people in the queue who are qualified and anxious to do more to keep the economy growing, when 50-somethings like Lynch and Joy decide to spend less time doing the same. Let's not forget that there are plenty of people so hooked on wealth accumulation that the economy will keep humming even if a few affluent people take a step back and start asking about the quality of their lives, in addition to worrying about their standard of living. And more than a few zillionaires will choose to continue rolling merrily along making themselves unhappy, adding to the GNP, and covering for you and me as we slack off a bit, earning less but learning more.

To Aristotle, there is nothing wrong with making more money unless doing so eclipses other, morally higher concerns. In fact, the issue isn't economic. We all aren't going to quit being *Homo economicus*. The issue is that we are also social, political, and philosophical animals. So Aristotle asks us to consider how we might spend our time in useful and rewarding ways in addition to making money. Balance and moderation as a way of life may be out of the question for a few driven souls, but is it beyond the reach of the rest of us who now have just enough to ask if, indeed, we have enough?

109

CONTEMPORARY ARISTOTELIANS

Most of the examples cited in these pages are males because, historically, men far more than women have been conditioned and expected to sacrifice other goods for wealth, honor, and power. Since before the time of Aristotle, the highest material prizes in Western societies have gone to men or have been reserved for men. This is now changing, and, as a result, there are growing numbers of Aristotelian and anti-Aristotelian women. For example, Hewlett-Packard's CEO, Carly Fiorina, has much in common with her peers in the corporate world in terms of her focus on power at the expense of other ends. Based on her many public pronouncements, the anti-Aristotelian Fiorina is an extremely capable and successful leader who casts every issue in terms of marketing. Indeed it is a positive sign of gender equality that there is a growing number of examples of women executives who behave in the traditional ways established by men.

Although the behavior of professional women is as diverse as that of their male peers, some of the best illustrations of contemporary Aristotelianism concern choices made by women. In the 1980s, Sue Bender was a successful commercial artist in New York, juggling two careers and two children the way so many professional women do. She valued accomplishments and results, and got them living a frenzied, fragmented life of "frantic energy," starting each day with a lengthy "to-do" list, and measuring her success by the number of items she had ticked off by midnight. Then, one day she asked herself, "Success at what cost?" In her book, *Plain and Simple,* she recounts how she then set out to answer the question, *Is there another way to lead a good life?* Her hard-won answer was to stop doing what "everyone said" successful people do. She got off the frenetic merry-go-round, but, importantly, she didn't abandon her career, her family, or New York. Instead, she describes how living with an Amish family for a few weeks helped her to quit trying "to be a star," to quit trying always to achieve "more," to quit engaging in "busyness" for the sake of busyness, and to slow down and take in the full richness of life, deriving happiness from the intrinsic pleasures of artistic creation instead of from sales and praise. In sum, she chose Aristotelian moderation and balance.

In *The Last Gift of Time: Life Beyond Sixty,* author Carolyn G. Heilbrun (aka, mystery writer Amanda Cross) offers a series of insights that led her "to choose each day for now, to live." Opting to move away from a successful university career while at the top of her game (because of poisonous faculty politics and the narrowness of academic life), she chose something other than retirement: a fuller life. Unlike those who find nothing to do after a lifetime on the job, she discovered leisure/work that needed to be done and an array of valuable ways to invest her time:

> It is not easy to decide what to undertake, what endeavor or activity will reward the devotion of one's hours in learning a new skill or acquiring new knowledge. Sadly, in our society there is a grievous need for individuals willing to dedicate their time

and energies in a serious manner. There are the dying in hospices, the hungry in soup lines, the homeless in shelters, battered women and their children, the newborn abandoned to exist as "boarder babies," desperately—for their life may depend on it—in need of company, affection, being touched or talked to. There are numerous opportunities for tutoring and teaching, projects that require patience and skill. And for those whom "social" work does not appeal there is politics, the grassroots politics, the work in local elections, on school boards and other important bodies. There is time now to read, in a serious, organized way—all of Shakespeare, novels of a single century or country, the works of a single poet or novelist. I have a friend who at the age of sixty took up playing the piano.

She argues that one needn't be rich to do any of the above, only "comfortable." In proper Aristotelian fashion, she says, "I am fortunate in that I have seemed never to wish for what I could not afford."

A summer 2004 issue of *Fortune* contained a retirement guide promising "Retire Rich: How to Get Set for Life." In it, the editors claimed to provide a method by which readers could calculate "The Number," the exact amount they would need in order to retire in style. A few weeks later, reader Rhoda Blecker wrote the following contemporary Aristotelian words to the magazine's editors:

> Despite having an MBA, I have always tried to live by the Talmudic precept that states a rich person is one who treasures what he has. I have always saved rather than acquired, because it is the way I was brought up and because my self-image is not tied to a bigger house, an upmarket car, or Ferragamos. When my husband retires next year, I will still work, not for financial reasons but because I believe I can be of value. For those who need more and newer possessions, there may never be enough money; there may never be a "number."

5

VIRTUE WON'T HURT YOU

WHO MADE ME WHAT I AM? ENGLAND? MY FATHER? MY SCHOOLS?
MY PATHETIC, TERRIFIED MOTHER? OR SEVENTEEN YEARS OF LYING
FOR MY COUNTRY? "WE REACH AN AGE, SANDY," YOU WERE KIND
ENOUGH TO INFORM ME, "WHERE OUR CHILDHOOD IS NO LONGER
AN EXCUSE. THE PROBLEM IN YOUR CASE IS, THAT AGE IS
GOING TO BE ABOUT NINETY-FIVE."

—*JOHN LE CARRÉ*, THE CONSTANT GARDENER

Although I found Aristotle's guidance to be practical in thinking about how much money is enough, it wasn't as clear how his golden mean applied to my insatiable desire for approval. I wanted all the respect and recognition I could get, but how much did I really need? I went back to Aristotle for further guidance, only to discover he was silent on the particular question that troubled me. What I found, instead, was an exegesis on the subject of virtue containing the reminder that, when in doubt about what will make us happy, we should return to an examination of basics. When we are having a problem finding our way, Aristotle says it is usually because we don't know where we are going. And if we are dissatisfied when we get to where we think we want to be, it is because we are seeking the wrong ends. It comes down to what he calls "right desire."

Aristotle defines virtue as the disposition to desire "the right things." The right things are those naturally good for humans, things we all need in order to develop our potential. He says a person who routinely desires and acts to obtain what is good for her is virtuous. She has disciplined her high-level reasoning powers to overcome her low-level passions so that, as a matter of course, she desires what she truly needs. Because her wants have become "right desires," she is seeking excellence and is on the path to happiness.

Two contemporary Aristotelians illustrate what the Ancient had in mind. In their late fifties, George "Skip" Battle and Benjamin Dunlap committed themselves to spending a full month every year teaching and mentoring young leaders from the public and private sectors, frequently traveling as far as Africa to do so. The discipline involved in keeping their commitments to this nonprofit leadership program cannot be overestimated. Unexpectedly, soon after agreeing to participate in the program, Battle was asked to be CEO of the then-failing dot-com, Ask Jeeves, and Dunlap was chosen president of then-struggling Wofford College. Although it has required them to give up vacations, placed considerable strain on their families, and, in Dunlap's case, created a financial burden, both have planned their complicated lives in order

113

to meet all their responsibilities. Seven years later, they both continue to volunteer their time to the benefit of society and, while so doing, also have led successful turnarounds of their respective organizations. To put what they have done in perspective, imagine Jack Welch having taken a month off annually from GE to do community service or Lawrence Summers not phoning in to his presidential office at Harvard because he is in Ghana teaching the fundaments of democratic leadership.

When I thought about how I allocated my own time, I saw I failed miserably when it came to identifying what was good in the long run, and even when I had good ends in sight, I lacked the discipline to stay the course. Truthfully, most of the time I actually chose to pursue things that were bad for me. I found Aristotle reassuring on this point. He says my problem is a common one and identifies its source: *Vice is exciting whereas virtue is, well, a bit tedious.* That's why most people associate hedonistic pleasures with happiness, and developmental activities are linked with piety and boredom. Who wouldn't want to spend time sailing on a yacht, especially if the alternatives were such activities as analyzing the complex issue of health care in order to become a more informed citizen or tutoring African civil servants?

But how do we come to desire "aright"? How do we come to know what is good for us, and then discipline ourselves to pursue it? In my fifties, it dawned on me that I didn't do things that were good for me because my inappropriate desires for recognition were so powerful that I couldn't imagine being happy without their being realized. Instead of enjoying a healthy hike, a good book, a conversation with a thoughtful friend, or signing up to teach in Ben and Skip's leadership program, I retreated to my study to brood about the happiness (recognition) I was missing. When I was really brooding, I actually became angry that my efforts hadn't been appreciated. Now, thanks to Aristotle, I am beginning to see that I was the author of my own unhappiness. As Emerson observed, "Every minute you are angry, you lose sixty seconds of happiness." What I wasn't ready to accept was Aristotle's contention that if I learned to desire "the right things," those developmental and com-

114

munity activities would bring me greater happiness than I would find in a glowing book review.

Aristotle believes that most men and women habitually choose the wrong short-term activities, and that's what leads to our long-term discontent. We needn't do so, he says, but it will only be otherwise if we come to see that virtue isn't necessarily painful. Contrary to common wisdom, he believes that virtue, when properly understood, can be pleasurable. The problem is that we think about happiness in mistaken terms.

CONFUSING PLEASURE WITH HAPPINESS

For the vast majority of men and women, the great tragedy of life is not getting what we want. Few of us are as rich, successful, or respected as we would like, and many of us fail to find all the sensual pleasure we desire. Paradoxically, there is a similar want among those who are the most rich, famous, and powerful, those who thus have sensual pleasure most at their command. On one hand, it's nice to know that those at the top still have something to strive for; on the other hand, it's disconcerting to think happiness may be unattainable, and we are all doomed to a life of discontent.

Aristotle has a slightly different take on this. He says the observed paradox is explicable if we see there is a logical error in confusing happiness with other "goods" like pleasure. He tells us not to despair. Happiness is attainable in this life; it only seems hard to come by because we mistake it for other things.

Here Aristotle says we need to make some clear distinctions between related concepts that we tend to blur in casual conversation. He asserts there are separate and distinct categories of "goods"—the pleasant, the useful, and the noble—and we are led astray if we confuse them. The pleasant category includes base things, pleasures of the body that hedonists enjoy in the manner of animals. The useful category includes goods like money and power, which are means to the pursuit of either pleasure or nobility; they also have some intrinsic elements of satisfaction. In Aristotle's view, happiness is found neither in the pleasurable category—wanton sex, six-packs, and $4,000 Armani suits—nor in the useful—which includes the power inherent in being a CEO and the honor of having one's picture on the cover of *Time* magazine—as much as we may believe these are the most desirable goods.

Instead, Aristotle says that happiness is found in the possession of *noble* goods, ones of intrinsic moral value. Although he doesn't offer a simple definition of noble goods, he implies that they are contemplative and developmental. What he does say is that people of good character, like Ben and Skip, can discern the difference between noble goods and goods that are merely pleasant and useful. Moreover, virtuous men and women habitually choose to pursue noble goods to the exclusion of others. Those choices entail the practical decisions we make concerning how to allocate and organize the time of our lives. Aristotle calls such choices "ethical" and asserts that they are the most important decisions we make in our lives because, all told, they constitute one's life plan.

VIRTUE AS A MATTER OF CHOICE

According to Aristotle, life isn't about rules or imposing rules. Rather, it is about choices and tradeoffs, about setting priorities, doing this instead of that and that before this. Amused, he observes us as we explicitly and implicitly, consciously and unconsciously, go about setting scores of small priorities: "In the theater, people who eat sweets do so most when the actors are poor." The ethical question then is, How should one decide what to do and when to do it? Aristotle admits that rules or rules of thumb sometimes help ("Don't act like an animal"), but they are by nature imprecise and, thus, take us only so far. The key to ethical decision-making is to ask ourselves the right questions, to explore our options from different perspectives, particularly perspectives opposed to ours and, if the decision is not a personal one, from the perspectives of all those who would be affected by the outcome of our decision. Doing that is what makes a decision ethical.

When choosing what goods we will pursue and, in the process, planning how we will spend our time, Aristotle assumes that most thoughtful people begin at a common starting point: a minimal sense of what is right and wrong based on the exercise of reason. First, he assumes we share a commonsense objection to excesses of bodily pleasures, such as too much food, drink, and sex. Second, he believes we can agree that there are excess desires for goods that, though worthy in moderation, such as victory, honor, and wealth, may be bad for us in the extreme. Third, he says there is a near-universal repugnance of bestial and morbid pleasures, things that are always bad, like murder and mayhem. Because choosing not to do things in the latter category is easy, he applies himself to helping us make more-informed decisions relating to the first two categories. In so doing, he returns to an analysis of our animal natures.

Like other animals, humans experience sensations, the broadest and most general categories of which are pain and pleasure. Like other animals, humans have appetites, which are developed in us as the complex feeling called *desire*. Aristotle says sense perception drives bovine behavior: Cows see grass and are driven by the appetite to eat it; bulls smell cows in heat and are driven by the biological urge to mount them. Humans share such beastly proclivities but can also desire things we don't see or smell ("the very thought of you"), and we can wish for things we never can see (abstractions like love, truth, and happiness). We also have the ability to apply our intelligence to the pursuit of our desires. Though animals can't help themselves when they pursue their appetites ("don't blame the wolf for devouring a lamb"), the conduct of humans is different. Due to our unique capacity to reason, only we among animals can choose the ends we pursue and the means to pursue them.

Although we have an innate capacity to make such moral choices, it is not natural to do so. Unlike animal instinct, the human ability to reason—to ask what is right or wrong for us—is not automatically or naturally developed. Considerable effort is required to develop the capacity for moral choice, and it takes many years from birth to maturity to develop it. In Aristotle's construct, physical sight is natural, but ethical insight is learned. And virtue is a question of seeing things clearly and correctly: in his words, "seeing aright." He means that people who fail to notice and reflect upon the moral implications of their actions are, in a sense, feeling their way through life blindly.

Whereas physical blindness is the inability to see things in the external, material world, moral blindness is the absence of insight. Aristotle asks what chance a morally blind person has of discerning the difference between a noble goal and one that isn't? Fortunately, he tells us that moral blindness is unlike physical blindness in that the morally blind can learn, under certain circumstances, to see. The rub is that they first must acknowledge their blindness. Next, they have to decide what it means to be a seeing, morally perceptive person. They must come to understand what it means to have insight, and then commit to developing that capacity. Finally, they have to learn to use their insight to size up ethical situations, then make effective choices about how to behave given the circumstances. Unfortunately, there are no laws or rules concerning moral choice. Through experience and practice, we learn to use reason to read situations and other people and especially to see ourselves.

"INTO THE WOODS"

If Aristotle's thoughts about virtue and desire seem vaguely familiar, that's because they're the stuff of fairy tales. In such children's stories as Cinderella and Rapunzel and, especially, in the Greek myth of Oedipus, the physical loss of sight is a metaphor for moral blindness. Blind characters in those stories wish for and chase after things that are bad for them. In 1977, child psychologist Bruno Bettelheim examined texts of familiar myths and traditional children's stories and showed that they are, in effect, morality tales based on the common theme of trying "to find meaning in our lives." In *The Uses of En-*

chantment, Bettelheim explains that this search for meaning is a lifelong process in which finally "gaining a secure understanding of what the meaning of one's life may or ought to be . . . constitutes having attained psychological maturity." Bettelheim says childlike illusions prevent us from perceiving reality, and we can't grow up until we come to terms with the world as it is as opposed to how we wish it to be. Fairy tales help us by explaining the conscious and unconscious fantasies of youth, the universal human problems that get in the way of seeing life as it really is.

Myths are our collective desires. Children deal with the terrifying realities of life through fantasy and wish fulfillment. To brighten and make bearable the scary and troubling world of childhood, boys and girls wish for a pot of gold, a Prince Charming, a fairy godmother, or a gingerbread house. What these good things have in common is that they are unattainable in real life. Searching for these unrealizable goods, young people embark on a psychological journey through "the woods." Significantly, Bettelheim uses the same dark, foreboding metaphor that the poet Dante uses to describe the midlife crisis in *The Inferno:*

> *Midway in our life's journey, I went astray*
> *from the straight road and woke to find myself*
> *alone in a dark wood. How shall I say*
>
> *What wood that was! I never saw one so drear,*
> *so rank, so arduous a wilderness!*
> *Its very memory gives a shape to fear.*

Like the fairy-tale characters Little Red Riding Hood, Hansel and Gretel, and Jack (of beanstalk fame), real youngsters get "lost in the woods" while pursuing their fantasy wishes. In order to get what they think they want, kids lie, like Ms. Riding Hood, and they steal, like Master Jack, and then pay a price for their moral transgressions in the form of cruel and unusual punishment. Fairy-tale kids are blinded by birds and eaten by wolves. In fairy tales, the very pleasures youthful characters pursue turn into beasts, giants, witches, and ogres, which then devour them.

Of course, they (children) grow up to be us (adults). And, if we are lucky, during this painful journey through the woods, we become *dis*illusioned—we abandon fantasies and come to see the world as it really is. We are then transformed, made different than we were, changed into mature, wise, practical adults. And so the story ends in the words of the Brothers Grimm: "They lived for a long time afterward, happy and in pleasure." Note that people don't "live happily ever after" because eternal life is also fantasy; instead, the fairy tale ends in an adult life of emotional security and inner confidence. To Bettelheim, this is also the process of psychotherapy. He adds that it is also the philosophy of Aristotle, whom Bettelheim quotes as saying, "The friend of wisdom is also a friend of myth." In essence, the philosopher and the psychologist agree: Those who understand the moral lessons of myths can become wise.

Aristotle's *Ethics* draws a clear distinction between wishes and choices. The Ancient says we often wish for the impossible, for ends like immortality, which are not under our control. In contrast, we choose things we can control, such as the means we pursue to achieve our intended ends. "We wish to be healthy and we choose the things that will give us health." A key distinction between the two is we wish "for whatever strikes our fancy," but we choose our actions with deliberation. Thus, choice is an activity of mature minds involving reason and careful thought. Because wishes are fantasies, they are products of immaturity; because they are made absent deliberation, they may entail bad ends for the wisher. Here is another instance of modern psychology reinventing Aristotle's ideas and putting them in the context of contemporary scientific and social thought. Bettelheim, like Freud and Jung before him, echoes Aristotle's treatment of "adult dreams"—wish fulfillment with regard to winning over all competitors, finding the pot of gold at the end of a rainbow, attending a ball and finding Prince Charming. And, I might add, becoming a famous writer.

The theme of Stephen Sondheim's musical play, *Into the Woods,* is that fairy tales aren't just for children and that our understanding of them deepens as we grow older. Based on Bettelheim's work, this popular show is about wish fulfillment in adulthood. Indeed, the first words sung in the play are "I wish." The songs describe how immature people are attracted to the unattainable (a princess in a tower), "Agony beyond power of speech, when the one thing you want is the only thing out of your reach"; how we wish for things that "are not to be touched" (a giant's pot of gold), "The harder to get the better to have"; and how we wish for things that are bad for us (a wolf-man desires sex with an underage Little Red Riding Hood), "Are you certain your wish is what you want?" The show is funny, the music beautiful, but the ultimate effect is sadness. Adults in the audience are frequently in tears at the final curtain because they identify with the characters who never grow up, some of whom die in futile pursuit of childish fantasies.

This is practical stuff. Those in 2003 who saw clips on television from the home video of the Tyco orgy in Sardinia saw the excessive and unethical expenditures that the 55-year-old Dennis Kozlowski made with his shareholders' money as the acting out of adolescent wrong-desire. When I recently saw *Into the Woods,* I experienced a gut-wrenching realization that my own, less expensive, desire for public recognition was a youthful fantasy I had carried into my sixth decade. Would I never outgrow it?

Alas, it is possible to take our unfulfilled wishes to the grave. At age 79, Pierre Cardin is the most successful clothing designer of his generation and doubtless the wealthiest. He lives in a Xanadu-like circular Bubble Palace near Cannes and has some 31 other pleasure pads spread around the globe. Cardin proudly proclaims that noble goods are not for him. He does not desire fulfillment as a creative artist. Instead, he says, "I want to die the richest man in the world." He may still be emotionally in the woods because he spent an unhappy childhood moving from one factory town to the next as his family looked for work in the aftermath of World War II. But philosophy is concerned neither with identifying the deep-rooted causes of misbehavior nor with providing excuses for why people do things that harm themselves. Instead, the purpose of philosophy is to clear our heads so we can make rational choices now.

HAVE WE MENTIONED SEX?

Though it is difficult to analyze the role adolescent fantasy plays in the lives of adults with regard to such useful goods as money, power, and respect, it is relatively easy to do so with regard to carnal pleasures. It is certainly more entertaining. Aristotle says there are men and women who spend their entire lives seeking base pleasures. We need only cite play "boy" Hugh Hefner, only a few calendar years younger than Cardin but with the emotional maturity of a teenager. Aristotle and Bettelheim agree that the object of moral development is to free ourselves from the endless, immature quests to which men like Hefner devote their lives. The philosopher and the psychologist are in accord that a universal part of growing up is getting ourselves out of the fantasy-cluttered woods of our youth. Where they disagree is on the means and methods to make this escape. For example, what, if anything, might be done about Hefner's lingering immaturity depends on one's disciplinary perspective. No one, except an ayatollah, would advocate forcing Hef to be virtuous, and nearly every realistic person would recognize his behavior as extreme, particularly for one his age. And surely it would be as hard for him to kick his hedonistic habits as it would be for a lifelong heroin addict to give up drugs. Those caveats registered, Plato would say, "Forget about him. He's an inferior being, incapable of virtue." Bettelheim would say, "He needs about five years of therapy, three sessions a week, and we'll cure him of his obsessive behavior." Aristotle's take would be different. He might say, "If Hefner is at all capable of change at his age, it would be through a process of reflection on experience. In order for him to understand satisfaction has eluded him for seventy-plus years because he has wished for the wrong things, he would have to learn the art of reasoned choice, of moral deliberation." Or, to put it in the immortal words of the Sage of Minnesota, Garrison Keillor:

> Some luck lies in not getting what you thought you wanted but in getting what you have, which once you have got it you may be smart enough to see is what you would have wanted had you known.

FIRST STEPS OUT OF THE WOODS

To the likes of Hefner, Aristotle would say that the first step on the path to virtue is acknowledging that beastly behavior, though natural, is not appropriate for humans.

> Each animal is thought to have a proper pleasure, as it has a proper function—that is to say, that which corresponds to its activity. If we survey them species by species, this will be evident: Dog, horse, and man have different pleasures. As Heraclitus says, "Asses would prefer sweepings to gold, for food is pleasanter than gold to asses." By extension, the reasoning function of mankind is also the source of our proper pleasure.

Although some people may act like animals, in fact they are not. However, as long as they rationalize their bad behavior as driven by uncontrollable instincts, they will never change and will have no chance of raising their moral horizons from the sty to the sky. Yet, Aristotle believes that even an inveterate voluptuary knows the difference between animal and human behavior. Without having to deliberate the difference, almost everyone knows it is not good to act like a beast, nonetheless some still do. Why?

Aristotle's least-controversial example of a virtue that almost all people recognize is *generosity*. Perhaps universally, a generous person is defined as giving: She gives of her time, sharing with friends, family, or colleagues at work her advice, wisdom, experience, information, knowledge, praise, help, encouragement, gentle admonitions, and support. In every culture, the *capacity* for such generosity is innate, but nowhere is its *exercise* automatic. Those who have observed children at play appreciate that one has to build a disposition toward generosity. Even as we mature, we sometimes have to remind ourselves not to be selfish when someone comes to us for help or advice. But, at a certain point, we may overcome the natural tendency to selfishness and start to become habitually generous. Aristotle says this happens when we learn to find greater pleasure in giving than in selfishness. Then, Aristotle says, we are on the path to virtue and happiness.

But is it true that we all share a common view on what is virtue and what is vice? For instance, isn't Aristotle wrong about sensual pleasure, which many people think of as every bit as good as generosity? If it is, all other considerations aside, why isn't Hefner virtuous when he engages in it? By extension, why aren't the possessors of wealth, fame, praise, honor, and power virtuous? Aristotle takes no position for or against the possession of such goods because, from an ethical perspective, they are intrinsically neutral. Instead, he believes "their goodness depends on the goodness of their possessor," as the noted Aristotelian scholar Sir Anthony Kenny explains. In the hands of a good person—say Lincoln or Gandhi—power might well be a good thing, but in the hands of a megalomaniac—like Alexander or Napoleon—power is not good for them or for those who stand in their paths to glory.

It might be useful for possessors of pleasant and useful goods to know that the things they value might be made noble by their personal virtue. This is where character comes in. Because Aristotle believes that people can make conscious and rational choices about their behavior, virtues are thus states of human character, traits we can choose to develop. Yet most of us don't choose to do noble things because, Aristotle tells us, we are not purely rational beings. According to the Ancient, our souls have both rational and irrational elements, the latter being the home of our passions. He defines passions as innate and instinctive and offers a list of examples:

> appetite, anger, fear, confidence, envy, joy, friendly feeling, hatred, longing, emulation, pity, and, in general, the feelings accompanied by pleasure or pain.

Where appropriate, such passions have a rightful, even necessary, place in our lives; however, moral problems arise when passions aren't kept in their place. A person who is driven by the passion of appetite has poor character by Aristotle's definition because he is not in control of his life. A person lacks virtue when he lets his passion for a sybaritic lifestyle overcome his rational understanding that he ought to be engaged in things good for him and society in the long run. Although this is admittedly a value judgment, Aristotle says we can't avoid making it about ourselves if we choose to pursue virtue and happiness.

In my own case, following Aristotle, I am not behaving virtuously when I choose to make an extra buck, watch a basketball game on TV, have a glass of wine, or engage in some other useful or pleasurable activity *when I could have chosen* to use the same free time in a noble, developmental pursuit, such as tutoring, writing, or studying. Again, there is no vice involved in my choosing pleasurable and useful goods for recreation, but if I do so habitually, I exclude doing the virtuous things that are good for me and, thus, I reduce the likelihood of my finding long-term happiness.

And how do I know what is "good for me"? By continually applying the deathbed test. Here's my personal version of the test: Will I assess my life more positively at the end if what I have to show for it is (a) an × amount of dollars in the bank, 10,000 NBA games watched, and a like number of glasses of chardonnay consumed, or (b) an × number of books read and written, a contribution to the welfare of my community, and many hours spent with friends, family, and colleagues in serious discussion? Here's the question for Hef: Does he want the measure of his life to be the number of his bedmates?

As this illustrates, the particulars of the deathbed test depend on each individual's personal set of wishes and vices. In my case, to get out of the woods and stay out, I have found I must do this self-assessment on a regular basis. Having done so repeatedly, I now realize that, because of a combination of pleasure-seeking and moral inertia (a) is the default scenario for me, and (b) will become possible only if I habitually choose to make it so. But here's the hard part: I will not make the right choices as a matter of course until I come to find the (b) activities as pleasurable as the (a) activities.

So, in my late fifties, I have come to the harsh realization that I have to begin to "desire aright" and that requires making hard choices. And I suspect that for Hefner and others like him, such a conclusion might be as comfort shattering as it has been for me. Indeed, it is understandable why many people reject both Aristotle's conclusions and the implications for their behavior. After all, who wants to choose (unpleasant) virtuous activities over (pleasurable) vices? No wonder people resist doing what is good for them. I know how hard I have resisted.

SEARCHING FOR EXCELLENCE IN THINKING AND FEELING

Fortunately, Aristotle makes his case for virtue positively, equating it with "excellence," a virile characteristic Hefner might relate to more easily than wimpy (and boring) "morality." Excellence is the habitual disposition of striving to achieve all one is capable of doing and becoming. To achieve excellence, one obviously must be in control of one's life. Hence, Aristotle and Bettelheim both say young people are incapable of excellence because they are controlled by their passions. And adults act like immature children when they organize their lives around the pursuit of lower-level pleasures. In contrast, because "reason rules over the passions" of mature adults, Aristotle says we become capable of planning our lives based on moral deliberation; thus, around midlife, we start to become capable of excellence.

Implicit in Aristotle's construct is a natural and lifelong struggle between passion and reason, between feeling and intellect. Here, he is said to part company with psychologists. Bettelheim called Aristotle the "master of pure reason," implying that the Ancient overlooked the importance of feelings. Although Aristotle does divide the human soul into two hemispheres—reason on the one side, passion on the other—he does not slight the emotional side in favor of the intellectual:

> For we say that some excellences are intellectual and others moral: philosophical and practical wisdom being intellectual; generosity and temperance moral. For in speaking about a man's character we do not say that he is wise or has understanding, but that he is good-tempered or temperate.

Aristotle is saying we must develop both sides of our nature: our mind (related to the use of reason) and our character (related to passions or feelings). Hence, when he cautions against behavior ruled by passion, he doesn't say that such "animal" instincts as anger, fear, lust, grief, and envy are wrong and can or should always be avoided. He instead says there are appropriate times for, and appropriate levels of, such emotions. In the next chapter, we explore a practical use of that insight with regard to anger.

Some psychologists scoff at Aristotle for advocating "right reasoning" as a key to happiness, dismissing him as being all head and no heart. In fact, there is a duality in his thinking, again reflected in the writings of history's greatest Aristotelian, Jefferson, whose famous "dialogue between my head and my heart" illustrates the essential tension between emotions and reason. Psychologists ignore this and draw a sharp dichotomy between the realm of feelings (positive) and the realm of reason (negative), arguing that Aristotle's emphasis on rationality means he ignores the important domain of emotions.

127

Psychologists do so probably because they observe that many emotional people are uncomfortable in the realm of complex ideas, so those who exercise great intellect, ipso facto, must be bereft of feeling.

Aristotle's insights in this regard are related to a major issue in modern psychology: *how to unleash locked-up emotions we cannot rationally command.* Psychologists say that males, in particular, have trouble "getting in touch with their feelings." Doubtless true, but does it follow that those who are insufficiently emotional are, therefore, in control of their reason? Although Aristotle believed that practical leaders of his own era needed to build such emotional habits as empathy and compassion, he also argued that they needed to learn to overcome their poisonous passions with reason. In essence, he believed that "practical" people were seldom as rational as they prided themselves on being or as observers thought them to be.

Here Aristotle anticipates the work of Daniel Kahneman, the psychologist who recently won the Nobel Prize for economics. Kahneman challenged the dominant assumption of economists that people are "rational actors" who make choices based on cold logic. He discovered that, when making economic decisions, people suffer from the same kind of psychological myopia, if not blindness, that infects decisions they make in other parts of their lives. For example, perfectly rational businesspeople will see the same business deal more positively if it is presented in terms of prospective gain as opposed to potential loss. In essence, even the most rational people making the least emotionally charged decisions are influenced by their feelings.

Aristotle believes virtue comes into play in the exercise of choice, and Kahneman's formal study of how people make choices attempts to find the rules of thumb we use when trying to "make a wise decision." He finds that most of us are not "rational" with regard to the goods we buy. In effect, he finds that people don't do a sensible cost/benefit analysis when choosing to buy a new Mercedes. Because Aristotle didn't live in a consumer society, he never addressed himself to such questions. But he did observe that few people are rational when making much more important choices, for example when choosing with whom to spend their time and in doing what. The Ancient argues that such choices need to be informed by reason because they add up to a plan for how we allocate the times of our lives. He would say that if we irrationally choose to buy, say, a Mercedes instead of a Ford, the consequences aren't all that great in the long term. However, if we choose to devote a large chunk of our time to making enough money to buy a fancy car we cannot afford, as David Denby did and I am tempted to do, we consequently may miss out on the good life.

To Aristotle, ethics are not about choosing what make of car to buy, but about how to decide what activities to engage in. He believes that, when push comes to shove, ethical considerations are typically omitted when major personal, business, and political decisions are being made. In my own experience as a business professor, I spend hours teaching students how to make rational decisions—that is, how to get the most bang for a buck. For example, when teaching a class about real estate development, I'll cover all the issues that need to be raised in order to maximize the return on a new shopping mall. What I don't teach is how one decides if it is virtuous to build the mall in the first place, or how to choose where to locate it so it will do the least environmental and aesthetic damage. In business school, such soft, ethical considerations are viewed as irrelevant to hard decision-making. Aristotle reminds us they aren't soft or irrelevant, and Kahneman's recent research illustrates that even what we think of as hard aspects of business decision-making are actually soft! If nothing else, this points to the need to make practical decisions in a more inclusive, holistic fashion.

When it comes to making personal decisions, there is the danger of similarly excluding ethical considerations from our deliberations. In this realm, virtue entails engaging in a process of continuous self-questioning and self-evaluation. When we continually stop ourselves in the middle of making an important decision to ask such ethical questions as, How much is enough? and What do I really need?, we are exercising the virtuous habit of seeking self-knowledge. And both the psychologist and the philosopher believe that developing that habit is the first step in the pursuit of happiness.

Although Aristotle's views are usually consistent with those of the great minds of psychology, and are often up to date with their latest thinking, we deny ourselves a valuable source of insight if we assume that psychology and philosophy always arrive at the same ends and, hence, that we can safely dispense with the latter. For example, the distinctions between how psychology and philosophy define happiness are few and subtle but nonetheless important. In measuring happiness, psychologists will ask people to indicate (on a seven-point scale) the degree to which they agree with the statement, "If I could live my life over, I would change almost nothing." That, of course, is a restatement of Aristotle's deathbed test. The difference is that psychologists see this question as a measure of how we feel at any given point of time rather than as a measure of a complete life well led. Similarly, they ask the extent to which one agrees with the statement, "I am satisfied with my life." In contrast, philosophers have a hard time answering such questions for any point in time. Had Aristotle been asked if he was satisfied with his life right after he lost his young wife, he might well have marked a low "1" on a seven-point scale. But that didn't mean he wasn't living a good life, or that he wouldn't find fulfillment in the end.

A major difference in the two perspectives is that psychologists define happiness as "subjective well-being," which is closer to the meaning of euphoria than it is to the philosopher's eudaimonia. Aristotle's eudaimonia is usually translated as "happiness," but as we have seen, it has little to do with the feelings of pleasure and contentment we usually associate with that word. What he means is something more akin to "the deep sense of satisfaction one gets when one grows as a human being." Eudaimonia is thus the well-being that comes from living a life of continuous self-development. Hence, if I am "fat, dumb, and happy," I may satisfy the psychologist's, but not the philosopher's, definition of happiness. Eudaimonia requires the continual pursuit of knowledge about oneself and the world, and such knowledge doesn't necessarily make us feel good. In midlife, when Aristotle undertook a thorough self-examination of his desires and behavior, he probably didn't "feel good" about himself in the short term. When he then chose to discipline himself to pursue the good, he found he had to make hard choices, to give up things he liked doing—perhaps playing faculty politics, going to the chariot racetrack, or having wine at lunch. He probably didn't feel good about making such sacrifices and trade-offs. As a result of his adult self-reflection, he may even have discovered things about himself that made him feel miserable, and seeing that he had to abandon adolescent wishes could hardly have given him a feeling of "subjective well-being." As a result of becoming sadder, he became a bit wiser and, thus, opened the possibility of finding long-term fulfillment. Without that self-knowledge, he had been groping blindly in the dark. Now he could see himself and make informed, rational, and adult choices. Outside of fairy tales, that's what "finding happiness" means to the philosopher.

Finally, psychologists do not equate happiness with virtue and excellence. But Aristotle does so because he doesn't want us to confuse it with any other goods, particularly feelings of pleasure. He wants us clearly to see happiness as a "godlike" activity. He says animals can experience pleasure because pleasure is a feeling, but they can't experience eudaimonia because that's related to the godlike ability to reason. In Aristotelian terms, psychologists are interested in our animal feelings, and philosophers are interested in our godlike reasoning. Thus we develop appropriate feelings through psychological processes, and we learn to develop our heads through philosophical reflection. Effective life planning depends more on the latter than the former.

BUT ARISTOTLE NEVER SAYS WE CAN'T HAVE A GOOD TIME

Because Aristotle associates the greatest happiness with activities involved in pursuing noble goods, he says the truest bliss derives from pursuing wisdom. Nonetheless, he doesn't say there aren't worthy pleasures to be found on lower ranks of the hierarchy of goods, as well. He's not an unfeeling prude or wet blanket. He says: "All men enjoy in some way dainty foods and wines and sexual intercourse; but not all men do as they ought." What they oughtn't do is to enjoy those pleasures to excess, to the extent they preclude the pursuit of noble goods, or to enjoy them in a beastly manner: hearty sex with your mate is virtuous; orgies are a vice. *But he isn't saying we can't have a good time.* He simply warns that we have entered the arena of excess if our pursuit of pleasure is so consuming that it prevents us from achieving higher goals.

Rejecting bodily pleasures is not what Aristotle has in mind when he speaks of virtue. They have a place in the good life, and those who deny them cannot be truly happy. Quite the opposite. To Aristotle, defects of sensual and sensible feelings are nearly as much a vice as are excesses. People who are without passion, people who do without bodily pleasure, people who make a religion of goodness are not virtuous, and they are not excellent. Again, the issue is moderation. A health nut who eats nothing but organic carrots and spends 16 hours a day exercising is not only excessive in his behavior, he fails to distinguish ends from means. Health is a means to happiness, not happiness in itself.

Rereading Aristotle on this point, I began to have a glimmer of insight into my unease concerning the virtuous lifestyle of writer John Jerome. Although it was the ascetic aspect of his life I found off-putting, there was also a hint of excessive goodness that bothered me in ways I couldn't explain. Because I am unable to identify with those who are "too good," I racked my brain for examples of too-perfect virtue to better understand such behavior. I didn't have enough information to fairly evaluate Jerome's virtues, but I finally was able to come up with another near saint whom I know rather well, a colleague I shall call Alan, a man who does not drink, smoke, swear, or display bad habits. As far as I know, he is honest, faithful to his wife, and treats his children in an exemplary way. He works hard, eats healthy food, saves for a rainy day, does not spend money frivolously, and gives generously to charity. He never speaks ill of others and is a dependable worker. He goes to church regularly and prays daily. He pays his taxes, obeys the law, and behaves ethically in activities where the reach of law doesn't extend.

Even though Alan avoids the vices and excesses Aristotle warns against, he is not the kind of person the Ancient has in mind when he describes virtuous people. Because Aristotle's goal is temperance, abstinence and other forms of asceticism become moral failings when they lead to a life of prohibitions. As nice and as gentle as Alan is, he is nonetheless a limited being. His limitations are found not just in the normal pleasures he denies himself but, more important, in the areas where he has not developed his potential. His defect is manifest. Almost everyone who comments on his saintliness also says it is unedifying to be with him because he has never taken any risks in his life, particularly intellectual risks which come with learning new things, trying out new ideas, or advocating unpopular causes. In short, you can't learn anything from being with Alan. He has not developed his talents or his intellect; he is not curious, not involved in exploring the many and mysterious facets of the world around him. Hence, to the extent he partakes in community affairs, he has little to bring to the table. That's why virtue, in the Ancient's reckoning, is most clearly associated with positive actions.

Alan is now in his mid-seventies, and I have known him for some 30 years. During that time, I have never noted a hint of growth or development on his part. In short, he lacks excellence. And if he ever comes to apply Aristotle's deathbed test without blinders—an unlikely eventuality—I doubt he will consider himself happy. If nothing else, thinking about Alan increased my admiration for Jerome and helped me to distinguish between virtuous behavior that is rooted in a clear commitment to the highest good, and saintly behavior that is largely irrelevant to virtue in Aristotle's eyes. Indeed, Hugh Hefner is much like Alan in that he has not developed over the years. There is nothing more tiresome than reading a current interview with Hefner in which he repeats his 1950s' playboy "philosophy."

TEMPERANCE AND SELF-DISCIPLINE

We may be able to easily dismiss Hefner, but it is much harder to reject the idea he represents: Vice makes us happy. After all, many people define a good time as a Vegas vacation. Aristotle assumes most people can tell the difference between an occasional weekend at Caesar's Palace on the one hand, and habitual gambling and partying on the other. Yet, if we instinctively know virtue from vice, why do so many sensible people pursue happiness by way of the latter? Why do so many otherwise reasonable people choose to follow a path they know will not lead to happiness?

Aristotle tries to unravel this paradox by drawing a distinction between the virtues of temperance and those of self-discipline. Temperance is the virtue associated with the golden mean. The conduct of temperate people is moderate. They know what is bad for them, and they avoid it. In distinction, self-discipline is the virtue of controlling one's behavior, staying true to one's convictions. Self-disciplined people don't give in to impulse, appetite, or temptation. To Aristotle, the difference between the two concepts is clearest in the negative: *Intemperance* is symptomatic of failure to identify the good, and being *undisciplined* is a symptom of those who do not pursue the good they have identified. People who consciously pursue pleasure, hedonists whose sole aim is to have a good time, Aristotle calls "intemperate." He sees intemperance as the adult equivalent of a temper tantrum: the desire for something not worthy of excessive passion.

Socrates says that if one knows the good, one will pursue it. But Aristotle begs to differ. He sees many men and women who know what is right for them but still do not pursue it, undisciplined people who desire the noble but nonetheless are seduced into pursuing the pleasant. He says that's because their appetites are stronger than their self-control. Virtuous people thus develop the willpower to control their appetites.

Two charmingly adolescent U.S. presidents illustrate the difference between being intemperate and lacking self-discipline. Because George W. Bush has never made the effort to identify what the good entails (he is not interested in contemplation), he would be intemperate in Aristotle's eyes. Doubtless, he religiously obeys the Ten Commandments, but no one would accuse him of personal introspection or philosophical enquiry. Although William J. Clinton seems to have struggled to understand the good, he has thus far lacked the moral discipline to pursue it. He is undisciplined. Aristotle sees this as a particularly childlike failing. Children fail to see how what they do now relates to their future happiness. Knowing it is wrong to do so, Jack nonetheless climbs the beanstalk and steals the giant's golden lyre, ignoring the consequences. Likewise, President Bill knew he was playing with fire to make hanky-panky in the Oval Office. Knowing it was wrong to do so, and repressing the obvious fact that he was unlikely to get away with it, he went ahead anyway, displaying the moral discipline of an adolescent.

Less dramatically, the hard-to-keep-in-mind (for me, at least) relationship between the immediate intake of fatty foods and longevity illustrates the point about self-discipline. This yummy piece of greasy Italian salami gives me so much pleasure now that I forget its impact on my ultimate lifespan. Indeed, as long as salami gives me short-term pleasure, I will continue to consume it and to clog my veins with cholesterol, even though at some level I know it is bad for me (sorry, Dr. Atkins).

Economists have their explanation for undisciplined behavior: *We discount the future.* Because, in fact, one piece of salami won't hurt me, I find myself back again dealing with a variation of the complex question, *How much is enough?* Aristotle's short answer, again, is moderation. A diet of salami will necessitate a coronary bypass one day, but forever denying myself its marvelous garlicky taste is to miss a distinct pleasure. The complex challenge is to define how much salami is harmful and to discipline myself to stop when I reach that hard-to-determine amount.

But salami is easy. Sex, for example, is a much more difficult issue, as Hefner and Clinton could attest. Determining how much sex is good, how much is enough, and with whom is a major moral problem for many good people. Aristotle's golden mean doesn't provide precise guidance. If temperance is the mean between abstinence and depravity, should one have sex twice a month, twice a week, twice a day? Aristotle's conclusion is that intemperance occurs when sexual activity interferes with living a good life. A Don Juan who spends all his time arranging assignations and engaging in seductions is not going to have occasion to develop other, higher aspects of his life. So reasonable people might conclude that having sex with multiple partners is excessive. But that's just a beginning. The issue then becomes one of self-discipline. How do we behave when an opportunity for casual sex with an attractive person comes along? To answer, "It all depends," doesn't cut it with Aristotle. He says we have to define what precisely the answer depends on if our moral reasoning is to be effective.

In sum, Aristotle calls a person who is not attracted to vice "temperate" and one who does what is right despite the temptation to stray "disciplined." So who is the more virtuous, the temperate or the disciplined person? Aristotle surprises us with his answer:

> Both the disciplined person and the temperate do nothing contrary to the rule of moderation for the sake of bodily pleasures, but the former has and the latter has not bad appetites. And the latter does not feel pleasure contrary to the rule, while the former feels such pleasure but is not led by it.

We can see why Aristotle concludes that it is better to be temperate than self-disciplined. Who is likely to be happier, the person who struggles all day with temptation, or the one who has overcome unhealthy appetites to the extent that they are no longer tempting? If we are temperate, we are free from the ongoing struggle to remain disciplined!

To understand this tricky point, it helps to know that the literal translation of the Greek word for *temperance* is "soundness of mind." The word has connotations of mastery and moderation, but most saliently, it relates to having full knowledge of both one's limitations and one's capabilities. Aristotle thus saw temperance as the ability to acknowledge our moral weaknesses and then identify our internal capacity to overcome them. This insight was reinvented by the psychiatrist Karl Menninger, who wrote, "To 'know thyself' must mean to know the malignancy of one's own instincts and to know, as well, one's power to defeat it." Hence, the first Aristotelian test with regard to temperance is to honestly ask oneself, *What are my malignant desires?* The follow-up question is: *What can I draw on to overcome those desires and to learn to desire aright so I won't be tempted by them?*

RIGHT DESIRE

Aristotle says that when people of sound mind learn to examine critically the nature of their desires, virtue becomes part of their character. They won't be tempted by a box of chocolates, a loaf of salami, or a quickie on their neighbor's couch; instead, they "seek the noble." Virtuous people thus develop "a general disposition to do what is best, all things considered." Why don't we all have that "general disposition"? Again, Aristotle explains there is a discrepancy in our lives between what is noble on the one hand, and what is pleasurable on the other:

> What is noble must be pleasant; but when the two do not co-
> incide a person cannot be perfectly good; when there is such
> a discrepancy between the good and the pleasant in the pas-
> sions a lack of self-discipline may arise.

Unless there is a coincidence between virtuous behavior and pleasure, the inconsistency between the two gnaws at us. When I eat salami, I get great pleasure even though I know fatty foods are killing me in the long run. If

I give in to my passion for salami, I will be undisciplined; and when I don't practice what I know to be right, I feel guilty (unhappy). On the other hand, if I force myself not to eat the cholesterol-producing goodies I crave, I also will be unhappy because I am denying myself what I truly want; fasting is no one's idea of happiness. As Shakespeare wrote, "Dos't thou think because thou art virtuous there shall be no more cakes and ale?"

The problem with vices is that they give us short-term pleasure. Smoking, drinking, overeating, and sexual indulgence are hard to give up simply because we enjoy them. And there are similar pleasures and problems associated with pursuing excessive amounts of fame, wealth, power, recognition, and other useful goods. Thus, breaking the cycle of pleasure seeking and substituting habitually virtuous behavior is no small feat. Aristotle never claims it is easy. All he says is that the starting point must be a conscious "choice of the good."

On second thought, Aristotle *was* a bit of a prude, but he had seen the moral consequences and physical aftereffects of the all-night food, drink, and sex orgies frequented by wealthy and successful Athenians, including Plato and Socrates. He concludes that people will be truly happy only when they come to enjoy things "good for them."

To understand this, I have had to personalize it. So as long as I crave salami, I am going to be unhappy. Because salami tastes so good, Aristotle recognizes that I am going to have a near-impossible time trying consciously to kill my desire for it. Hence his secret: *Not until I learn to like carrots and celery will I be temperate.* When I have that "right desire," I may still enjoy a piece of salami at the office Christmas party, but I won't be tempted to have two, and I may discover I really don't like salami as much as I once thought. Aristotle says we don't have to make the onerous choice between doing the right or the pleasurable thing. When we understand the true source of happiness, we will find pleasure in doing what is right.

STILL IN THE WOODS

To summarize, Aristotle's discussion of right desire helped me understand that I was still a prisoner of youthful fantasy, and undisciplined when I attempted to pursue mature goals. I learned that I behaved irrationally because I wanted to avoid pain and because fear of the loss of comforting illusions was stronger than the possibility of the gain of happiness. So how should I develop "right desire" and then learn to enjoy what is good for me? Aristotle says it is through the repeated exercise of reason that I would begin to see that my desires for approval are what are making me unhappy. But how could I manage my conflicting desires for Aristotelian happiness on the one hand, and conventional career success on the other? How could I be like Skip Battle and Ben Dunlap, and find pleasure in helping others, without feeling like I was making a huge sacrifice? How, after decades of pursuing things that were bad for me, could I develop the discipline needed to finally get it right in my fifties?

139

6

MORAL EXERCISES: BREAKING THE HABIT OF MAKING OURSELVES UNHAPPY

VICIOUS ACTIONS ARE NOT HURTFUL BECAUSE THEY ARE FORBIDDEN, BUT FORBIDDEN BECAUSE THEY ARE HURTFUL. . . . IT WAS THEREFORE IN EVERYONE'S INTEREST TO BE VIRTUOUS WHO WISHED TO BE HAPPY. . . . [HENCE] I CONCEIVED OF A BOLD AND ARDUOUS PROJECT AT ARRIVING AT MORAL PERFECTION. . . . I SOON FOUND THAT I HAD UNDERTAKEN A TASK OF MORE DIFFICULTY THAN I HAD IMAGINED. . . . THO' I NEVER ARRIVED AT THE PERFECTION I HAD BEEN SO AMBITIOUS OF OBTAINING BUT FELL FAR SHORT OF IT, YET I WAS BY THE ENDEAVOUR A BETTER AND A HAPPIER MAN THAN I OTHERWISE SHOULD HAVE BEEN.

—*BENJAMIN FRANKLIN*, AUTOBIOGRAPHY

In striving to achieve happiness through "moral perfection," Ben Franklin identified 13 virtues he swore to practice:

1. Temperance: Eat not to dullness. Drink not to elevation.

2. Silence: Speak not but what may benefit others or yourself. Avoid trifling conversation.

3. Order: Let all your things have their places. Let each part of your business have its time.

4. Resolution: Resolve to perform what you ought. Perform without fail what you resolve.

5. Frugality: Make no expence but to do good to others or yourself; i.e., waste nothing.

6. Industry: Lose no time. Be always employed in something useful. Cut off all unnecessary actions.

7. Sincerity: Use no hurtful deceit. Think innocently and justly; and if you speak, speak accordingly.

8. Justice: Wrong none by doing injuries or omitting the benefits that are your duty.

9. Moderation: Avoid extremes. Forebear resenting injuries so much as you think they deserve.

10. Cleanliness: Tolerate no uncleanness in body, clothes, or habituation.

11. Tranquility: Be not disturbed at trifles or at accidents common or unavoidable.

12. Chastity: Rarely use venery but for health and offspring—never to dullness, weakness, or the injury of your own or another's peace or reputation.

13. Humility: Imitate Jesus and Socrates.

According to Franklin biographer Walter Isaacson, the Sage of Philadelphia established a disciplined regimen (see item 3, above) for integrating each of these virtues into his life, concentrating on the first until he mastered it, then moving on to conquer the second, then the third. Isaacson says Franklin ultimately admitted to failure in this enterprise. But who could live up to his standards of virtue? After all, Moses only promulgated 10 prohibitions, and his were a lot less demanding than Ben's stringent 13.

Although Aristotle would agree with the desirability of the virtues on Franklin's list, and applaud the resolute linkage of virtue with happiness, the Ancient would question the practicality of "shall nots." In contrast, Aristotle seeks to portray virtue in positive terms of how we live. He says virtue is a state of the soul, much as health is a condition of the body. Moreover, virtue derives from the motivation, the preference, to choose to act rightly. Franklin clearly had that motivation, but he misunderstood the process by which virtue is achieved and underestimated the amount of work involved in the effort. As Aristotle notes, we have to build our capacity to see the difference between right and wrong, better and worse, then habitually act on the better choice. Virtue comes about when we are *predisposed* to act properly as a matter of habit, when we find pleasure in the good.

142   But what kinds of behavior are included in Aristotle's general "predisposition"? His concept of virtue is vague and abstract; in contrast, Franklin's list is a model of precision and clarity. And, in practice, the Ancient's construct doesn't really seem much different or more helpful than Franklin's more precise prohibitions. But is Aristotle's concept of virtue, like Franklin's, simply concerned with the seven deadly sins? Do all of his ethics merely come down to saying petty vices, like eating too much salami, make people unhappy? After reading Aristotle, David Denby concluded:

> I was bored by his shrewd, very sane advice in the *Nico-machean Ethics* that we avoid the extremes of behavior and choose the "golden mean" or middle way, a mode of existence practiced by the virtuous man as a way of taming the excesses of appetite. True enough, but so what?

Indeed, so what if all Aristotle is talking about is curbing excessive desire for fatty sausages. Like Denby, I found myself so caught up in the Ancient's

Franklinesque examples that I lost sight of his deeper message. But when I recently went back to reread the *Ethics*, I experienced a little epiphany: Offering advice to intemperate snackers is not the point of his moral exercises.

IT'S NOT ABOUT SALAMI

As my wife will attest, I have numerous bad habits: watching too much basketball, drinking too much chardonnay (it complements salami), avoiding exercise, tuning out when she tells me news about our relatives, and refusing to take vitamins. These vices and others like them make her unhappy. But they don't make me unhappy. What makes me unhappy is that my career has not been as successful as I would like: My books aren't bestsellers, nor are they often cited in scholarly tracts. And every time I think about this absence of approval and recognition, I get depressed. I assure you, I try not to let it get me down that my last 12 books were not reviewed in the *New York Times,* but every time I pick up the goddamn paper, let me tell you, I remember. And I get really unhappy.

But after rereading Aristotle, I finally understood how his thoughts about virtue relate to breaking the most serious of my bad habits. I suddenly understood that the day will never come when I won't want praise, honor, and approval, because those things are, in fact, *goods*. The reason I could never convince myself otherwise, could never shake my desire for affirmation and approval, was because those useful goods have undeniable extrinsic value. Who wouldn't find it rewarding to be praised by others? My problem was that I mistook praise for the highest end, and getting it became my goal. It led to my unhappiness because, when I failed to get the praise I sought, I became miserable. Moreover, it's not too great an exaggeration to say my desire for approval was insatiable; no matter how much I received, I could never get enough. Now, thanks to the threshold test, I saw that whether or not I received the desired praise and approval had little to do with me. There was little I could do to regulate its supply because the granting of it was under the control of others. Hence, after years of making myself miserable, I understood that I had to shift my focus to attaining other goods, noble ones that were not only good for me but over which I had control.

Thus my little epiphany: If the secret to overcoming my craving for salami was to learn to find pleasure in carrots, the secret to overcoming my far more consequential craving for approval was to learn to find pleasure in other, higher, goods. This was consistent with my earlier insight about the pleasure of "getting into the zone" when I was in the act of writing. It was obvious to me in hindsight that happiness is the intrinsic reward that comes from challenging work itself, and not the extrinsic good of praise from others who might consider my work well done. Yet I had failed to make that connection, and missed it with regard to my initial evaluation of John Jerome, because I was still resisting acting in a way that would make me happy. Even after undertaking several Aristotelian exercises, I still was not ready to let go of my 50-year habit of seeking approval. But with this new understanding, albeit obvious now, I was ready to move on.

And with that in mind, we, too, can better understand what Aristotle is talking about when he speaks of virtue, what he means when he speaks of breaking the habit of making ourselves unhappy by refocusing our efforts on the pursuit of higher goods. Aristotle doesn't care much about the many little vices to which we, and Dr. Franklin, are prone. The primary habit he wants us to break is *intellectual indolence,* and the most important new habit he encourages us to form is *self-development.* Virtuous people learn to enjoy things good for them: contemplative goods like science, history, music, drama, poetry, painting, and the discussion of moral and political ideas, pursuits that elevate humans from the lifestyle of animals.

In fact, the reason Benjamin Franklin is ranked among the most respected of the nation's founders is not that he lived by his 13 commandments; rather, it's because he lived a life fully engaged in politics and philosophy. His curiosity was unbounded; he read widely and applied his learning in all manner

144

of practical ways. He invented the lightning rod and bifocal glasses; he founded America's first public subscription library and the American Philosophical Society, where he discussed scientific and social ideas with the likes of Jefferson, Adams, and Benjamin Rush. He founded a hospital and university, published a newspaper, and served as ambassador to France. In the words of ethicist Randy Cohen, "For Franklin individual virtue was inseparable from civic virtue." He was virtuous because he pursued both the highest good of self-actualization and the complete good of community service. And that's what Aristotle tells us we must do if we want to be truly virtuous. In effect, he tells us to try something most of us would prefer not to do.

THE PROBLEM WITH "GOING TO THE GYM TO WORK OUT"

The reading of Aristotle's books might serve as an example of why we resist   *145*
the true pursuit of happiness. Most people today do not want to read Aristotle because the task seems unpleasant, even tedious. In fact, many people who read him for the first time find him incomprehensible. Even on second reading, he is difficult to follow. But by the third time through, almost everyone finds the exercise rewarding, and those who continue to reread him receive great pleasure because, with each reading, they find something new and profound that they had not noticed before. So the challenge is to get through those initial readings.

In terms of our development, Aristotle says, "Try it, you'll like it. Try it more than once, and you may even find it pleasurable." Moreover, the experience of growth is self-reinforcing: Those who get pleasure from a hard physical workout are more likely to exercise regularly than are those who view exercise as drudgery. And those who exercise regularly are most likely to become fit in the long run. Similarly, those who find the pursuit of excellence pleasurable are most likely to engage in it and, thus, are most likely to find true happiness. In fact, it was through disciplining themselves in this way that Ben Dunlap and Skip Battle were able to maintain self-discipline in the face of temptations to stray from their pursuit of happiness. The trick is to learn to find pleasure from habitually developing one's potential.

But how do we learn to enjoy what is good for us? Certainly trying to con people into believing vice isn't pleasurable doesn't work. But is the opposite any easier? Try telling a child that eating spinach can be pleasant. Kids, hell, try convincing me I can enjoy carrots as much as salami! By extension, it's hard for many adults to believe that it can be as rewarding, more so in fact, to spend a day learning a hard subject as it is to spend a day at the beach drinking Sam Adams. Obviously, it will do no good telling such things to kids, to me, or to you. The best way to get the point is to experience it for ourselves. But before risking displeasure, we prudently inquire if anybody else has tried it and survived to tell the tale.

CONTEMPORARY ARISTOTELIANS

After examining numerous examples of the lives of sultans and voluptuaries, I became convinced that I could not become happy continuing to pursue the pleasurable and useful ends they desire. But that was a relatively easy call. It was much harder to convince myself I could become happy if I disciplined myself, instead, to do things typically associated with bitter medicine, say organizing the performance of a Shakespearean play for hospitalized seniors. So I cast around for an example of a contemporary Aristotelian whose behavior I could try on for size, much as I had analyzed the careers of anti-Aristotelians. I looked for someone, like them, with whom I could identify, someone roughly my age with similar professional interests yet more successful than me; that is, not someone like the reclusive and unsuccessful writer John Jerome. If I were to emulate a virtuous person, I would need to feel I wasn't giving up too much in terms of useful and pleasurable goods.

About the time I was writing this chapter, I read several glowing profiles of Stephen Carter, professor of law at Yale and author of seven books on such diverse topics as politics, ethics, race, and religion, in addition to scholarly articles in his academic specialty, contract law. I had known Carter professionally for a decade and was aware of his diverse interests and broad range of abilities. Yet, like many who thought we knew him, I was awed when, in 2002, I learned that he had written a masterful, bestselling novel, *The Emperor of Ocean Park*.

My acquaintance with Carter was through his occasional work in adult education, and I was impressed that the business and government leaders he taught invariably described him in terms of modesty, civility, thoughtfulness, and virtue. Carter not only reads and teaches Aristotle, he lives the Ancient's good life; in fact, Carter indirectly quotes Aristotle on the foundation of government in a *New Yorker* interview by David Owen: "I see the family as prior to the state." According to the article, Carter, his wife, and their two children are a close-knit family who pray and study the Bible together. Carter explains his family-oriented values to Owen:

> My life is pretty simple, in many ways. I spend time with my family, I read the Bible, I go to church, I write, I teach my classes—and that's my life. I play chess, but I don't have any spectacularly interesting hobbies.

"He has no discernible vices, either," Owen observes. Like my aforementioned colleague, Alan, Carter abstains from the seven deadly sins while practicing all the cardinal virtues. Unlike Alan, Carter is virtuous in Aristotelian terms: *He takes intellectual risks and is engaged in important political issues.* In fact, his life isn't "simple." He is an outspoken defender of the right of religious people to practice and espouse their beliefs in public forums and institutions, a conservative position that often puts him at odds with academic colleagues. But Carter doesn't worry about gaining the approval of the likes of us; instead, he is interested in making the strongest rational case possible for what he believes, even if that makes him unpopular. Not coincidentally, one of his finest books is on the subject of integrity. Most important, in his quiet way, Carter practices what he preaches. When Owen asked him about the moral dilemmas created by the $4 million advance he received for his novel, and by the fame and fortune attendant to a related movie deal, Carter answered:

> One element of the old-fashioned way in which I was raised is that you don't talk about money. . . . I will say this, though, and I want to put it delicately: We are . . . of the traditional Christian view that from those whom much is given much is required. Whenever we have financial good fortune, our first obligation is to recognize that we are supposed to give a lot of it away—and really a lot of it. That is just an absolute obligation of the faith.

What intrigues me most about Carter is that, unlike many university professors today, he uses his academic career to become a truly educated person. Until quite recently, the position of professor afforded the finest opportunity for an individual to live Aristotle's contemplative "life of the mind." But overspecialization and the anti-Aristotelian desire to make all fields "scientific"— even such imprecise disciplines as the humanities, social sciences, and particularly the Ancient's own field of philosophy—has caused the professoriate to dig deeper and deeper into narrower and narrower channels of inquiry. As a result, over the years, fewer and fewer scholars have viewed an academic career as the vehicle for becoming broadly educated men and women.

The trend has been limiting to the lives of professors, bad for students, and ultimately self-defeating in making some disciplines irrelevant to the practical world, and for exactly the reasons Aristotle anticipated 25 centuries ago. Carter understands that Aristotelian virtue requires something more than an academic career. Merely to be educated is not the same as to be happy, and many professors, perhaps most today, do not lead good lives by Aristotle's standards.

Indeed, narrowly focused academics are no more virtuous than people who narrowly pursue wealth or do repetitive technical jobs. So in an era when many professors choose to burrow in academic foxholes, it's heartening to learn of a few, like Carter, who choose to use their privileged profession to develop a full range of serious interests. Moreover, my assessment of Carter's successful career is that he demonstrates that it is possible to be both happy and productive. The way he has chosen to live illustrates that one can excel in one's technical or professional field and, at the same time, be a complete human.

I concluded from analyzing Carter's behavior that I, too, had a choice. He showed me there is no necessary trade-off between being productive in the economic sense on the one hand, and pursuing noble goods on the other. What was required of me was the moral imagination to make the combination of the two work and the discipline to stick with the behavior needed to get me where I wanted to go.

But, whoa, had I again loaded the dice by choosing such an extreme example of Aristotelian virtue, as I feared I had done earlier when choosing the extremely un-Aristotelian Clark and Ellison? Certainly, that would be the case if Carter had been "born virtuous." But I know him just well enough to detect signs of the character flaws that afflict us all. More telling is the subtext of his novel: The book portrays the lengthy and painful struggles of a middle-age law professor to overcome his misplaced desires and discipline himself to choose aright. In interviews, Stephen Carter may make the possession of virtue appear easy, but in his fiction writing, he shows us that it is extremely hard work for everybody.

Yet, it is obviously easier for a professor to pursue happiness than it is for a person who has "a real job and career," particularly someone like the CEO of a big company who is doing the socially necessary work of wealth creation. It may seem that people in their shoes have no choice but to pretend vice is virtue. As Lord Keynes wrote in the 1930s, only after we are all rich can we "once more value ends above means and prefer the good to the useful." "But beware!" Keynes warned,

The time for all this is not yet. For another hundred years we must pretend to ourselves and to everyone that fair is foul and foul is fair: for foul is useful and fair is not. Avarice and usury and precaution must be our gods for a little longer still. For only they can lead us out of the tunnel of economic necessity into daylight.

In this view, economic progress depends on continuing to choose useful over noble goods, and career/economic success depends on making oneself unhappy.

But don't the facts belie Keynes's contention, even among those who are not fabulously rich? For example, married couple Isabel Geffner and Peter Guzzardi were enjoying successful editorial careers in the high-stress world of New York publishing when, in their late forties, they decided the quality of their lives would improve if they moved and took lower-paying jobs in family-friendlier Chapel Hill, North Carolina. Explains Geffner:

I felt like I could reinvent myself. I didn't have to be one thing as an adult. I had been a book publishing person, and that was great, but now I was going to do something different. I loved being in school. The sense of being engaged and alive was like a fountain of youth. I didn't worry about getting hired at my age when I got my degree—I figured if I'm good at what I do and I care about it passionately, I'll get a job. If I choose to go back to grad school again at age 65, I'll have a similar attitude then.

Having now earned a master's degree in social work, she is running a nonprofit agency, spending more time with the kids, and contemplating a lifetime of more learning and career changes:

When I went back to school I fell in love with learning in a way that I hadn't when I went to college the first time. I came home one day and said to my husband, "Maybe I'll get a master's in biochemistry and art history."

Out on the West Coast, another contemporary Aristotelian, Sheena Paterson Berwick, recently followed in Geffner's shoes, also without benefit of being rich. Growing up in a poor family in Glasgow, Scotland (her parents were soldiers in the Salvation Army), Berwick was forced to leave school at age 16 and enter the competitive world of journalism in order to support herself. Gradually working her way up the ladder over the next 30 years, she eventually became editor of Toronto's *Saturday Star* and an editor of the Los Angeles *Herald Examiner*. Most people at that point would either have congratulated themselves on a job well done or reached for the gold ring: a job with one of the prestigious national dailies. Not Sheena.

Berwick wanted an education, and she wanted it for purposes other than credentialing, status, or making up for youthful deprivation. She wanted an education clearly and simply because she hadn't fully exercised many aspects of her potential. So, in her early fifties and with only modest savings, she enrolled as a full-time undergraduate at the University of California, Santa Barbara, and has since graduated Phi Beta Kappa, summa cum laude. Significantly, she didn't major in finance or computer science. With the wisdom that comes from experience, she realized higher education is too valuable an opportunity to waste on learning a trade. As she had observed, people who look back most positively on their undergraduate experiences often are those who had pursued a liberal education and later got their career training in graduate school or on the job. She simply did it backward. At an age when most of us would say, "Hey, I'm too old to learn this stuff and, anyway, what practical good would it do me to try?" she majored in English and won the UCSB Italian Department's Dante Prize for her essay on *The Divine Comedy*. Moreover, while earning her degree, she volunteered her managerial skills to help a community center pull out of an administrative mess.

What Aristotle means by virtue is exactly Sheena Berwick's self-discipline and willingness to test her mind in new fields and new ways. Likewise, Aristotle encourages all of us to challenge and stretch ourselves, learn new things, and ask tough questions about the way we live. Yet, because we fear that the experience will be unpleasant, we resist his call and studiously avoid asking ourselves difficult questions about the way we conduct our lives. Worse, we fear if we read and think deeply about moral questions and about the consequences of such for our own behavior, the process will lead us to make unpleasant choices about how we should then act. So why should we work hard to do something that doesn't seem fun? As Canadian songwriter/poet Leonard Cohen writes, "You are locked inside your suffering and your pleasures are the seal."

A PRACTICAL EXERCISE: CONTROLLING THE COMPLEX EMOTION OF ANGER

Where Ben Franklin thought virtue could be acquired quickly and by obeying rules ("Tranquility: Be not disturbed at trifles"), Aristotle says it takes time and effort to build the habit of right reasoning and subsequent right behavior. In order to break the comforting seal that habitually locks us into self-defeating behavior, the Ancient says we need to embark on a series of exercises to develop our moral muscles. To illustrate what he means, he cites the practical case of a man who must struggle to control his anger. Aristotle starts by acknowledging that everyone gets angry from time to time, so if a person's face occasionally turns red, that doesn't signify anything about his character. Nor should we be concerned with inherited traits: It is morally inconsequential if someone's face is red all the time. But if a person habitually becomes inflamed with anger, and those who know him are constantly on edge waiting for the tell-tale signs of red ears and cheeks indicative of an oncoming eruption, *that* is a valid indicator of a character flaw.

Aristotle then calls positive attention to the person who is prone to go red-faced with anger *but has learned to control it*. In general, he concludes that it is virtuous to be even-tempered. But he doesn't stop there. His discussion of the emotion is nuanced: He goes on to say there are times when anger is called for and appropriate. In fact, if one does not become angry over a grave injustice, he says one cannot be considered virtuous. The secret is in knowing when to be angry and then how to direct it usefully. The virtuous person, he says, becomes angry at the right time, over the right issue, and to the right degree. He then cites examples of questions we might ask of ourselves in order to develop the moral muscles needed to allow us to do that habitually. Properly understood, his example of anger management is not only practical, it serves to illustrate how we can free ourselves from the prison of whatever particular emotion might prevent us from behaving virtuously.

Here's a current example of what I think Aristotle is getting at on the subject of anger: In 2004, the Bush administration argued that charges leveled against it by counterterrorism expert, Richard Clarke, should be discounted because the ex–White House aide's judgment was warped by anger. That argument gained some traction with the public. Understandably, Americans expect a level of institutional loyalty from public servants and find unseemly those who kiss and tell (especially those "jilted" by their bosses and trying to "even the score"). And it did appear that Clarke had become seriously disgruntled when he found himself out of the loop at the White House and his advice ignored by then National Security Advisor Condoleezza Rice. But if we apply Aristotle's tests to the subject, we can ask ourselves if Clarke's undeniable anger was either justified or adequate reason to discredit the veracity of his critique.

A look at what is known about the behavior of indignant employees in public and private organizations provides a framework for understanding Aristotle's perspective. In the early 1970s, MIT social scientist Albert O. Hirschman posited that employees who disagree with company policy have only three options: "exit, voice, and loyalty." That is, they can (1) offer a principled resignation, (2) try to change the policy, or (3) remain loyal "team players." Experience shows that most people choose option three, the path of least resistance. They swallow whatever moral objections they have to dictates from above, concluding that they lack power to change things or, worse, will be punished if they attempt to do so. Indeed, such "loyalty" is assumed. Most executives expect that employees will be good soldiers and not question company policy (or, if they do, will go away quietly).

But sometimes employees find the actions of employers so unconscionable that they feel they have no choice but to resign and "go public" with their objections. Typically, this is the last resort for those who have voiced disagreement internally and exhausted channels of appeal but feel they were not given a serious hearing. On rare occasions, a respected organizational insider will proffer such a principled resignation; but, typically, those who quit over matters of principle are powerless outsiders, or those who have been pushed to the extreme of quitting by the disrespect shown to them by superiors. After all, how many employees would resign if they felt they were listened to and their opinions respected, even if they didn't get their way on a matter of principle? In general, people have to be angry as hell before they quit and go public. And because anger is such an unattractive, unsettling, and even frightening trait, angry people seldom have much influence and are easily dismissed by those in power as "out of control."

But anger can be a socially useful fuel, as the wrathful 2004 presidential candidacy of Howard Dean illustrates. Dean seemed legitimately angry over the Bush administration's decision to invade a country that he believed had no intent to attack America and presented no real threat to the nation's security. His anger-fueled campaign served the purpose of mobilizing his party to challenge the administration's war policies (those Democrats who weren't angry enough had acquiesced to the invasion of Iraq). Even though he was a member of the opposition party, whose supposed duty is to offer loyal criticism, Dean paid a price: His hostile demeanor was ridiculed by allies and foes alike. And when Dean ultimately went red-faced wiggy on national television after a primary loss, he obviously blew it by Aristotle's standards of appropriate anger: He got angry at the wrong place, to the wrong degree, and over the wrong issue.

In contrast to politicians, angry ex-employees risk a lot more than being mocked by late-night talk show hosts. They open themselves to attacks on their personal lives by the considerable force of their threatened institutions. That's why most workers have to be totally teed off before they violate the norms of organizational loyalty. To get angry enough to face onslaught on one's character and veracity requires not only fundamental disagreement over policy—typically involving the conviction that a moral principle has been violated—but also deep personal hurt. Such were the mixed motivations in recent high-profile corporate cases of whistle-blowing at cigarette-maker Brown and Williamson and at Unum Provident Insurance. In both instances, corporate leaders responded with the standard organizational defense that the whistle-blowers' testimonies should be discounted because the ex-employees were "disgruntled" (they were portrayed as angry "nut cases" with enough skeletons in their closets to outfit a Halloween ball).

Moreover, many institutional leaders argue that employees owe loyalty to them as individuals. In contrast, whistle-blowers typically say they owe their first allegiance to their organizations. Indeed, it is when employees believe their leaders betray their organization's integrity that their anger mounts sufficiently to justify the risks of whistle-blowing. Nothing makes formerly loyal employees angrier than values-betraying leaders who claim, *"L'etat, c'est moi."* In contrast, Aristotle says the organization takes precedence over its leaders.

Hence, to the administration's charge that such critics as former Treasury secretary Paul O'Neil, Ambassador Joseph Wilson, and Richard Clarke were "too angry" to be trusted, Aristotle would say, of course they were angry: "Those who are not angry at the things they should be angry at are thought to be fools." If they weren't angry, they would still be inside, loyally carrying out orders, or trying to voice disagreement through established processes. They had tried that, failed in their attempts to be heard, and then opted for vocal exits. Doubtless, it would be prettier if whistle-blowers weren't so angry, but anger is often a necessary spur to doing the right thing. Indeed, what might have happened had Secretary of State Colin Powell allowed his reported anger over the decision to invade Iraq to overcome his military-disciplined instinct to loyally fall into line with administration policies? Had he instead resigned and publicly voiced his concerns, would Americans then have been so accepting of the questionable evidence on WMDs? Who knows? But it does seem clear that if we too quickly ignore the angry words of disgruntled former officials, fewer of them will be willing to step forward, and there will be fewer safeguards of the public interest. Aristotle adds one important admonition: "The good tempered man is not revengeful."

As I read Aristotle, I couldn't help but recall the most difficult career issue I have struggled with: what to do when the leaders of the organization I worked for betrayed its essential values. Because I had firmly believed in those values, my response was over-the-top emotional: I became mad as hell. When I expressed that anger to colleagues and friends, their response was, "Cool it. They're not going to change, so it won't do you any good to get angry. If you can't live with the situation, then just quit. But don't burn bridges by making a stink." One friend went so far as to tell me that my anger was "unattractive." Frankly, I didn't know what to do. I didn't know how to think about the issue and didn't know how to behave. But because the only thing more damning that can be said about an employee than that he is "angry" is that he is "dis-loyal," I bottled up my emotions, quit, and went quietly away.

Years later, the organization was still in a tailspin, and I found myself still angry and not at all certain I had done the right thing. In retrospect, I wish I had been able to analyze the issue with the help of Aristotle's insights. After rereading what he has to say about anger, I now feel my response had been half-right, at best. I still believe I did the right thing by quitting when my bosses put themselves above the values of the organization, but I don't think I channeled my anger in a useful way. Before I quit, I should have tried to offer them a constructive suggestion by which they could have gotten back on track. And after leaving, I think I erred in not having had the moral courage to "go public" to call attention to what was happening. Had I reached out to powerful individuals who also cared about the organization, I might have prevented the leaders from damaging its integrity. For that course to have succeeded, I would have had to be clearly acting for the good of the organization and not in a "revengeful" spirit. Aristotle's insight that virtuous people become angry at the right time, over the right issue, and to the right degree now allows me to see that, by repressing my legitimate anger, the act of quitting not only had no constructive impact, I also made myself unhappy. Had I asked myself the questions Aristotle raises, I think I might have directed my anger more positively and gotten rid of it much sooner.

The ultimate end of all Aristotle's philosophical exercises is ethical: He wants us to learn how to spot a moral issue, weigh the consequences of staying on the current course of action, and then apply our moral imaginations to the task of creating better alternatives. To do so effectively, we must expand our moral capabilities, which we do by developing the most human (rational) side to control or channel the least human (emotional) side. He says we acquire virtue when we habitually learn to listen to our human side and come to desire morally good things. Hence, to become virtuous, we must engage in exercises that build a disposition toward "right reasoning." Because much of life is a matter of practical choice—*should I do this or should I do that?*—people who discipline themselves to view such choices as matters requiring conscious moral deliberation are those most likely to make right choices for themselves in the end.

ANOTHER PRACTICAL EXERCISE: KNOWING WHEN TO "GO WITH YOUR FEELINGS"

As in psychology, the process of philosophical deliberation begins with self-awareness, often with the realization that *I am not happy.* To Aristotle, as to psychologists, the reasonable man or woman then asks, *Why is it I am not happy?* Some may answer, *I am unhappy because of what others are doing to me.* If so, the reasonable person will put herself out of the way of harm from others. Having done that, both psychologists and Aristotelians suggest this person should also ask, *What am I doing that makes me so unhappy?* And both define folly as doing more of the same: An unhappy man drinks more to make himself happy; an unhappy rich woman seeks more wealth in order to be happy; and so on down the list of things typically expected to cure unhappiness. Instead, both Aristotle and the modern psychologist call trying a new course of action the beginning of wisdom. The Ancient says this is done most effectively by engaging in a planning process in which alternative ends and means are consciously and analytically evaluated.

Let me make this process concrete by way of another example. In early 2002, the great, former basketball player, Kareem Abdul-Jabbar, took a job coaching in the second-tier United States Basketball League. Significantly, he did not blame others for having failed to land a more lucrative and prestigious job in the NBA, where former stars of his caliber are more typically employed. Instead, he acknowledged that he had been a loner in his playing days, dour and standoffish, and that after he retired, he hadn't nurtured relationships with league owners and officials: "For the longest time, I didn't want to talk to the press or to management. . . . I guess I can look in the mirror and only blame myself for that." At age 54, Jabbar saw the consequences of his own behavior in a way he couldn't when he was younger, then he committed himself to a course of change.

When I read about Jabbar's transformation, it dawned on me that throughout my own career, I had behaved similarly. I hadn't attended professional meetings, hadn't formed relationships with people who could give me access to the resources needed for an academic writer to succeed, hadn't done most of the normal and expected things my professorial peers had done to advance their careers. It now occurred to me that this was a major reason I had never been as successful as I had hoped. Like Jabbar, in my fifties, I have been forced to conclude, "I can only blame myself for that." With this insight, I now have to choose whether or not to change my behavior. Do I want to start schmoosing with people I sought studiously to avoid for 3 decades or keep doing things "my way"? Either way, I have to live with the consequences of my now-conscious choice.

Here's another instance where psychologists and philosophers part company: The former believe making a choice about how we should allocate the time of our lives is related to our feelings, and the latter believe it is an intellectual and moral issue. Aristotle won't let Jabbar and O'Toole off the moral hook by copping the plea "we were prisoners of our passions." Many psychologists would counsel us "to go with our feelings," but Aristotelians worry our feelings may take us in the wrong direction. Doubtless, President Clinton went with his feelings when he chose to pursue his affair with Monica Lewinsky. In fact, the reason I hadn't done the things necessary to advance my career was that I *had* "gone with my feelings" of disdain for careerism and self-promotion. Like Jabbar, who went with his feelings about how and with whom he would spend his time off the court, I had avoided conferences and cocktail parties because I found the impersonal nature of such events painful.

The issue isn't whether my actions were right or wrong back then, but rather to understand how I immaturely had failed to think through the consequences of acting on my feelings. I hadn't made a conscious choice about how I should spend my time. Like a dumb kid, I had assumed I could thumb my nose at convention—and attending academic conventions—and still find conventional success. My fantasy wish was for success to come in a painless and easy way. Now I recognize that it was no one's fault but my own that things didn't work out as I had desired. The lesson for me today is that I must make conscious choices, and, to do so effectively, I must think through the probable consequences. In Aristotelian words, to become a mature person, I must "plan with my entire life in view."

159

PUTTING IT TOGETHER AND INTO ACTION

Aristotle is a great believer in personal responsibility. This should not be confused with the advice of pop psychologists who counsel each and all to be responsible *for our own lives,* which is true but limited. Because we were "abused children," some psychologists tell us that we have a right to behave as self-indulgent adults and that we will find happiness if we "listen to our inner child" and pursue the fantasy goods we were denied by our ogrelike parents. In distinction, Aristotle believes we are responsible *for our own character.* The issue is not "forget all others; I have a right to do my own thing," but "how can I develop my potential *and* be a virtuous and productive member of my community?"

To the psychologist, unhappy men and women need to think less and feel more. To the Aristotelian, they need to learn to think and desire aright. To become happy, they need to explore intellectually and rationally the nature of happiness. If they discipline themselves to engage in such moral deliberation, instead of assuming whatever direction their passions lead them is true north, they eventually might discover a coincidence between the pursuit of wisdom and virtue on the one hand, and a profound and lasting experience of real pleasure on the other.

Granted, getting out of the emotional woods involves a lot of hard work. We have to explore consciously the extent to which the pursuit of our passions leads to a good end. We have to think through what and how many material goods are necessary for a complete and virtuous life. We have to ask ourselves how we should use the time left in our lives. Finally, on discovering what we need to do to make ourselves happy, we have to commit to doing those things until they become habitual and pleasurable. None of these things is easy. But is it reasonable to assume our current course of intensifying the very actions that make us unhappy is more likely to succeed?

To quit making oneself unhappy, Aristotle says we have to ask what is ultimately good about being human, to identify which virtues are consistent with that end, to deliberate what actions we might take to live a virtuous life, and then to practice their pursuit. Most of us can't do that effectively because our moral muscles aren't adequately developed. Aristotle says that people in poor moral condition continue to act against their long-term self-interest, and continue to make themselves unhappy, until they engage in exercises to make themselves "fit."

Stated his way, the task seems daunting. Yet, in practice, a surprisingly large number of mature men and women turn the trick. David Heenan's *Double Lives* documents how 10 individuals with successful conventional careers decided in midlife to carve out second and third parallel vocations and avocations. For example, Lawrence Small was a senior executive in the financial industry when he decided to pursue his nonbusiness interests in anthropology, art, languages, and music. Small, now secretary of the Smithsonian Institution, divides the time of his considerably broadened life among such activities as playing flamenco guitar, collecting folk art, speaking four languages, wind surfing, scuba diving, and long-distance bicycling. He told Heenan, "I've done what I've done in terms of my many interests because I couldn't exist happily without doing these things."

Heenan also tells of Pat Williams, who decided not to let his relatively untaxing job as a front office executive for a professional basketball team limit his personal growth. He has written 18 books and run 13 marathons, in addition to being an active *pater familias* to a brood of 19 children, 14 of whom are adopted. Williams explains that leading such a full and fulfilling life requires planning: "To manage time, you've got to have your values lined up," he told Heenan. "Your values have to be written down and constantly reviewed and studied." Heenan, who has himself successfully pursued three parallel careers as a business executive, writer, and educator, suggests that the reason most of us choose to remain unidimensional workaholics instead of liberating our lives with discovery and experimentation is because we "let procrastinations, excuses, or regrets" get in the way of our dreams. His advice: "Don't just dream—do something. Set in motion a chain of activities" that will expand horizons. In true Aristotelian fashion, he concludes, "Most of us rely on a narrow field of expertise to support our ego and self-esteem. Learn to suspend what you know to discover what you don't know."

MID-COURSE SELF-EXAMINATION

If this sounds repetitive, it is, and that is the point Ben Franklin missed with his one-week virtue exercises. To change our behavior, we must repeatedly address the sources of our resistance until we finally wear them down and overcome them. We do so by surfacing the rationales we cleverly offer to protect and justify our current behavior, then logically and coolly dispel each of them over and over again in an iterative process for as long as it takes. In essence, that's what midlife psychotherapy is about. In our forties, psychiatrists help us to explain our self-defeating behavior in terms of what others did to us in our childhood. In our fifties, Aristotelian philosophical therapy gets us to think about the ways we make ourselves miserable and what we need to do to break those habits.

So what are we to do? Aristotle says virtuous people are those who learn to (a) spot a moral issue when they see it; (b) use a disciplined process for choosing both ends and means; (c) make choices "because of themselves" (for example, repay a debt because it is due and not because you will get a bad reputation if you don't); and (d) "proceed from a firm and unchangeable state."

Aristotle is a realist. He understands that we each have our own equivalent of the yacht or country estate that beguiles and entraps voluptuaries, even if it is only a new PT Cruiser or a Bang & Olufsen stereo system. We all have irrational material desires that get in the way of the pursuit of real happiness. Hence, we conclude, "I'll postpone serving on the school board until I've saved $400,000 for a condo in Vail." And he recognizes that we each have our own irrational desires for acceptance and honor that are as bad for us in ounce quantities as they are for sultans by the gallon. Nonetheless, Aristotle says we all have the capacity to change those desires, and we have within us sufficient capability to choose a right course of action no matter what our starting place may be and no matter how rich, powerful, or old we are. Moreover, we have the responsibility to do so. Foremost, we are responsible for choosing the right object of our lives. So, instead of engaging in a Franklinesque exercise to identify a list of moral prohibitions, Aristotle suggests that we ask ourselves a set of tough questions about how to make the best use of the increasingly scarce time of our lives:

- To what extent do I engage in moral deliberation about the ends I pursue and the means I use to pursue them?
- To what extent is my pursuit of goods driven by unconscious appetites? What passions rule my behavior? What can I do to gain control over those passions and appetites?
- To what extent do I behave in intemperate ways?
- How can I build the habits of temperance and right desire?
- When I set a moral goal, do I hold fast in its pursuit?
- How can I train myself to do those things habitually that will lead to the development of my highest-order human capacities?
- What moral capacity do I most need for developing self-discipline? How should I begin to develop it?
- What activities do I currently find pleasurable, but which prevent me from becoming happy in the long term?

As Aristotle observes, most of us spend the first 5 decades of our lives resisting the manifest need to ask such questions. And most of us direct our boundless powers of denial to avoiding the need to pursue those virtues that, alone, can make us happy. The overarching question is, *How do I start to develop the right desire to do so, and how do I then find the strength to stay the course?* The answer, in part, is that we begin the process "with a little help from our friends."

7

FRIENDS, FAMILY, RELIGION, AND OTHER GOODS

It is impossible, at least not easy, to do noble acts if one is unequipped. In many actions we take, friends, wealth, and political power serve as that instrumental "equipment." Furthermore, the lack of certain instrumental goods—such as being born to successful parents, having good children and good looks—will take the luster off our efforts to find happiness. For one who is extremely ugly in appearance, ill-born, solitary, or childless is not likely to be happy. And he is still less so if he has extremely bad children or bad friends, or if he lost good children and friends by their early death.

—Aristotle

While rereading Aristotle, I reached the point where I was ready to take on a subject more concrete than virtue. I was relieved to discover that he has a lot to say about a host of practical subjects ranging from leadership to philanthropy to business partnerships. I don't know why I had never noticed this before or why these ideas seem not to be cited in textbooks, but I was pleasantly surprised to find a practical side to the Ancient I hadn't been aware of. In fact, if it is utopia you're after, read Plato. Or if you think the material world is just an illusion, dip into the writings of the 18th-century philosopher Bishop Berkeley. Aristotle, in contrast, ultimately leads you to what is practical and real. For example, he asks how likely it is you will be happy if you are (a) born into wretched poverty, (b) so ugly you can't find a mate, (c) cursed with having thoroughly bad children, or (d) left alone because your good friends or children have died young? He says, no matter whatever else you might have, if you've got those woes, finding happiness won't be easy.

His positive scenario for happiness is equally nonidealistic and down to earth. He knows that practical people won't pursue a vision of the good life if it strikes them as abstract, unattainable, or unattractive. He understands that the only goals sensible men and women will pursue are familiar, attainable, and desirable. For most of us, those goals include a modicum of wealth, honor, health, family, love, friends, and, perhaps, good looks. Such instrumental goods can give anyone an advantage in the pursuit of happiness, as scions of the Rockefeller and Kennedy families demonstrate. Although those who come from the right families—those with wealth, powerful friends, and attractive children—have a leg up in the pursuit of happiness, those goods are not sufficient, as many a Kennedy and Rockefeller has shown. Nor are such inheritances necessary, as countless self-made Horatio Algers have demonstrated. Thus, the items on Aristotle's list of instrumental goods are nice-to-haves, but they affect happiness most significantly when they are absent from our lives rather than when present. However . . .

OUR LUCKY STARS

Aristotle says *everybody needs good luck.*

> Many things happen through fortune, differing in the size of
> their impact: among those with good fortune there are small
> things, and these obviously do not affect the scales of life. But
> when many great things turn out well they will make life
> more blessed, for by their nature they add adornment, and
> one's use of them turns out to be fine and excellent. But if
> they turn out the opposite way, they reduce and destroy
> blessedness, for they bring pain and impede many activities.

If we lose our wealth, or contract cancer, or our children die, it is hard to be happy.
Aristotle knows firsthand about Dame Fortune's fickle finger: Having buried a
young wife, he is sensitive to the fragility and contingency of happiness. He is no
Stoic. He recognizes that if a loved one dies, it hurts deeply, and you are dimin-
ished by the loss. Depending on circumstances, you may never again be completely happy. Conversely, good luck is always a boon, even to virtuous people.

But Aristotle also recognizes that good luck, in and of itself, doesn't necessarily bring happiness. If it did, there wouldn't be those stories about miserable lottery winners. In Aristotle's view, what matters is how one uses good
fortune. Luck may be necessary, but it is no substitute for virtue (somehow
Aristotle manages to sneak virtue into a discussion of luck!). He says we all
need enough good fortune to provide the financial freedom to decide how to
conduct our lives, but we still must choose to pursue the good. Moreover,
virtue can offer some security in the event of misfortune: Cyclist Lance Arm-
strong possessed the virtues needed to cope with the misfortune of life-threatening cancer, and Galileo's dedication to the highest good enabled him to brave
misfortunes in his old age that would have been debilitating to most people.

Aristotle wonders about the extent to which we make our own fortunes.
He sees examples of dumb luck: the equivalent of the village idiot who wins

the lottery or today's employee of average intelligence who is in the right job at the right time and is granted valuable stock options. Similarly, he puzzles over why fortune will smile on only one of several equally talented individuals. Numerous explanations are offered to explain that frequently observed occurrence: "Some people are naturally lucky," "people get what they deserve," and "life is a craps game." All things being equal, Aristotle goes with the latter explanation. Bad people, stupid people, mindless people, and lazy people may benefit from blind luck and win lotteries; good, smart, morally deliberative, and hardworking people may get struck with bad luck, lose spouses, have strokes, and see their wealth stolen from them.

Yet there are times when we make our own fortune or misfortune. In terms of doing the right thing morally, chance favors the prepared mind. A chronic adulterer might get lucky and never be caught in the act, but a faithful spouse runs no risk of such embarrassment. So, in some ways, we can control our fates. Through use of reason, we can choose to do things that are likely to lead to happiness and not do things that have a high probability of making us unhappy. The outcome isn't guaranteed, but such reasoning greatly increases the odds in our favor.

But no matter how lucky a morally lazy person may be, he or she has no chance of finding true happiness as Aristotle defines it. We confirm this by observing what happens when people with bad moral habits win the lottery and by reference to individuals who get rich through hard work but are morally unprepared for their success. So Aristotle concludes that luck is a necessary, if insufficient, requirement for happiness. But as important as luck is, it is no substitute for the highest of all instrumental goods.

FRIENDSHIP

"Without friends, no one would choose to live even though he had all other goods," Aristotle writes, adding that a virtuous person "does many acts for the sake of his friends and country and, if necessary, dies for them." Aristotle's strong views on friendship might come as somewhat surprising, particularly in light of what he calls the "highest good": the development of one's own individual potential. As individual development seems such a relatively self-sufficient activity, we might think Aristotle's good life would be a solo affair. But his advocacy of contemplation doesn't mean he favors isolation, monasticism, or ascetic retreat. He is no advocate of rugged or any other form of individualism; he is, instead, a communitarian. Although self-development is the "highest good," he reminds us that it is not the "complete good." To achieve completeness, we must be fully contributing members of a community. We develop our individual abilities not for selfish ends but because others benefit when we do so. To Aristotle, friendship is the bond in all human relationships, from the family through the community to the state: "Friendship seems to hold states together." This makes sense when we recall that Aristotle believes humans are "political animals" who, as members of a community, are all "friends," conscious of each other and solicitous of the desires and concerns of others.

To Aristotle, the cardinal virtue of friendship is a broad category including relationships in one's community, in political life, and at work. Ideally, one's spouse and children are also one's friends. The Greek word for friendship, *philia,* means "affection for one's associates," as in Philadelphia, "the city of brotherly love." Aristotle has strong opinions about the depth of affection one should have for, and how broadly one should define the category of, one's associates. Indeed, it is jarring when reading Aristotle for the first time to find that he applies the same Greek word for love to the various relationships of husband and wife, parents and children, leaders and followers, as well as to relationships among friends, neighbors, and coworkers. Yet, Jesus Christ spoke of love in the same broad way 400 years after Aristotle.

Aristotle says the essence of virtuous friendship is selflessness: With a true friend, "we wish what is good for his sake." But not all friendships are selfless and virtuous. Some are based on pleasure. Young people, in particular, seek pleasant relationships. They say, "Charlie's my friend because he's fun to be around." And many adult friendships, particularly business relationships, are based on utility. In friendships based on pleasure or utility, the individuals involved wish for what is good for themselves and not what is good for their friends. Aristotle says such relationships are fragile: "Those who are friends for the sake of utility part when the advantage is at an end, for they were lovers not of each other but of profit." He says that problems also arise in friendships when participants have dissimilar purposes for the relationship: for example, when one party loves the other virtuously, and the other sees the relationship solely in terms of utility. Such friendships are doomed to bad ends, as when we seek to be friends with famous or powerful people, hoping to have some of their honor rub off on us. There is neither virtue nor stability in such relationships.

True friendships, Aristotle asserts, are characterized by permanence, deep familiarity, frequency of interaction, and generosity. It helps if friends have similar interests, tastes, and desires, although they needn't agree on everything. The minds of virtuous friends need be in accord only on basic values and ends, on what the good life entails. Aristotle says you have to be virtuous to be a good friend, for such a friend will "desire the good for the other." In contrast, bad people have trouble keeping friends; they come into conflict and competition with others because they seek "more" for themselves. Ultimately, friendships are based on trust, the test of which is the conviction of each friend that the other "would never wrong me."

Equality is often but not always a characteristic of friendship. Similarity of age helps to build friendship because of the inherent equality of such relationships. Because young people are almost always unequal beneficiaries in relationships with elders, as in mentoring relationships, few young people are true friends with those who are far older; such relationships serve the utility of the younger. Indeed, when relationships are inherently unequal, as with parent and child, Aristotle says the one who has more power gives (loves) more. Likewise, when good people are in positions of authority, as leaders and

169

bosses, they give more than they get in return. A good leader "will look not to his own interests but to those of his subjects," and a "tyrant pursues his own good." Thus, the degree of virtue in the utilitarian relationship between leaders and followers "depends on an excess of benefits conferred" upon the latter.

WHY WE NEED FRIENDS

Aristotle says friends are indispensable. We need them because we aren't gods who can get through life alone, sitting in perfect contemplation. Instead, we are animals who, by nature, live in groups and need other people for purposes of survival. Practical work activities require social cooperation. But we also need friends for higher purposes because humans are "*political* animals," as well, with the quasi-divine capacity for speech. To Aristotle, speech is the outward manifestation of our reasoning capabilities, the purpose of which is to enable us to participate with others in political deliberations. Because politics is part of our nature, we have a moral obligation to engage with others, to participate in our own governance, and to share in collective deliberations about what is right and just for all members of our community. Thus, to govern best, we need virtuous friends with whom we come together to discuss the well-being of all members of the organization or system in which we participate. Such discussions are bridges between philosophy and politics, between thought and action, between the highest good (our personal moral development) and the complete good (creating justice in our community).

In such discussions, friends are also instrumental to our happiness. As we have seen, to gain wisdom one must devote considerable time and effort to discover what is good, just, and true for oneself. Each of us has to learn to "see aright." Because Aristotle believes that people, collectively, have a sense in common of what is good and bad and right and wrong, it is therefore useful to partake with others in our moral development. Friends are invaluable sources of right desire. We learn from friends through moral deliberation and discussion, and through them are better able to be ethical and virtuous than if we are socially isolated.

Humans become excellent, Aristotle says, when we learn to reflect on moral experience. He adds that we often do this best with help from our friends. In particular, friends help us overcome our lack of self-discipline. The biggest obstacles on the road to happiness are the distractions of apparent goods, distracting pleasures that cause us to lose sight of our real goals. Friends help us to stay on the high road, help us to habituate ourselves to pursuing the good. So it helps to have friends who are predisposed to virtue. Instead of saying, "Let's go to our local tavern for a brew," true friends will engage us in virtuous thoughts and activities. Aristotle says it's easier to resist temptations to go to the pub if your friends aren't interested in getting sloshed.

This is a not-so-subtle critique of the symposia, or drinking parties, frequented by Socrates and Plato. At those events, friends seeking pleasure would gather at a watering hole where the first business of the evening was deciding the degree to which their wine would be diluted; if they drank it without any water, everyone would get so drunk that there was little hope of serious conversation. Aristotle thinks wine always should be extremely watered down. He acknowledges that friends find pleasure sharing "bodily delights," but he adds that they find the greatest pleasure in sharing their virtue. The pleasure found in sharing a bottle of wine with friends is not getting plastered but, instead, the intellectual and moral benefits of good company. In all cases, he says that those higher pleasures of drinking with others far outweigh the apparent pleasure of drinking alone.

As my teacher, Mortimer Adler, never tired of reminding his students, Aristotle believes "reading alone is as bad as drinking alone." That's because Aristotle believes "life in common is . . . knowledge in common." Although the task of pure contemplation can be done alone, the virtuous person "can perhaps do so better if he has fellow workers." Aristotle suggests that conversations among equals over dinner can be profound learning experiences because, in such settings, we are willing to share our insights, take intellectual risks, and try out ideas whether fully baked or not. Hence, friends are necessary for the life of the mind because they act as sounding boards and critics of our bright ideas. That's why our best friends will be equals, people who are not reluctant to tell us when we are all wet or when we're slightly damp.

In this regard, Aristotle says we see ourselves most clearly through the eyes of others: "We can contemplate our neighbors better than ourselves, and their actions better than our own." We see the vices and virtues of others more clearly than we can see our own; and they, likewise, can see us better than they can see themselves. We learn what not to do when we watch friends screw up, and we learn the ways and rewards of virtue when we observe them behave well. Because so many of the choices people make are unconsciously self-destructive to happiness, a priceless value of friendship is that friends provide mutual mirrors in which they can see each other's actions, thus helping each other to avoid the pitfalls of denial and self-deceit. Consequently, a requisite of happiness is having friends who wish to be in a candid, sharing, intimate relationship:

> So the happy person needs to be conscious of the existence of his friends, and this will come about through their living together and sharing in discussion and thought; for this is what living together would seem to mean in the case of humans, not just browsing together side by side like cattle.

If we need such good friends, how many should we have? Aristotle answers, "as many as are sufficient for living together . . . sharing in discussion and thought." We need as many friends as can be close enough to have shared interests and can trust enough to engage in deep discussions. The number of virtuous relationships is thus limited by the bounds of intimacy: How many people can you really know who can know you well in return? A person with

172

"thousands of friends" is probably a person with no true friends. Or, if one is like Hugh Hefner, there is no limit to the number of "friends" one can use because they are being used for purposes of pleasure, not virtue.

Although the number of true friends is limited, Aristotle says it is probably insufficient to have only one because that overly limits the range of ideas and perspectives to which one is exposed. A person with only a single friend may not be willing to really have anyone challenge his ideas. Moreover, such a guarded person probably lacks the virtue of trust. In the end, Aristotle tells us that the right amount of friends is the number that most fosters our development. If we are always in a crowd, we will not have sufficient occasion to read and to contemplate; if we are always alone, we will never test our ideas, and we will not contribute to society. So how much time should we spend alone and how much time with friends? Again, the trick is finding the right balance: as much time in each activity as needed to maximize our self-development and our contribution to the community.

In sum, Aristotle says, "Virtuous friends are the greatest of external goods." We need them in times of adversity (for support) and when things are going well (to share our good fortune). A virtuous person will not turn to friends only when he is in trouble, because that transforms the nature of the relationship into one of utility. Moreover, virtuous people recognize that they need friends when fortune is kind, because they need others on whom to bestow the benefits of their wealth and power in order to ennoble those goods. He tells us we cannot be virtuous if we horde such goods, use them for selfish purposes, or use them merely as instruments to gain "more." We need friends to be the recipients of our good fortune; in effect, they are the objects of our virtue. Aristotle concludes that humans are social animals who need others; and, therefore, the person "who stands alone is a beast or a god."

After reading Aristotle on friendship, it clicked in my head in the middle of the night that I had basically been a loner all my life, and perhaps that accounted for some of my unhappiness and for the difficulties I was having breaking bad habits and learning to enjoy more virtuous ones. I remembered what the sports writer Jim Murray once said of Kareem Abdul Jabbar: "No man is an island, but Kareen gave it a shot." Perhaps not coincidentally, at the time of this insight, I had been reading about and even teaching about the merits of group over individual organizational leadership. My colleague and mentor, Warren Bennis, had cowritten a fine book, *Great Groups*, in which he and David Heenan described several dissimilar circles of "friends," all of which had in common the importance of the group to the success of its individual members. He cited such diverse examples as Walt Disney's early studio and the group of scientists at Los Alamos who created the atomic bomb. I also had read Louis Menand's *The Metaphysical Club*, in which he showed that the pragmatic American way of looking at the world, among both left- and right-wing thinkers, was developed by a "school" of friends in the era following the Civil War. All of this is in keeping with the thesis of Randall Collins's *The Sociology of Philosophies*, which argues that, almost without exception, all major thinkers and innovators throughout history have been members of movements of friends (and friendly rivals), from neo-Confucianism to German Idealism to French Impressionism. That thesis is further supported by Jenny Uglow's *The Lunar Men*, which deals with an 18th-century circle of friends including such noted inventors, scientists, and industrial innovators as Matthew Boulton, James Watt, Joseph Priestly, and Erasmus Darwin, who formed a kind of Aristotelian intellectual support group, encouraging each other and acting as sounding boards for the others' ideas. Moving from the sublime to the ridiculous, Tom Shales and James Andrew Miller's *Live from New York* recounts how the early *Saturday Night Live* cast of Dan Aykroyd, Gilda Radner, John Belushi, and Bill Murray were a close-knit group of friends who got by (and high) together. The more I read and thought about it, the "path-breaking" loner was a myth; and almost all the great philosophers, artists, writers, and religious thinkers had been a part of some group of friends, mentors, and disciples.

Friendship turns out to be yet another subject on which modern social science has reinvented Aristotle. Economist Richard Easterlin's data demon-

174

strates that earning more money doesn't make people happier, but spending quality time with friends and loved ones does; and psychologist Sonja Lyubormisky's research shows that happy people have more friends. In *The Pursuit of Happiness,* David Myer cites data correlating strong friendships with individual self-esteem and career satisfaction. Echoing Aristotle, he uses the methods of social science to show that "We humans are made to belong." And, like Kareem, I was trying to go it alone!

IMPLICATIONS FOR BUSINESS LEADERSHIP

Although I had been teaching the merits of shared leadership, I wasn't getting much traction with the notion among business executives. Indeed, the successful business leaders with whom I worked almost all subscribed to the belief that leadership is, by necessity, a lonely activity, a singular noun. Moreover, the dominant view among scholars in the field of leadership studies is that leadership is a one-person show. Plato had called it "a rare trait typically possessed by only one person" in any society, an individual with a unique lock on wisdom and truth.

Aristotle wrote *Politics* to refute his teacher. He thought Plato's view led to ineffective leadership at best, tyranny at worst. Because wisdom is never the sole province of one person, Aristotle argued that a good society would share leadership as broadly as possible, instead of concentrating power in the hands of a single person, no matter how smart or virtuous he or she might be. But Aristotle's arguments fell on deaf ears because Plato's view coincided with the kind of leadership most people saw in practice: one-man rule. Indeed, Aristotle's concept of shared leadership seems counterintuitive: For most of history and in most places, leadership has seemed to be an individual trait and activity.

But is it really? When we speak of leadership, the likes of Mohandas Gandhi and Martin Luther King Jr. spring to mind. Yet, in fact, during the struggle for Indian independence, Gandhi was surrounded and supported by dozens of other great leaders, including Jawaharlal Nehru, Vallabhbhai Patel, and Mohammed Ali Jinnah, without whose joint efforts Gandhi almost certainly would have failed. Lest we forget, far from doing it all himself, King's disciples included such impressive leaders in their own right as Jesse Jackson, Andrew Young, Julian Bond, Coretta Scott King, and Ralph Abernathy. As with Gandhi and King, ditto Franklin Roosevelt, Thomas Jefferson, and George Washington: Almost every great leader throughout history has listened to and shared power with "friends." When the facts are assembled, even the most fabled "solitary" leaders were supported by a team of other effective leaders. In his youth, Winston Churchill read the *Ethics* and consciously modeled his proclivity for shared leadership along Aristotelian lines.

In the business world, American corporations are often portrayed as shadows of the "great men" who sit in chief executive chairs. *Fortune* magazine cover stories are more likely to be about Jack Welch or Bill Gates than about GE or Microsoft. Business schools dutifully conform to the common wisdom: Leadership is studied and taught by focusing on the characters, biographies, and "charisma" of a single leader—the CEO. If team concepts are discussed at all, it is not in leadership courses. In terms of best practices, it is assumed a single person must be held accountable for the performance of a corporation and for each of its subsets. This individual focus isn't always wrong; rather, it blinds young executives to the existence of other models and causes them to discount the many examples of shared leadership running counter to received wisdom. Worse, it causes them to miss out on the value of having friends who can provide the all-important mirror reflection on themselves.

Aristotle identifies the main benefit of shared leadership: No one individual, no matter how gifted, can be right all the time. As the past CEO of Champion Paper, Richard Olson, explains, "None of us is as smart as all of us." In large corporations, there is simply too much work for one person, and no one individual is likely to have all the skills needed to do it all. History shows that businesses dependent on a single leader run considerable risk: If that individual retires, leaves, or dies in office, the organization may lose its continuing capacity to succeed. Witness the performance of General Motors after Alfred Sloan, ITT after Harold Geneen, and Polaroid after Edwin Land.

Amana Corporation's chief executive, Paul Staman, recently explained the benefits of shared leadership: "It allows more time for leaders to spend in the field; it creates an internal dynamic in which the leaders constantly challenge each other to higher levels of performance; it encourages a shared leadership mindset at all levels of the company; it prevents the trauma of transition that occurs in organizations when a strong CEO suddenly leaves." Significantly, Staman is one of four coleaders at Amana. When Amana's Gang of Four are asked what makes their unusual arrangement work, they identify an Aristotelian "shared set of guiding principles, and a team in which each member is able to set aside ego and 'what's in it for me' thinking." That's what the Ancient has in mind when he talks about friendship being selfless.

The practice of shared leadership, though rare, is not new. Despite broadly held views to the contrary, history provides successful examples of shared political power. In its declining years, the Roman Empire was ruled by two "caesars," one in Milan, the other in Constantinople. In imperial China, real power was wielded not by the person on the throne but by the meritocratic Mandarin class of leaders. And there are examples of shared leadership in major U.S. corporations, as well. The aura of high-profile operators like Jack Welch and Harold Geneen causes the general public to believe that leadership is an aria sung by a prima donna, obscuring the famous duets of the business world sung by HP's William Hewlett and David Packard, and Berkshire Hathaway's Warren Buffett and Charles Munger. Intel has been run by leadership teams from day one. Various combinations of "friends"—Robert Noyce, Gordon Moore, Andrew Grove, and Craig Barrett—have shared leadership roles, offering constructive criticism much in the way Aristotle describes.

If Aristotle is right about this, why do so many American businesspeople

177

try to go it alone? For example, after driving Oracle's chief executive, Ray Lane, out of the company, Larry Ellison began to centralize his control of the organization, transforming the nature of its leadership more and more into a one-man show. This is paradoxical because, questions of virtue aside, Ellison's behavior seems self-defeating in terms of his own goals. The business press in 2002 was full of reports that investors were growing wary of owning Oracle stock because of his increasingly one-man rule. Ellison seems unaware that his stand-alone posture causes some observers to say he identifies with the gods! Why has Ellison done so? We cannot know his motivations, but we do know that talented, successful people often subscribe to the myth that they are, by nature, self-sufficient. In fact, such people often believe they have no choice but to stand alone. To them, good, trustworthy friends are nearly impossible to find.

FINDING A CIRCLE OF FRIENDS

How and where can one find the depth and breadth of friendship Aristotle found during his formative years in Macedonia? Because communities of virtuous friends are unlikely to form naturally in modern, impersonal societies, they must be sought out or, failing that, created. For example, between 1950 and 1996, groups of 15 to 20 professional men and women would gather at the Aspen Institute for 2-week seminars created by Mortimer Adler to replicate the Aristotelian model of virtuous friendship to the extent possible and practical. Participants were typically in their late forties to early fifties, roughly Aristotle's age when he found his own community of friends. They read philosophical, political, and literary texts and discussed their relevance to creating a good life for themselves and a good society for others. Because the seminarians were away from work and other distractions, they were able to focus on what each other had to say, learning to listen carefully in a way that is unusual among busy folk today. They met in the mornings to formally discuss the readings, then spent afternoons and evenings in informal discussions during hikes and over meals. The seminars were not touchy-feely therapy groups; nonetheless, honest and close relationships were formed that often lasted long beyond the end of the seminar. One group continues to meet annually to refresh themselves some 25 years after their first trip to Aspen.

Although such seminars may sound like the pastime of retirees, dilettantes, and humanists, in fact busy professionals not only can engage in them, they can benefit greatly from interactions with others from different backgrounds. For example, contemporary Aristotelian David Eisenberg is a distinguished professor of biology at UCLA, a true scholar who publishes in his field's top journals. Yet he doesn't let the narrowing demands of academe prevent him from becoming truly learned and, then, applying his learning to the needs of the broader society. He is a first-rate teacher at a research university not known for its undergraduate teaching and is actively involved as a leader in LA's cultural and political life. David is also the founder of a high-tech start-up company and a serious bike rider (in his fifties, he and his daughter pedaled across the breadth of the entire United States). He and his wife, Lucy, a successful lawyer, not only read novels and serious nonfiction, they discuss them in "salons" they host for their Aristotelian "friends"—professionals, politicians, and scholars. The Eisenbergs' example illustrates how seminars, study groups, reading clubs, literary salons, and the like can be designed to meet the need identified by Aristotle for friends to engage in collective deliberation. Indeed, I wonder how many readers of this book are regular members of such "good groups."

There is no reason to wait until one is middle-aged to join a circle of virtuous friends. The stated purpose of the Henry Crown Fellowship program is to help high-potential business leaders in their thirties and forties to develop their leadership skills and to encourage them to ask Aristotelian questions about community service while still young enough to pursue the complete good in the middle of their professional careers. Each class of Crown Fellows assembles regularly to read and discuss classic works by the likes of Plato,

179

Locke, Hobbes, and, of course, Aristotle, along with modern texts on leadership and ethics. The seminars afford these busy young leaders the opportunity to think about and discuss what it means to lead the good life. But at a deeper level, the real value of the program is that it allows those who are too-often solo operators to interact rigorously with a group of peers, much as Aristotle did with his friends in Macedonia.

Crown Fellows don't just talk about their experiences; they work together to find ways to create a good society in their businesses and communities. Each accepts responsibility to initiate a community project under the mentorship of a more experienced leader, then they share with each other what they learned from their efforts. According to program founder and director, Keith Berwick, the Fellows often learn that giving money is relatively easy; they find it much harder to make effective gifts of their time and talents. Indeed, their discussions often turn to the difficulties they experience defining what people in their communities really need. My favorite of these projects was initiated by economist Peter Reiling, CEO of the nonprofit TechnoServe, who started a program to develop leadership skills among entrepreneurial people in Africa.

When I have spoken with some of these young executives, I have found it encouraging that so many of them have a better grasp of the ethics of helping others than do most business leaders of my generation. Crown Fellows are Aristotelians-in-waiting, often citing friends, family, and "making a contribution" as being as important as money in their personal searches for happiness. Here's how Reiling defined happiness:

> For me, the key components of happiness are a strong and happy family, good health, a comfortable but not lavish physical existence, good friends, intellectual stimulation (the ability to pursue my curiosity), and the ability to use the opportunities afforded to me, by luck of birth and circumstances, to help others realize their own potential. Did I

mention my 1962 Chevy Impala convertible on a sunny fall day? A heaping pile of Maryland steamed crabs? Bob Dylan's *Blonde on Blonde*? Or a hike in the Marin Headlands?

Crown Fellow John Rogers, CEO of Ariel Capital, seeks to lead a life balanced between family, friends, work, sports, and community service: "I measure happiness by the length and quality of friendships, and the measure of that quality is mutual respect." Unlike many busy executives, Rogers will drop everything in the middle of a workweek to travel out of town to compete in a 3-on-3 basketball tournament. When he stays home, the native Chicagoan serves on four private and four public boards, including the board of commissioners of the Chicago Parks District. He seeks to be an unobtrusive and unselfish civic leader and believes he can be most effective to that end by creating wealth: "Money gives me options I wouldn't otherwise have." And Rogers seems to exercise those options often and thoughtfully, as in his creation of the Ariel Education Initiative to provide quality educational options to inner-city kids, including the Ariel Community Academy, a fully-funded primary school. Rogers also has cut all of his employees into the financial action of his investment firm so they, too, can contribute to their community, and they, too, can become virtuous.

Another young business leader, Laurence Belfer, COO of Belco Oil and Gas and cofounder of Harvest Management, a money management firm, also attempts to divide his time meaningfully between work, family, friends, and community activities. For example, he serves on the board of HELP, Housing Enterprise for the Less Privileged, the nation's largest provider of housing for homeless families, with an annual budget of $40 million. A voracious reader, Belfer says the most important lesson he has learned from books is that happiness is not something to be put off until tomorrow. As he puts it in Aristotelian terms, "Happiness is a journey, not a destination."

Crown Fellows are neither naturally nor accidentally leading virtuous lives. Aristotle's point, and the purpose of the Crown Fellowship program, is that it takes conscious effort over a period of years before one can become disciplined to seek the highest and complete goods, and to do so, we need a little help from our friends. The Crown Fellows I've interviewed demonstrate that it isn't necessary to wait until middle age before getting started.

ANOTHER LITTLE TEST

When I took the mid-course examination at the end of the previous chapter, I was pleased to give myself improved grades in terms of my personal development. When lost in the act of writing, I was slipping into "the zone" and, in the process, often was able to forget about my needs for approval. Thanks to Aristotle, I was learning that my personal route to happiness was to scribble, scribble, scribble. But I also saw that I was only halfway there; although I was working on achieving the "highest good," I was not yet pursuing the "complete good." How could I effectively address this shortcoming? If a test of the highest good is one's ability to get into the zone while doing something, what is the comparable test for the complete good? In other words, how would I know if I were engaged in a virtuous activity that entails true friendship? As I furiously leafed through the *Ethics* trying to find Aristotle's test of the virtue of activities we engage in with others, it occurred to me that he might say I should begin by asking myself the following kinds of questions:

- What activity do I engage in with others that gives me so much pleasure that I lose my intemperate desires in the process?
- While engaging in that activity, do I learn moral lessons about myself from observing others?
- Is the purpose of the activity "for the sake of others," for the benefit of friends?
- While taking part in this activity, do I apply the fruits of my individual growth to the development of others?

As I tried to answer those questions, I saw that I was missing the kind of friendships Aristotle found when he participated in an intimate relationship with equals who, to their mutual benefit, shared ideas and experiences. In modern society, one might expect to form such friendships at work; but when I thought about it, I had to admit I seldom found such friendship among my university colleagues. In particular, most interactions with individuals from my own discipline amounted simply to work/work and did not involve elements of mutual growth or leisure/work. Worse, professorial meetings often deteriorated into exhibitions of power, ego, and mutual contempt; and academic one-upmanship is not what Aristotle had in mind by friendship. The few rewarding experiences I have had in academia were with individuals from different fields who came together to study a cross-disciplinary problem. Unfortunately, such gatherings don't occur naturally at large research-based universities, where working outside one's discipline is associated with dilettantism.

Nonetheless, a few contemporary Aristotelians in the academic community have the courage to create truly developmental activities across departmental boundaries. For instance, English professor Ronald Gottesman is known in his field as an editor of the *Norton Anthology of American Literature* and author of numerous books and articles related to literary criticism. But Ron's friends and students also know him as an expert on cinema (he has written about Orson Wells, Sergei Eisenstein, and King Kong); a clinical psychoanalyst; a lecturer on aesthetics, robotics, jazz, and Native American art; and a consultant to the National Council on Aging and the Walt Disney company (he provided inspiration for the cover of one of their annual reports). He most recently served as editor in chief of the critically acclaimed three-volume encyclopedia, *Violence in America*.

In 1975, when Ron arrived at the University of Southern California, he put aside his specialized work to found USC's Center for the Humanities. While other professors were dedicated to careers of reducing useful learning to the point of irrelevance, Ron invited professors not only from the humanities but from the sciences and the professions, as well, to join him in making his center a truly Aristotelian community in which scholars worked together on significant interdisciplinary issues, ranging from business ethics to urban unrest. Outsiders to university life often assume such activities occur on campuses as a matter of course, but in fact Ron had to struggle mightily to overcome opposition from discipline-bound faculty and, especially, narrow-minded administrators who dislike threats to departmentalization. But for the sake of friendship, Ron was willing to bear the cost of such unpopularity. Here's what Ron said to his colleagues and students on the occasion of his recent retirement:

> Hundreds of millions of people the world over are concerned with an economy gone sour. It is to these perplexed and perturbed I wish to speak some words of economic advice: Invest in friends. There is no other instrument that pays such high returns. I figure that I have an average investment ratio of 5 to 1 based on the past 30 years that I have known many of you. Some years I have neglected certain items in my portfolio—neglected to call, to write, to e-mail, to console, to encourage, to hug—to simply say I love you.
>
> I can't tell you how much I regret this neglect, this all-to-human failure to imitate the dyadic dance that begins at birth and sustains us throughout life. We need each other, but perversely we neglect each other. Every day we have an opportunity to exercise friendship, to make huge returns on a tiny investment, but foolishly we relapse into sleep and forgetting. Please take my advice to heart—forget bonds, forget stocks, forget gold—invest in friendship.

At age 66, Ron left academia to start an online art gallery specializing in Australian Aboriginal art. He understands that if growth for a career businessperson entails adding an element of "the life of the mind," growth for a career intellectual may mean adding an entrepreneurial element to create a well-balanced life. His students call him an "edupreneur."

Ron's courageous efforts to bridge disciplines at USC were contagious: I recall a series of particularly rewarding meetings in the late 1970s with a group of professors from law, engineering, physics, mathematics, business, the humanities, and social sciences who gathered to search for creative solutions to the energy crisis. In the process, I learned a great deal about a broadening range of issues I would never have been exposed to had I stayed comfortably immured in my own academic department. It was then, more than at any other time, that I loved being a professor, loved university life, and laid a foundation of nontraditional learning I have been building on ever since.

I also had gotten into a communal version of the zone at the regular meetings of the Board of Editors of the *Encyclopaedia Britannica*, chaired by Mortimer Adler. Clearly, I was in over my head with that distinguished circle of friends, the most remarkable aspect of which was that they listened to each other and felt free to respectfully disagree. As accomplished as they each were in their respective fields, they nonetheless were equals in the group, engaging in a process of mutual teaching and learning. But as great as that experience was, it is impossible for me to recreate it, and it isn't the kind of friendship most of the businesspeople I deal with on a daily basis would find rewarding. As was I, they would be intimidated.

Indeed, the more I thought about it, the most rewarding groups of friends I have had were the "ordinary" people I met at Aspen seminars. There, I have been fortunate to spend time with men and women, roughly my age, from business, government, labor, and nonprofit organizations who, collectively, shared in the high of mutual intellectual discovery. And it was just such deep human interaction that I found missing from my current life. It also occurred to me that such opportunities are missing, in general, from the lives of most members of my generation. Few of us have places where we can gather in a structured setting with friends our age to discuss issues that matter to us.

So I committed myself to finding a way to interact more often with new friends in a formal way. I soon adopted as my model a group of 10 couples, most in their fifties and sixties, who for the last 5 years have been gathering, once or twice a year for a few days each time, to discuss plays, poems, novels, and other works of art. Led by two remarkable contemporary Aristotelians, Geraldine and Charles Van Doren, this group of true friends has met in culturally stimulating locales in Europe and the United States to engage in shared reflection and renewal. Following the Van Dorens' example, in the summer of 2004, I joined with author Joan Peters to gather a group of new friends with the intent of working together to write our life plans. We began our effort the way in which I suggested readers should begin thinking about their life plans: by each of us drawing a map of the trajectory of our lives and sharing it with the group.

We then spent most of the next 5 days discussing works of literature that explored the major milestones and landmarks on life's journey that Aristotle identifies as important. We discussed plays (Euripedes' *Medea*, Shakespeare's *King Lear*, Miller's *Death of a Salesman*), short stories (Joyce's "The Dead," Melville's "Bartleby the Scrivener," Hemingway's "The Big Two-Hearted River"), poems (Shakespeare's sonnet "like as the waves make toward the pebble shore / So do our minutes hasten to their end," Eliot's "The Love Song of J. Alfred Prufrock," Shelley's "Ozymandias," Dickinson's "I died for beauty"), films (*Wild Strawberries, Holiday, The Barbarian Invasions, City Slickers*), and books (Iris Origio's *The Merchant of Prato*, Simone DeBouvier's *The Second Sex*, Budd Schulberg's *What Makes Sammy Run?*). We also found it useful to discuss readings by H. D. Thoreau, John Muir, and Aldo Leopold about how nature consoles and delights us. In particular, we benefited from discussing Helen and Scott Nearing's *Living the Good Life*, which describes how the couple created a new life apart from urban pressures and modern technology (we decided that wasn't for us). And it helped us to discuss works that caused us to see the familiar afresh and make the familiar foreign, such as John Berger's *About Looking*, Italo Calvino's *Mr. Palomar*, Anthony Storr's *Solitude*, and Sue Bender's *Plain and Simple*. As Proust said, "The real voyage of discovery consists not in seeing new landscapes, but in having new eyes."

In discussing these works, we found ourselves raising some profound questions we never had imagined we would be exploring in the company of others:

How important is proving oneself?

Is ambition necessary, or is it a trap?

What is appropriate ambition?

How can art and nature heal us and prepare us for our next adventure?

How can we learn to live bravely in the face of adversity?

What gives coherence to our lives?

When is it time to return to the less practical interests we put aside early in our careers?

What should we now learn to do and to do well?

In trying to answer such questions, we each candidly confirmed that our own pursuits of happiness hadn't been cakewalks. But we also concluded, in hindsight, that our various struggles, setbacks, and sacrifices were best seen as inescapable potholes and detours on what were ultimately satisfying journeys along the road to maturity. As we each made our ways along that path, we had come to appreciate what T. S. Eliot meant when he wrote, "Old men ought to be explorers." Middle-age women, too, we found. At the end of the week, we all were able to work more confidently on our life plans and, with a little help from our friends, were able to flesh out the parts of our maps that dealt with our futures. We helped each other to create life plans designed to transport us, in Ron Gottesman's words, from the youthful activities of accumulation, ambition, and achievement to the satisfying renewal, realization, and redemption of maturity.

FAMILY

Aristotle, a sexist by contemporary standards, nonetheless believes that spouses can be "true friends." He writes that men and women form natural bonds for the purposes of pleasure (sex) and utility (sharing familial workloads) and that adding the presence of children strengthens those bonds. He says childless couples "part more easily." He also observes that some marriages go beyond pleasure, utility, and the raising of children to become true friendships. On marriage, Aristotle writes, "This friendship may also be based on virtue if the two parties are good." If a man and wife have a relationship based on intellectual equality, and if they act out of mutual respect "for the sake of the other," he concludes that they can become true friends and "will delight in the fact."

It turns out that Aristotle, often accused of being "all head and no heart," believes in the possibility of romantic love (within marriage, yet!): "Love is a sort of excess of feeling, and it is the nature of such only to be felt towards one person." Of course, Aristotle had sown wild oats in his youth; but, by all accounts, he was loving and faithful to his wife, Pythias, and, after her death, to his companion, Herpyllis. There is some evidence that both women helped him to identify the good and to habituate himself to temperance and self-discipline. In the final analysis, that may be why he includes the marriage relationship in his category of friendship, claiming there is nothing more positive one can say about a spouse than that he or she remains a close and true friend throughout one's life.

Aristotle recognizes that having a bad marriage, like having selfish and ungrateful children, will tarnish an otherwise happy life; nonetheless, he thinks marriage and family are both worth the risk. Although he had made the acquaintance of happy single people and childless couples, on the whole he feels they are at a disadvantage compared with married people, particularly those with kids. He thinks it would be hard to pass his deathbed test with flying colors if one is alone. Experience leads him to conclude that older, single people almost always regret not having found a life partner, and childless people usually regret not having kids, if only for the instrumental good of having someone to care for them in their old age.

But to Aristotle, family members, like all friends, are not merely instrumental goods who serve our needs. We also have responsibilities to them, in particular, to desire what is good for their sake. He says this starts with how we raise our children, what we teach them, and how we model the roles they will someday play. It is through familial interactions that children first see the consequences of right desire and through which they begin to form an ethical conscience, even if it will not be developed fully until long after they leave their parents' care. We return to some implications of that in subsequent chapters. Modern psychologists, of course, have similar things to say about families, and many of their studies show a correlation between family life and happiness. But again, Aristotle isn't concerned about whether or not we "feel good" about our families. Instead, he wants us each to ponder the question: "What role does a family play in a complete life well led?"

RELIGION: A GOOD UNTO ITSELF

Among contemporary men and women who, in my reckoning, live Aris-
totelian lives, some are rich, others not, some are well educated, others not, some are Republicans and some Democrats, and some are very religious while others are not religious at all. Of those defining characteristics, religion is the most problematic. It might appear that religion fulfills exactly the same ethical role as philosophy, and, if so, one could find virtue and happiness simply through religion and skip the intellectual work involved in philosophical analysis. Indeed, we have noted the compatibility of Aristotle's thinking with the ethical precepts of monotheism that led early Moslem and Christian scholars to adapt his teachings to the tenets of their respective religions. Moreover, his writings are compatible with the new religious ideas of his own era—Zoroastrian, Confucian, and especially Buddhist. With regard to his "Way of Practical Attainment," the Buddha taught, "A man is foolish to desire privileges, promotion, profits, or honor, for such desires can never bring happiness but will bring suffering instead," which, in language and intent, is almost identical to what Aristotle teaches a hundred or so years after

Siddhartha Gautama's death. Moreover, the general consistency of Aristotelian and Buddhist thinking is apparent in the Dalai Lama's contemporary writings on happiness: In both Buddhism and Confucianism, following the "middle way" of moderation and temperance leads to virtue.

Such similarities also can be noted between Hinduism and Aristotelianism, particularly in the writings of modern Indian sages Swami Vivekananda, J. Krishnamurti, and, of course, M. K. Gandhi. The *Bhagavad Gita* says Hindus must perform their karma (duty) in line with their dharma (moral philosophy governing all actions to do good) and do so to the very best of their abilities without reference to whatever rewards may follow. In other words, Hindus must act not for praise, honor, money, or public opinion. Their actions and the logic behind those actions should be reason enough to perform at the very highest level their minds, bodies, and souls can deliver. Dharma is, it seems, akin to virtue, and the Aristotelian lesson of the *Gita* is that it is morally fraudulent to do something, even the right thing, for the wrong reason.

Thus, one can be an Aristotelian and also be a believing Buddhist, Christian, Moslem, Hindu, or Jew. (In Chapter 10, we see how Aristotle's thoughts are consistent with a bit of Judaic theology.) Yet one also can be an Aristotelian and, at the same time, unreligious and nonbelieving. That's because Aristotle was a philosopher and not a prophet or priest. In the final analysis, religion is based on faith and philosophy on reason. The two paths to finding meaning may end up in the same place, but their methods are distinct and shouldn't be confused. It is enough for the Buddha to assert that greed is a vice; it is necessary for Aristotle to demonstrate that it is so. And the act of moral reasoning is not the same as obeying a religious precept. In sum, religion is no more a substitute for philosophy than philosophy is a substitute for religion. Aristotle found the two to be necessary, instrumental goods in his own virtuous life.

PART TWO

VIRTUE IN ACTION: APPLICATIONS OF ARISTOTLE'S CONCEPTS

8

COMMUNITY LEADERSHIP

"THE END IS NOT KNOWING, BUT ACTION."

—ARISTOTLE

Here's the conventional wisdom on how to find happiness:

- ❧ Stop to smell the roses: "Who ever regretted *not* having spent an extra day in the office?"
- ❧ Spend more time with family and friends.
- ❧ Stick to your knitting: Hang in there, do what you do best, hone your skills, and eventually the world will come around to appreciate the value of your special contribution.

Conventional wisdom is useful because, for the most part, it's true. Aristotle himself not only agrees with the maxims above, he lived his life accordingly, devoting adequate quality time to the enjoyment of nature, family, and friends and holding true to his beliefs and career goals to his dying day. Yet, as accurate and useful as such popular advice was in Aristotle's day (and is still) he notes that even the few people who follow it faithfully often fail to find deep, lasting, and meaningful happiness. Yes, he concludes, a good life requires leisure/family/work balance, and true satisfaction entails conventional career success, but those are just the obvious things one needs in order to live a good, happy life.

Aristotle says we can't become truly happy unless and until we apply the fruits of our personal self-development to meeting the needs of others. As we each must find our own route to what the Ancient calls the highest good of self-realization, we also have to choose our own paths to the complete good of using our knowledge, skills, and wisdom to the benefit of our communities, workplaces, nations, and, perhaps, even to humanity. As we cannot begin to achieve self-realization until we acquire sufficient experience, expertise, resources, and judgment, he notes that only mature people can understand the necessity of applying what they have learned to the benefit of others.

We need only observe the behavior of those approaching or having just passed their fiftieth year to understand the nature of the biological and moral imperative Aristotle describes. In their fifties, multimillionaires Michael

Bloomberg, John Corzine, and Steve Forbes each decided to leave successful business careers and run for high office. Although not quite as rich as the members of that trio, when approaching their fifties, Dianne Feinstein and Jane Harman chose to forgo lives of leisure in favor of the burdens of service in the United States Congress. Without great personal wealth, mid-centurians Patty Murray, Louise Slaughter, and Blanche Lambert likewise threw their hats into the same Capitol Hill ring. And need I mention the 150 or so boomers (including the winner) who vied against each other in the 2003 California gubernatorial recall election? Across the nation, countless other, less well-known men and women in their fifties are running, or are considering a run for, public offices ranging from statewide positions to local school boards. And more impressive to an Aristotelian are the thousands of ordinary men and women who, on reaching their mid-centuries, are stepping out of their lifelong careers to serve in nonprofit organizations or to teach in public schools.

At the same time, many people in and around their fifties who can afford to retire nonetheless are opting to stay in business in search of the traditional career fulfillment still eluding them: among them Scott McNeely (Sun), Carleton "Carly" Fiorina (Hewlett-Packard), John Chambers (Cisco), Steve Jobs (Apple), and Larry Ellison, to cite just high-tech CEOs. Many such businesspeople believe they still can serve society best simply by creating wealth. But in the same industry, hundreds, if not thousands, of wealthy semiretired mid-centurians are turning to philanthropy in search of personal satisfaction, including Netscape's Jim Barksdale, International Data Group's Patrick and Lore Harp-McGovern, Microsoft's Paul Allen, PeopleSoft's Dave and Cheryl Duffield, and Jim Clark.

Like you and me, each of these boomers has an itch to scratch. What we don't know is which tree—public office, business leadership, or philanthropy—is likely to provide the most effective scratching post. This is a practical question even for someone like me who has no bent for high office, will never be a CEO of anything, and will never have enough money to qualify as a philanthropist. For in thinking about Aristotle, I was forced to admit that it had been some 20 years since I made an altruistic commitment of time to any community activity, including jury service. The consequences of this hit home in October 2003, when it dawned on me and many other Californians that the cumulative effect of our failures to be involved in our communities was that we were being governed by a "terminator." My wife's immediate response was to own up to her civic responsibility and volunteer her time to work in the forthcoming presidential campaign for the candidate she found most virtuous. Me, I hemmed and hawed. How could I decide what was the best contribution I could make to my city, state, and nation? Indeed, the open question is whether members of my generation can find the fulfillment we seek most effectively through community service, wealth creation, charity, or a combination of each.

Aristotle's view is that *it all depends*. Clearly, men and women take the first steps toward realizing the complete good when they choose to participate in endeavors that contribute to the public weal, but he says it's not a foregone conclusion they will achieve their goal. Their happiness ultimately depends upon the degree to which their pursuits, whether in politics, business, or community service, are virtuous. And the complete good of virtuous participation in such activities is no easier to achieve than the highest good of personal development. Both require hard work, and both must start with rigorous thought about the ends one chooses to pursue.

To appreciate why, we first need to review a few pages of rather complex Aristotelian theory. When I recently reviewed it, I not only found it useful in helping me to decide how to act more virtuously in my community, I also was amazed to find that the Ancient resolves the main issue that bedevils students of leadership today: how to evaluate a "great" leader who is obviously effective but clearly a bad person. In doing so, he offers guidelines that help us make meaningful, appropriate, and moral judgments about the leadership of contemporary political and business leaders. After all, Enron's CEO, Kenneth Lay, was *Fortune*'s "most respected" CEO! More directly, we can apply Aristotle's test of leadership virtue to our personal motivations to serve our communities.

PRACTICAL WISDOM: THE SINE QUA NON OF VIRTUOUS LEADERSHIP

Aristotle says the good of a community is "greater and more perfect" than the good of any one individual. *What is better, one (or even a few) excellent individual(s) or "a cityful?"* he asks. He answers: A good community provides the environment in which *everyone* has the opportunity to realize his or her personal excellence. Hence, the role of the "statesman" (*leader* in modern parlance) is to create the conditions in which his fellow citizens all can find happiness. In order to create those conditions, a statesman needs special traits and skills, among which are intelligence and technical knowledge. To gain such intelligence, one needs first to master some discipline, whether a science or an art. People who do so effectively are said to possess *intellectual excellence,* a trait measured by their skill in calculations (designing a computer chip) or in theoretical reasoning (making investments in futures markets). Possessing, then developing and effectively using, this kind of intelligence is necessary to succeed at work, make contributions to knowledge, create wealth, and realize one's personal potential. It is also a prerequisite for political leadership. However, Aristotle adds, those necessary technical skills aren't sufficient.

More important, Aristotle says a leader also needs *practical wisdom.* Practical wisdom has "nothing to do with calculating magnitudes," nothing to do with science, theory, disciplinary knowledge, or knowledge of facts in any way. It is concerned "neither with eternal and unchangeable truth nor with anything and everything that comes into being (and passes away again). Instead, it deals with matters where doubt and deliberation are possible." In particular, practical wisdom is not concerned with the way things are but with "how things can be other than they are." In other words, it is about how conditions in society and organizations *could be made better*. And "it implies the use of one's faculty of opinion in judging matters" relating to what is right and wrong for a group, or society as a whole.

In Aristotle's eyes, such practical wisdom is the prerequisite of "moral excellence," the sine qua non of *leadership:* "That is why we say Pericles and men like him have practical wisdom. They have the capacity to see what is good for themselves and for humankind." The practical wisdom possessed by Pericles, Athens' most brilliant and virtuous leader, had nothing to do with his ability to calculate or even his ability to administer; instead, it related to his moral excellence, his capacity for effective deliberation about human affairs. Practical wisdom is the skill Pericles used to identify the policies and programs that would make Athenians collectively happy, the actions required to create a good society characterized by justice for all. Hence, though virtuous leaders have skill-based *intellectual* excellence, more important, they possess the *moral* excellence that derives from practical wisdom.

198 Aristotle concludes that virtuous leaders in the Periclean mold are rare, but their scarcity is not due to a shortage of leadership capacity in the human race. Instead, he believes the virtue manifested by those rare leaders is an acquired trait; he believes leaders are made, not born. Indeed, they are self-made. He concedes that many leaders aren't virtuous and even grants that it is possible for leaders entirely lacking in virtue to be successful. Today, we need only check the daily paper to find examples of leaders who lack virtue but who do the right thing, at least on occasion. But, Aristotle adds, "While people may perform just acts without actually being just themselves, they do so either involuntarily or through ignorance." Such leaders are neither virtuous nor can they be depended on to do the right thing again tomorrow.

Aristotle also acknowledges that leaders lacking in virtue can be effective. His pupil, Alexander, was an effective conqueror as, in modern times, Mussolini was noted for having made Italy's notoriously inefficient railroads run on time. Yes, a morally weak or even bad person blessed with great intellect (Osama bin Laden, perhaps) might effectively calculate how to achieve a bad end and might even attain a good end by the wrong means. But Aristotle argues there will be no virtue in either act because *effectiveness is not the sole measure of leadership.* Instead, virtuous leaders *are those who are effective at pursuing a moral end.* At all times, the conscious goal of a just leader is to help followers achieve what is good for them, which, on occasion, may be something different from what they think they want. Hence, in addition to effectiveness, leadership has a moral dimension: the capacity to discern and provide justice.

JUSTICE: THE MEASURE OF SOCIAL ACTION

In Aristotle's view, justice is the virtue associated with achieving the complete good. Indeed, justice is "the complete virtue," the measure of all public actions, not only the actions of leaders but of every action people take in relationship to their community. All public actions must be for the benefit of others if they are to be considered virtuous: "Justice alone of all the virtues is thought to be the good of others." Even the virtue of friendship has self-serving elements, because friends provide that "mirror reflection" of our own behavior. In contrast, the goal of justice is solely to benefit others. But Aristotle fears he will be misunderstood. We might think he means that leaders cannot or should not derive personal satisfaction from their virtuous public acts. But who will act justly if such acts involve no pleasure or, worse, if they are painful? He thus amends his assertion slightly, saying justice is the "complete virtue because he who possesses it can make use of his virtue not only for himself but also in his relations with his fellow man." Virtuous leaders like Pericles, Gandhi, Lincoln, and Churchill govern for the good of others; yet, and this is Aristotle's point, they are not entirely selfless because they become happy in the process.

But what is justice? To Aristotle, justice has to do with people getting their fair share of goods: their just proportion of money, power, honor, and all other social rewards and benefits. Unfortunately, there is no simple or mechanical way to calculate the just proportions of such goods. He says an equal distribution of goods will not be just because the social contributions of individuals aren't equal; clearly, he is no Marxist. And basing the distribution of social goods on heredity isn't fair, either. He would ask why unqualified sons of Yalies should be entitled to attend Poppy's alma mater. So Aristotle goes down the list of possible principles of distribution and concludes that the fairest is merit. Ergo, individuals deserve rewards proportionate to the contributions they make to society. Alas, he admits such a reckoning is easier said than made.

VIRTUOUS LEADERSHIP

Because social contribution is a complex, multifaceted concept, evaluating it fairly requires reasoned deliberation, *the exercise of practical wisdom.* When they undertake such deliberations, leaders are "the guardians of what is just." When allocating social goods, virtuous leaders make their decisions based on reason and not on self-interest. Virtuous Yale alumni don't attempt to get their own low-achieving kids admitted ahead of better students. Especially, just leaders don't take for themselves disproportionate shares of social and economic benefits; instead, they are recompensed for their efforts in terms of due "honor and privilege." For example, the president of the United States is not the highest paid person in America; instead, he gets the honor of being addressed, respectfully, as "Mr. President" and the privilege of living in a big house, rent free. But those honors and privileges adhere to the office, not to the person, and they are revoked at the end of service. But even those relatively great honors are a small thing to "the magnanimous man," the true leader who derives happiness from serving the common good. Indeed, service to others comes close to being Aristotle's definition of leadership. Leaders *give:* like good friends, they are generous to others. In contrast, injustice occurs when leaders take more than their share of the good and less than their share of the bad, taking as much power, praise, and compensation as they can, and avoiding responsibility by passing the blame when things go wrong.

Justice, Aristotle notes, is one of the few virtues that cannot be measured with reference to his golden mean: It is impossible for a person to be "too just." Too much leadership, however, can be bad. When one person has too much power, Aristotle says the overall interests of the community are harmed. Measured on his scale of moderation, a society in which power is concentrated in one person is out of balance, and the result is the excessive condition called tyranny:

DEFECT	VIRTUE	EXCESS
PASSIVITY	LEADERSHIP	TYRANNY

In a tyranny, the populace is justified in ousting its leader. Because the good of the community has priority over the interests of any individual, Aristotle says even a benevolent dictator—one who has no evil intent but who nevertheless exercises too much power—should be ostracized (exiled from society). He concedes there can be extremely wise and benevolent dictators, but he adds such persons are not easy to find. Even when found, the very nature of benevolent dictatorship hinders the development of the citizenry because people are political animals who need to participate in their own governance in order to realize their full humanness. Because all people have the capacity to reason, he concludes they all need the opportunity to exercise it. Thus, paternalistic leaders lack virtue because they impede the development of those dependent upon them. In Aristotle's view, such leaders forfeit their right to lead when they deny the citizenry the political power they need to grow through the process of making moral choices for themselves.

Aristotle sees leadership as a duty rather than a privilege, a duty of the best and brightest individuals. Since such individuals must forgo their self-interest while governing, the duties of leadership can be burdensome. Hence, he

201

proposes that the burden should not be exercised by a single individual but, instead, rotated among all those qualified to lead, among the circle of virtuous friends described in the preceding chapter. This would prevent not only tyranny but also an unfair distribution of responsibility in society. And if there are personal benefits to leadership, like the opportunity to learn by making important decisions, those opportunities should be shared, as well.

And where does leadership begin? Because the purpose of governance is to serve the needs of the citizenry and not the ruler's interests, virtuous leaders must have a clear view of community needs and goals: the common good. The leaders of Sparta, much like Napoleon and Hitler in later eras, thought military conquest was the goal of the state. Consequently, they made decisions designed to attain it: for example, funding military training. Had they, instead, viewed the end of the state as the development of its citizenry, they might have made quite different policy choices, like funding the arts and sciences.

While it is essential for leaders not only to identify a goal worth pursuing, they must also communicate it clearly and constantly to their followers. That's why Jefferson wrote (in the second paragraph of the *Declaration*) that the goal of the country being founded in 1776 was to provide conditions in which all its citizens could pursue happiness—realize their full potential— and that the justice of its government would be measured by the extent to which it facilitated that end. Those virtuous goals were quite different from the ends of power and aristocratic privilege sought by Britain's George III and, in Jefferson's Aristotelian eyes, justified ostracizing the king.

Like friendship, Aristotle says, "Justice in political matters is found among people who are free and equal and who share a common life in order that their association will bring self-sufficiency." So the role of a just leader is to create the conditions in which a community of free and equal people may work together for the common good, conditions in which each and all can find happiness. In sum, virtuous leaders create justice, defined as the opportunity for all members of the community to realize their potential. As Aristotle explains, "Things that are just create happiness for the social and political community." One can see how Jefferson found his inspiration for the *Declaration* in Aristotle.

There is an important principle implied in all Aristotle has to say about leadership: The activity has two dimensions, practical and moral. He recognizes that most leaders are measured by the practical yardstick of effectiveness. In his day, that usually meant effectiveness at obtaining and maintaining power. He does not deny that effectiveness is a legitimate metric, but he argues it is not the only standard by which one should take the measure of leaders. In addition to effectiveness, there is a moral dimension: Virtuous political leaders also are concerned with providing justice. The tyrant who ruled Sparta was effective; Pericles was effective and just; hence, Pericles was virtuous. Measuring political leadership both by a standard of effectiveness and one of justice makes it possible to clarify the difference between the performances of leaders who would otherwise seem to be equal: Mao was effective; Gandhi was just. The application of the Aristotelian principle to contemporary leadership allows us to raise useful questions. For example, in 2004, when U.S. Attorney General John Ashcroft justified the Patriot Act, he did so in terms of its effectiveness in fighting terrorism. Aristotle would ask, to what extent did Ashcroft also weigh issues of justice in his evaluation of the law? As we see in the following chapter, Aristotle's principle is also useful in evaluating the virtue of contemporary business leadership.

MOTIVATION: "RIGHT DESIRE" REDUX

Appropriate motivation is also inherent in what Aristotle says about the practical wisdom of leaders. Much as right desire is the primary measure of virtue in one's private life, desiring the good for others is the primary metric of public virtue. In his view, leaders cannot be "accidentally just," nor can they be just if they merely appear to be serving the interests of followers when, in fact, they are not. To illustrate the ethical centrality of right motivation,

203

Aristotle cites a fragment of brilliant dialogue from a lost play by Euripides:

Character A: *I killed my mother, brief is my report.*

Character B: *Were you both willing, or neither she nor you?*

As difficult as it is to set aside the relevance of this 2,500-year-old exchange to the current debate about the morality of physician-assisted suicide, we need to focus on the reason Aristotle cited it: to call attention to the significance of motivation as a factor in ethical analysis. In this ethical mini-case, Euripides implies three different situations, each morally quite distinct from the others:

First Situation: A mother is murdered ["in cold blood"] by her child.

Second Situation: A mother's request for a mercy killing is granted by an [unloving] child who is only too happy to comply.

Third Situation: A mother [perhaps dying from a terrible disease] asks her child to end her pain. [With great sadness and reluctance] the child grants the mother's wish.

Only the latter situation contains the possibility of ethical virtue. Although the moral choices most of us face are less dramatic than these, Aristotle says motivation is a powerful indicator of the degree to which virtue is present in all our social acts. For example, one might say, "Michael Bloomberg serves as mayor of New York, brief is my report." But is Bloomberg's service virtuous? To answer that question fairly and properly, we would need to know the unknowable: his motivations. Is he serving for his own sake or the sake of others? Is his goal the good of the New York citizenry, or is it to satisfy his own needs for fame, power, praise, or whatever? Similarly, did Steve Forbes and John Corzine run for office in order to enhance the good of the citizenry, or did they run in order to enact legislation to serve their own interests or the interests of members of their tax bracket? Obviously, no one but Bloomberg, Forbes, and Corzine could answer such questions with certainty. Aristotle's point is not that *we* should assess their virtue, but that *they* should engage in the introspection and ethical analysis involved in assessing their own motivations. Especially, we each should question our own motivations whenever we choose to run for office or engage in other community activities "for the good of others."

However, when it came to evaluating the candidacies of those three gentle billionaires, it's safe to assume that many voters wondered about their respective motivations for wanting higher office because followers know motivation has a powerful impact on the behavior of their leaders. Sooner or later, the reasons a leader chooses to serve become apparent to all. For example, Senator Robert C. Byrd of West Virginia is, by all accounts, not in the political game for the money. In general, he is an extremely thoughtful and courageous representative of the citizens of his state and nation. Yet there are indications that he harbors desires for undue honor and recognition. In displays of narcissism unusual even by the ego-inflated standards of the U.S. Senate, Byrd has managed to have nearly three dozen federally funded public projects named after him. Although West Virginia's state policy dictates that individuals must be dead for 50 years before their statues can grace the statehouse, Byrd is the sole exception, as he is with the two Robert C. Byrd courthouses, four Robert C. Byrd highways, the Robert C. Byrd Green Bank telescope, the Robert C. Byrd Locks and Dams, and 20-plus other products of federal pork bearing his name. While Byrd has mastered the technical skills of leadership and most often does the right thing, he seems to fall a bit short of possessing Aristotelian moral virtue.

Motivation also is related to the exercise of political decision-making. Aristotle asks if a leader's motivation is the desire to create a good society for the benefit of others, or is it the desire for the personal satisfaction derived from solving problems? While those may not be mutually exclusive activities, Aristotle says that a problem solver, at best, may stumble on the good, while a leader with practical wisdom is focused at all times on the good of the community and, thus, is more likely to achieve it. Of course, when leaders are engaged in decision making, observers can't tell if they are merely exercising intellectual excellence (treating social issues as technical problems with calculable solutions) or utilizing practical wisdom (asking what is best for society and engaging in the tough moral deliberations attendant to such choices). Only the latter is virtuous in Aristotle's eyes.

Consider Michael Bloomberg. In a 2002 article in the *New Yorker,* Elizabeth Kolbert portrays the mayor as a quintessential problem solver who sees "his primary role as managerial" and measures his political success by the same calculations he formerly used to assess his performance as a businessman. According to Kolbert, the mayor treats each problem on his agenda as technical and discrete, and the measure of his performance is the degree of his effectiveness in solving it: "As far as he is concerned, the only reason to talk about a problem is to solve it, the corollary of which is that only problems that can be solved are really worth talking about."

When presenting his first city budget, Mayor Bloomberg said, "I am going to show you how we got into this situation . . . and a solution to work our way out of this situation." The mayor's motivation for public service seems to be, in part at least, gaining pleasure from solving problems (like a budget deficit). Aristotle says there is nothing wrong with that; indeed, by applying the financial skills Bloomberg developed in his business career to the problems of his city, he may be halfway along the road to virtuous leadership.

What seems missing is the exercise of practical wisdom, the conscious deliberations about justice and what constitutes a good end *from the perspective of others,* the citizens of New York. According to Kolbert, the mayor "rarely addresses the emotional or moral complexities of life in the city." Which isn't to say he doesn't entertain diverse, even opposing, views about what the policies of the city should and should not be. To his credit, he holds regular salons at his Manhattan townhouse, where it is said he carefully sounds out the opinions of influential people on the pressing issues of the day. Nonetheless, published reports about those salons describe them more as networking opportunities than Aristotelian seminars among true friends. Apparently, what doesn't occur at the salons is candid discussion about why or why not the mayor is effective or whether or not he has a clear concept of the good.

Bloomberg donates his own money generously to worthy causes, but he seems less giving of himself. For example, in his first year in office, when he spoke in public, he typically cited a few numbers and facts, then abruptly left without engaging in discussion with his constituencies. He seldom attempted to address the needs of his various audiences and seemed not to inquire what those needs might be. He brings to mind King Creon, the tragic hero in one of Aristotle's favorite plays, *Antigone*. Creon's flaw was a lack of empathy, a trait that begins with listening. In the end, Creon brings down his own throne because he cannot hear what his people want; he is too sure that he is right. The message Bloomberg often sends to the citizenry is that the mayoralty is about him and not about them. In this way, his behavior in public office is a continuation of the way he ran his company, Bloomberg L.P., as a former employee explained to Kolbert: "When you get hired, you get this stack of publicity. Every single article is about Mike Bloomberg. Every article . . . it's all about Mike, and it always has been about him."

To summarize and oversimplify, in his first year in office, Michael Bloomberg displayed uncommon intellectual excellence but seemed not yet to have acquired the proper motivation and practical wisdom needed to be a virtuous leader by Aristotle's standards. Even though he is in his sixties, it is not too late for him to grow and develop his capacity to put his followers' needs first. To do so would require some introspection on his part, beginning with asking himself some hard questions about the choices he makes. In particular, he would have to ask, *For whose good do I serve?* There were signs he was growing in office in this second year. His decision to ban smoking in restaurants and bars was morally courageous, and, while we cannot know his motivation, a strong case can be made that he acted for the welfare of others.

MATURITY AND PRACTICAL WISDOM

Another prominent New Yorker, Bill Clinton, often displays a lack of practical wisdom and adamant resistance to the self-analysis needed to acquire it.

In 2002, even some of the best Friends of Bill were observed shaking their heads in dismay when it was revealed the former president was entertaining the idea of becoming a television talk show host. In so doing, he provided additional grist for his continuing ridicule by critics. David Letterman mused that Clinton "could become the first president ever to be impeached and canceled"; and Maureen Dowd opined "the spectacle of Bill" on daily TV would be "gratifying for him, giving him all the attention and love he craves." She pictured him "ordering a *vente* white chocolate extra-whip mocha at the Starbucks in Harlem, complaining to the cashiers that his post-presidential life is not being taken seriously enough." To that very point, friends and foes alike were left wondering why, with Jimmy Carter serving as a living example of virtuous ex-presidential behavior, the undisciplined Clinton would choose, instead, to model his post–White House life on show biz celebrities.

On this score, most Americans appear to be unconsciously Aristotelian: In their judgment, Clinton's behavior manifests "wrong desire." Although he is in his late fifties, many see him as immaturely chasing sensual pleasure, cheap fame, and easy money. They are waiting for him to grow up and become the statesman he is capable of becoming, to serve others, and to promote the collective good at home and in the world. Given Clinton's manifest intellectual excellence and potential for working for the benefit of his nation and humankind, it hurts us to see continuing evidence that his leadership is still all about him.

In 2001, a friend sent me the following e-mail:

It's a pity for the country that Bill Clinton wasn't mature enough to be President when he was elected in '92, or even in '96. Imagine how great a president he would have been if he had been sworn in for the first time in 2001. Given what he's learned, what he's been through, he may now be wise enough to meet the challenge of the job. Maybe we should change the Constitution to bar anyone under the age of fifty from serving

as President. Wasn't it Plato who said the earliest one can become wise—and be a good leader—is age fifty-five?

To Clinton's credit, when his autobiography was published in 2004, he began
to show some insight into his own motivations. When asked why he had
risked everything on the fling with Monica Lewinsky, he answered, "Because
I could." He went on to admit that it was "the worst possible reason" because
it represented an abuse of the power of high office. He finally seemed to recognize that virtuous leaders are not voluptuaries or sultans; instead, they are
temperate, self-disciplined individuals who serve for the good of others. He
seemed to be growing up.

AH, YOUTH . . .

Aristotle raises the important issue of maturity in the context of the behavior
of leaders and their pursuit of the complete good. On Aristotle's long list of instrumental goods, youth is a missing element. Today, we say, "You can never
be too rich, too beautiful, too thin, or too young," but Aristotle saw youth
mainly as a phase one should seriously endeavor to outgrow. His low opinion
of youth was doubtless influenced by his relationship with the young
Alexander. Try as Aristotle might to instill an ethical conscience in the young
prince, Alexander went to his early grave giving in to every temptation that
came along. If ever there was a slave to animal instinct and passion, it was the
young master from Macedonia. Alexander wanted nothing but fame, power,
wealth, and sex; and those who resisted his desires, he slaughtered. As he
dashed across the world indiscriminately slaying and/or screwing nearly
everyone he encountered, he was a lousy advertisement for Aristotelianism.

From his bad experience with the Great One, Aristotle concluded that philosophy is wasted on the young. The teenage Alexander lacked the experience to make sense of his teacher's complex moral arguments. Alexander was

a brilliant lad who, with but little effort, could repeat back to his teacher whatever he had been taught, be it history, Greek grammar, or geometry. But he was not mature enough to internalize moral lessons. He lacked the experience needed to link Aristotle's discussions of virtue to his own behavior and thus failed to retain what he had been taught. Fifteen centuries later, Shakespeare read Aristotle's thoughts on the subject of youth and, in *Troilus and Cressida,* summarized poetically the Ancient's timeless insights:

> Paris and Troilus, you have both said well;
> And on the cause and question now in hand
> Have glozed, but superficially; not much
> Unlike the young men, whom Aristotle thought
> Unfit to hear moral philosophy.

Even Aristotle's best young students, the class stars most proficient in the abstractions of mathematics, were unable to understand issues of ethical conduct. After observing his brightest students' moral failures, he concludes that finding the good is not like finding answers to math problems. While Aristotle considers mathematics atop the hierarchy of intellectual disciplines because it requires the highest-order abstract reasoning, he also sees it as a young person's game requiring the creative application of rules and principles, an exercise at which facile, energetic young minds are especially adept. In contrast, the pursuit of the good requires experience rather than rules and moral deliberation rather than principles. Further, and counter to the essence of mathematics, it requires *right desire.* Developing the kind of practical reasoning used in math and science will not lead to virtuous behavior until and unless it is directed toward the achievement of some good. Aristotle explains the complex relationship between practical and ethical forms of reasoning:

> The element of desire partakes of reason in so far as it listens
> to and obeys it; this is the sense in which we speak of paying
> heed to one's father, or to one's friends—and not that in which
> we speak of the rational in mathematics.

I think he means that well-brought-up young people will apply moral rules and do the right thing because that is what their parents told them to do. But, only later, when they have sufficient life experience, will they learn how to apply their reasoning abilities to ethical concerns and thus be able to choose aright. The two rational processes are related but not the same. In the words of Oliver Wendell Holmes Jr., "Life is painting a picture, not doing a sum."

And philosophy is about making distinctions between things that seem to be the same but aren't. We all use words in a general fashion, which is fine in daily discourse but dangerous when it comes to public matters. Unless leaders are precise, they will not know what ends to pursue or what to do to obtain them. Nonetheless, when engaged in making necessary distinctions, leaders must be careful not to slip into sophistry, that subtle, tricky, superficially clever way of making a fallacious argument. Aristotle calls our attention to the difference between being clever and being wise. He says we should not confuse clever reasoning, calculating, and logic on the one hand, with wisdom, judgment, and understanding on the other. Alexander was extremely clever: When attracting followers to join him in making war, he overwhelmed his opposition with brilliance. He had a high IQ, but he asked the wrong questions, omitted matters he couldn't calculate, and ignored inconvenient consequences and costs. He was the Classical era equivalent of an analytical whiz kid logically demonstrating with pie charts and overheads the most effective way to commit mayhem. Since clever men can fool us with bad arguments, Aristotle advises that we should look instead to "sympathetic judges," wise people who in their deliberations about public affairs look to fairness as well as efficiency, explore both long- and short-term consequences, and consider the costs and benefits to all those who may be affected.

In particular, he says we should be wary of young people who varnish foolishness with impressive displays of data and clever arguments. Ever since Donald Rumsfeld and I were both young men in the Nixon administration, I have marveled (usually at a safe distance) at how he uses his quickness of mind to run intellectual roughshod over men and women who, in my opinion, hold more ethical positions. According to Chuck Colson, another Nixon staffer, in seeking to ingratiate himself with the president in 1971, Rumsfeld volunteered to be the White House's "go between" with the respected polling organization run by his Princeton classmate, George Gallup Jr. Rumsfeld wouldn't actually ask Gallup to juggle the numbers in national polls, mind you; he would try only to influence the way questions were asked and when results were released! Indeed, few who have served in high public office in my lifetime have been as good at splitting ethical hairs as Rumsfeld. Who else could so confidently and quickly draw distinctions between prisoner "abuse" and "torture" and between "prisoners of war" and "unlawful combatants"? The issue isn't politics: Rumsfeld's parsing of the truth reminds one of nothing more than Bill Clinton's explication of the verb "is." Plato taught Aristotle that you can't win an argument with a sophist, and Aristotle later added that being smart isn't the same as being good, or doing good.

Examples of immoral cleverness are found at both ends of the ideological spectrum. Throughout the 1990s, the majority on San Francisco's Board of Supervisors were moral relativists who advanced postmodernist arguments for why the city should allow "street people" to sleep on its sidewalks, in public places, and in private doorways and why it should support them with regular cash payments. In question were thousands of drug and alcohol addicts, able-bodied people capable of making reasoned choices, not the mentally ill or those temporarily homeless for economic reasons. The majority on the board argued that the desire of the addicts to live on the streets was as legitimate as the desire of the majority to live under a permanent roof, and that neither choice (or "lifestyle") can, or should, be assumed "normal."

In contrast, the Aristotelian minority on the board had few qualms about calling the desire to sleep on the street abnormal behavior because a basic characteristic of *Homo sapiens* at all times and in all cultures has been to seek shelter. All normal humans need shelter, so it follows that people who do not have shelter cannot be happy, and it is the responsibility of those with the authority and wherewithal in society to give those without sufficient power and

212

wealth the opportunity to pursue happiness. Thus, they argued, if San Francisco were a Good Society, it would provide shelter and addiction treatment for all those who seek it. Of course, no one would be forced to seek the things needed by all normal humans, and, indeed, some lone wolves would choose not to. The choice would be theirs; but, if they chose to stand alone, they would not be allowed to infringe on others' pursuits of happiness (they would not be allowed to urinate in public, sleep on private property, aggressively cadge for drug money, and engage in other forms of behavior that transferred the costs of their chosen lifestyle to others). In particular, the city wouldn't continue to give them the cash that subsidized their chosen way of life.

These politically incorrect conclusions were unpalatable to the majority of supervisors, who cleverly argued that there is no such thing as "normal" behavior and that it was impossible to make normative generalizations about all of humanity ("Who are we to say they are wrong?"). Basing their decision on such moral relativism, the city fathers and mothers defended the rights of the homeless to sleep wherever they chose and, for over a decade, refused to enforce statutes relating to trespassing, vagrancy, and loitering. The young chairman of the board was so adept at making these arguments that, in 2003, he was almost elected mayor in the closest election in my beloved hometown's history. Aristotle reminds us that when leaders reason well but lack an ethical core, they are smart but not virtuous. In my view, a great many San Francisco voters didn't make that distinction.

ETHICAL REASONING
AND VIRTUOUS LEADERSHIP

Only after years of observing the actions of others, experiencing the consequences of our own actions, studying and discussing the customs and habits of society—and through repeated efforts to find and do the good—are we finally able to overcome our immature impulse to deal with ethical issues as if they were practical problems solvable by the logic that informs mathematics. The intelligent but immature person might conclude, logically, "We would all have more money in our pockets if we didn't pay taxes." But justice, the goal of leadership, is not so easily arrived at. Justice is not the product of a facile mind but, rather, the result of wisdom. Good moral judgment is displayed by mature people who are able to bring together all they have learned and then to apply it imaginatively to issues for which there were easy answers when they were young. Lingering immaturity shows when individuals of great intellect fail to consider the effects on others of their public acts, when they fail to consider the moral as well as technical implications of the choices they make.

To illustrate, many wealthy and powerful people who have lobbied successfully for a reduction in taxation have not stepped forward to volunteer their time and talent to take up the slack in community services resulting from budget cuts in federal, state, and local agencies. Despite repeated calls from both Presidents Bush, Colin Powell, Nancy Reagan, and other influential advocates of a "thousand points of light," Americans seem not to be stepping to the plate to volunteer their time and money to offset the shortfalls in essential public services. In fact, most of our volunteering is of the once-a-year kind we are all proud and guilty of: slicing turkeys for the poor on Thanksgiving (my own last benevolent act). Convenience seems to be the prime criterion for our volunteerism. MSNBC's Eric Alterman observes that most of the effort and time volunteered by wealthy people goes to help local operas, museums, hospitals, and, particularly, their children's schools: "In this respect, volunteerism helps the rich get richer." Arianna Huffington sees things similarly, explaining she once believed "the private sector—especially conservative multimillionaires who want less government involvement—would rise to the occasion and provide the funding needed to replicate the programs that work, sustain them, and bring them to market." But now she has concluded that such individuals were not interested in supporting "groups who were good at saving lives but not at raising funds," and says she "sadly discovered how much easier it was raising money for the opera or a fashionable museum."

In Aristotle's view, the pursuit of the complete good entails more than service in public office. The virtuous person needs to be an "enlightened seeker" of happiness. Men and women who are just, who possess practical wisdom, consider the consequences of all their actions on the good of others and adjust their behavior accordingly. To get to the point where one acts virtuously as a matter of course takes time and hard work because there is no way to shortcut the process of maturation. Happily, Aristotle claims it is never too late for us to begin, although he implies that maturation gets harder as we enter old age. The obvious question is, *How old do we have to be to begin the process?*

People in midlife may experience deep regret when they look back to discover that, in their youth, they unwittingly had laid the foundation for their present unhappiness. Indeed, through a lengthy process of youthful error and subsequent reinforcement, we build layers of defenses that prevent us from learning how to behave virtuously. But Aristotle believes there isn't much one can do about avoiding the follies of youth while one is young. Instead, we must learn later from those experiences, then devote years of conscious effort to overcoming their residual effects. In midlife and in the company of true friends, we need to reflect on our experiences in order to discover why acting on the certainties of our youth didn't lead us to where we now need to be. Out of that often-saddening process comes wisdom.

Leadership is beyond the grasp of the young, Aristotle concludes, largely because the essence of leadership is acting for the good of others, and the chief characteristic of immaturity is narcissism. Years after his tutoring experience at the Macedonian royal palace, Aristotle finally came to understand why the teenage Alexander hadn't gotten it. When he had explained to his famous student that virtuous leaders create conditions under which their followers can realize their potential, those were just words to the adolescent's ears. Indeed, almost all of moral philosophy is nothing but words

215

until one has lived long enough to be able to reflect on the consequences of one's own habitual actions. Alexander died at age 33 and, thus, didn't live long enough to look back in horror at the consequences of his monstrous behavior, behavior in no small part responsible for his early death. The modern mystery is why so many of us, as we push on toward our sixties, don't learn more from the, albeit smaller, mistakes of our own immature actions.

ETHICAL TESTS OF PUBLIC SERVICE

At midlife, when we have the intellectual skills and experience needed to participate effectively in public affairs, evaluating the behavior of leaders like Clinton, Rumsfeld, and San Francisco's supervisors may help us to plan our own future courses of public action and to define what we should be doing now to prepare ourselves for pursuing the complete good. While most of us act on smaller stages than presidents and mayors, let alone world conquerors, Aristotle says the challenges that the famous and powerful face are, in essence, the same as those before us all. The process of ethical analysis is the same for Bill and Hillary Clinton as it is for you in deciding whether to lead the local United Way campaign, or for me as I decide whether to run for the school board. As we each plan how best to scratch our own itch for public service, the questions we need to ask about our goals, motivations, and behavior are identical to those Bloomberg, Corzine, and Forbes asked, or should have asked, before choosing to run for office:

＊ Am I engaging in political actions for my personal benefit or for the benefit of others?

＊ Do I have some notion of the good that I am trying to help my community to realize?

＊ How can I best apply my technical knowledge for the benefit of the community? How can I make sure I am using those technical skills to achieve a higher end, and not just using them as an end in itself to keep me busily employed in an ego-satisfying activity?

For the mature man or woman who has developed moral excellence, answering such questions is not difficult. I once worked for the distinguished public servant Elliot Richardson, who served his nation as Undersecretary of State; Secretary of Health, Education, and Welfare; Secretary of Defense; and Secretary of Commerce. I observed that he was a true Aristotelian: a skilled leader, lawyer, writer, and artist constantly engaged in learning and doing new things. He was also an appropriately ambitious politician who made no bones about his desire to be president. Yet he would not sacrifice virtue for the honor he so passionately desired. Rather than obey President Nixon's order to fire Watergate prosecutor Archibald Cox, Richardson resigned as Attorney General of the United States, saying that it was "one of the easiest decisions in my life." It also ended his political career.

As philosopher W. F. R. Hardie summarizes, the ethical distinction Aristotle draws between one person's search for the complete good and another's "is the difference between the objects which they value and seek to achieve." Virtuous leaders discipline themselves to put good ends ahead of their ambitions for power and honor. In this regard, Elliot Richardson had done his moral exercises.

MY FAVORITE ARISTOTELIAN BOOMER

Few of us have Richardson's level of talent, ambition, and opportunities for service. Though most of us want to serve our communities, we don't want to run for public office, and we don't hanker for the spotlight. Most of us are more like David Guggenhime, my former classmate at San Francisco's Lowell High School, who could be an inspiration to all boomers who aspire to achieve Aristotelian excellence through public service. I remember admiring Dave's energy and enthusiasm when I last saw him back in the early 1960s; nonetheless, until

I recently learned what he has been up to, I would have considered him an unlikely candidate for Aristotelian virtue. Indeed, he struck me then as one of those slightly overprivileged nice guys who at that time were routinely admitted to Stanford. After graduating from The Farm, he confirmed my prejudices when he pursued a conventional career in investment management.

However, in his late forties, he underwent a remarkable change. In 1991, he abandoned his business career in order to make a 12-year commitment to enriching the education of 29 underprivileged children, pledging to help them get the brand of first-rate schooling he had enjoyed while growing up in toney Pacific Heights. Working with these youngsters as their tutor, mentor, and counselor throughout their elementary and high school years, Dave also met monthly with their parents to reaffirm their commitment to the educational goals of his program. Obviously, this job is too big for any one person, and Dave has recruited some 60 volunteers to help, each of whom dedicates three or four afternoons a week to afterschool mentoring and tutoring. Dave also has hired a few college students to tutor advanced subjects. Depending on how well Dave's students are doing in school, they spend from 6 to 9 hours per week with their tutors. Saturday sessions are arranged for those who need additional help, and during the summer, all the kids attend a 6-week program tailored to each of their needs. For his efforts, Dave has received the Marin County Martin Luther King Humanitarian Award and the 2000 United Way of the Bay Area Volunteer Merit Award. To those I would add the highest compliment I can think of: Dave is the truest Aristotelian I know.

WHAT ABOUT ME (AND YOU)?

Clearly, it was easier for Aristotle than it is for me to participate in virtuous public activities. He lived in a small-scale community where the opportunity for meaningful political participation was far greater than it is for one living in a modern, impersonal metropolis. To participate, all he had to do was head to the local acropolis and engage directly in the democratic process with his fellow citizens. I couldn't do the same with the San Francisco Board of Supervisors; they are unlikely to welcome the unsolicited sharing of my Aristotelian ideas about the city's homeless problem. Indeed, true citizen participation in political processes is extremely rare today in all large societies. Perhaps the best opportunity for ordinary individuals to effectively participate in philosophy and politics is the way Aristotle himself engaged with his own community: as a teacher. For boomers, teaching in an elementary or high school is the most practical way in which those of us currently working in technical, managerial, and professional jobs might simultaneously develop our potential and make our greatest contribution to our communities. That assertion is based on several assumptions:

- A critical shortage of teachers, particularly in urban schools, and primarily but not exclusively those skilled in math and science.
- Most smart, educated people can be effective when teaching small groups of students. Chris Cecil, for 16 years a Manhattan commodity trader, gave up his six-figure salary to teach science to kids, no more than 20 at a time, in a suburban elementary school. Says Cecil, "I had been thinking of going into teaching for 5 years, then my father died suddenly of a heart attack. He had told me, 'Do it now.' My income has been reduced, but the rewards are more time with my family and less stress. Most of all I'm having a good time." Cecil probably wouldn't be having so much fun if he were facing 37 kids in a class, as some teachers do in inner-city schools.
- Good teaching is not correlated with having a degree from a school of education. Instead, teachers' outlooks and attitudes are more important than training. In general, good teachers are those who are enthusiastic about their subjects and who believe in the capacity of their students to learn. In his mid-forties, Tom Meschery (also a Lowellite, I'm proud to say) decided he wanted to teach high school English. Al-

though his first love was poetry, he had rather unorthodox credentials to teach the subject. His résumé consisted of 10 years in the NBA, during which the 6-foot-6 forward averaged 12.9 points and 8.6 rebounds per game. Good stats, but not the sort most school districts are looking for in one applying to teach Eliot and Pound. Yet Nevada school officials were willing to take the gamble and hire a long shot. They did so and, some 20 years later, big Tom is still teaching English and is one of the most popular teachers in his high school, particularly effective with kids who think poetry (and learning) is for sissies.

❧ Many boomers who, in their twenties, chose teaching as a profession are now burnt out and ready to retire. I recently met a 55-year-old who had spent his entire professional career teaching high school math. He confided he simply had had enough after 30 years in the classroom and had recently retired to become chief financial officer for a start-up business. He explained, "I'm having a ball keeping the books, managing the company's funds, and providing a little gray-haired wisdom to the two 25-year-old techies who own the business." There's an important Aristotelian lesson here: The process of continuing development differs according to individual experiences and needs.

❧ Many more boomers who, in their twenties, chose careers other than teaching are now more than willing to relieve their age peers who have been at it for the last 3 decades. However, to draw on this reserve army of teachers, state legislatures and local school boards would have to change many outdated administrative policies, including an array of union, licensing, and credentialing barriers.

But the main barrier discouraging mature men and women from making the switch to teaching is the job itself, as now constituted. Natalia Mehlman recently left a career in investment banking to teach in the New York City public schools. She admits that she has had, literally, one hell of a time in the classroom:

220

Lack of parental support, lack of experienced teachers, lack of a safe environment for teachers and students: these are terrible and familiar problems in the city schools, and for all these reasons this first year of teaching will be my last.

Three thousand miles away in inner-city Los Angeles, new teacher Jeff Porter discovered that his charges had never done any homework:

I expected them to read at night, so we could discuss in class. It never happened. I assigned them two chapters to read over Christmas vacation. When they returned only two students had done the work . . . The kids are adaptable and smart enough, but they had never been pushed hard enough.

Building on what Dave Guggenhime has done, I believe it's possible to overcome these and other barriers that currently prevent experienced and knowledgeable individuals who want to teach from doing so. Many thoughtful and mature boomers currently burned out in other careers would love to teach—if the students involved want to learn and if there are none of the discipline problems associated with a large classroom of unruly kids. Indeed, most boomers are appalled that public schools fail to teach so many young boys and girls how to read, write, and compute. The source of our collective dismay is the conviction many of us have that, if we were charged with teaching just one or two young people, we could teach them to read; many of us taught our own kids to do so even before they went to kindergarten. Moreover, many of us believe that, given a few uninterrupted hours each week over a couple of years, we could teach almost any youngster arithmetic and, with a little more time, algebra and geometry, as well. Those of us who have engineering and science backgrounds know how fast young people can pick up statistics and even calculus—if they are not in a large classroom, if there are not too many nonacademic distractions to compete against, and if

221

the teacher understands the subject matter and how to apply it to real problems.

That's where Guggenhime's program comes in. I believe it succeeds for three reasons: First, he and his tutors work with their students on a one-to-one basis (or in small groups). Second, they set challenging academic goals, refusing to believe that poor kids are necessarily poor students (in Robert Hutchins's Aristotelian words, the program is predicated on the belief that "the best education for the best is the best education for all"). Finally, Dave and his tutors are supported by their students' parents.

Dave's model might serve as a challenge to others of our generation to create variations on what he has done, perhaps to find ways of overcoming some of the barriers even his fine program has failed to surmount. Politically skilled boomers might be able to convince school boards to allow mature, experienced volunteers to come into schools in the mornings (when kids are fresh) to tutor small groups on academic subjects. The regular teachers could monitor and coordinate this activity. Moreover, relieved of the impossible task of teaching 30 kids at a time, the regular teachers might have the pleasure themselves of teaching one child or a small group of children. The problem isn't that most current, professional teachers are incompetent; they are simply overwhelmed and worn down. When the real work of learning was done, the volunteer teachers could go home, and the afternoons at school could be dedicated to the countless nonacademic activities and programs that don't require high levels of concentration.

One can imagine dozens of variations of Dave's program. It might become possible in some states and districts for skilled people in their thirties and forties who aren't credentialed by schools of education to be licensed to teach and, perhaps, to be paid for it. I don't pretend to understand all the problems involved, let alone to have the answers. But I know one thing: Nothing will happen unless many more of us follow Dave Guggenhime's example and commit ourselves to the true pursuit of virtue, excellence, and happiness. I now see that it is what I have to do in the long term (in the short term, in 2004, I signed up for jury duty and decided to work alongside my wife in the upcoming presidential campaign).

As Aristotle causes us to rethink conventional distinctions between work and leisure, Guggenhime's efforts instructively blur common demarcations between virtuous leadership in public service, paid work, and philanthropy. In the following chapters, we see how all those activities require the identical element of practical wisdom, no matter how rich we are, or what our profession may be.

THE ARISTOTELIAN
WORKPLACE

I HOLD THAT WHILE MAN EXISTS IT IS HIS DUTY TO IMPROVE NOT ONLY

HIS OWN CONDITION BUT TO ASSIST IN AMELIORATING MANKIND.

—*ABRAHAM LINCOLN, SPEECH IN CINCINNATI, 1861*

SO IN EVERY INDIVIDUAL THE TWO TRENDS, ONE TOWARDS PERSONAL

HAPPINESS AND THE OTHER TOWARDS UNITY WITH THE REST OF

HUMANITY, MUST CONTEND WITH EACH OTHER.

—*SIGMUND FREUD,* CIVILIZATION AND ITS DISCONTENTS

W e all lead complex lives, playing many and diverse social roles. I am, variously, a teacher, writer, and consultant; but I am also a husband, father, citizen, and capitalist (more about the latter in the next chapter). In each of those roles, my actions affect others, and Aristotle has useful things to say about the way I should evaluate my performance in all those relationships. Among the social roles he addresses is that of "boss," a role that most of us play for at least a part of our lives, even if we have only one person who reports to us. He has practical advice for modern men and women about what it means to be a virtuous employer, and if you are at all like me, you may be a bit embarrassed when you measure yourself against his ethical yardstick.

Of course, Aristotle never heard of a corporation. Outside of armies, there were no large organizations of any kind in his world. Nonetheless, what he had to say about the political leadership of communities has great relevance to those who seek to be virtuous leaders of organizations. But we need to apply a little moral imagination to make the translation between his city-states and our workplaces.

THE SOCIAL CONTRACT

Aristotle writes that the unwritten constitutions, or social contracts, of the small-scale societies he observed were the prime determinants of the degree to which people in the ancient world led good lives. In the very few just societies he observed, the constitution provided opportunity for people to develop their natural abilities and, thus, pursue happiness. In such a society, the role of the leader was to create conditions under which followers could achieve their potential. Political leadership was therefore a task and responsibility rather than a privilege, right, or reward. Speaking of the characteristics of virtuous leaders, Aristotle says,

> It is the mark of a man of practical wisdom to be able to de-
> liberate well about what is good and expedient for himself . . .
> and about what sorts of things are conducive to the good life
> in general.

But how does a leader know what is conducive to the good life for others? This is tricky business. On the one hand, Aristotle believes Platonic pater-nalism is morally wrong and impractical, but on the other hand, he says it is virtuous and practical for leaders to place the good of others above their narrow self-interest. That's a fine line to draw. Usefully, he then shows how leaders begin the process of deciding what is in the interest of others without dictating how they should behave. Because no one wishes to be treated un-justly himself, Aristotle suggests that a virtuous leader start by putting him-self in the place of his followers, asking *How would I want to be treated if I were a subject of this state?* Next, Aristotle asserts the priority of the welfare of the whole community over the interests of its individual members. So the second question a virtuous leader asks is, *What form of social contract would allow all members of our community to develop their potential in order that they each may make their greatest contribution to the good of the whole?*

In posing such questions, Aristotle is like Lincoln (and unlike Freud) in finding no conflict between the good of a community and the good of its in-dividual members. Indeed, to Aristotle a prime task of leadership is to reduce as far as practical the necessity of painful trade-offs that pit the good of the whole against the welfare of individuals. Moreover, he says virtuous leaders seek to reduce or eliminate either/or situations that create conflict among their followers. Although he believes that some social goods—power, wealth, honor—are limited and scarce, Aristotle thinks all individuals in a group can develop their potentials in a non-zero-sum game: "It is clear that the best con-stitution is that organization by which everyone, whoever he is, would do the best things and live a blessed life."

How is this constitution to be determined? In keeping with his belief that wisdom is never the sole province of any individual, the practical and just way to determine the conditions of a social contract is through discussion among all the participants in the system. This should not be confused with political democracy. The Ancient is no enthusiast of democracy, believing, instead, that only the virtuous few who actively pursue both the highest and the complete good are fit to participate in political decision-making. Yet Aristotle's political oligarchs are not tyrants, nor are they ranked in one of his typical hierarchies. In his model of governance, all qualified people in a community come together to discuss rationally the issues and problems they face. Though that participation is limited to virtuous individuals, all those so qualified are equal in terms of their right to participate. These equally enfranchised participants nonetheless will be unequal in that some will be smarter, some wiser, some more articulate, and some will have more technical knowledge in particular fields.

Here's how Aristotle envisions such a system working: All qualified citizens gather regularly at the acropolis to participate in open and disciplined debate on matters of public policy. When considering what the school curriculum shall be, Plato might take the lead because he has made special study of that subject. Then, on the issue of the construction of a new building in the agora, the mathematician Euclid might have the most to offer, given his great learning in the field of geometry. But in every such discussion, all qualified participants will be equal in terms of being able to ask questions and then to evaluate the various policy ideas put forward by experts. No one person will dominate every discussion because political issues are so complex and varied that no one ever has all the information needed to make the best decisions in all cases, and no one ever has a monopoly on wisdom. Aristotle is not naïve: He understands that people have real and legitimate differences of opinion and that they're divided by competing and conflicting interests. Still, he cannot imagine a situation in which qualified people who come together to achieve justice for their community cannot, after free and rational discussion, eventually arrive at a rough agreement about matters that affect them. The

227

qualification, of course, is that all the participants have something to bring to the table as the result of their individual self-development.

In the late 18th century, James Madison identified the flaws in the Aristotelian model. In *The Federalist Papers*, Madison explains that people in small-scale societies often divide into permanent factions, or interest groups; and once members of the weakest faction see that they will never get their way, the system of direct democracy breaks down; the permanent losers pack up and go home, refusing to play a game in which the cards are stacked against them. Madison says the trick to overcoming this democratic gridlock is to create a large, diverse, and pluralistic form of representative government in which special interests are forced to compromise or risk losing their leverage. History has shown Madison's critique to be basically correct in the political arena. However, contemporary organizational theory shows that Aristotle has the last word when it comes to the governance of workplaces.

228

THE ARISTOTELIAN WORKPLACE

Modern workplaces are the moral equivalent of Aristotle's small-scale communities. As societies grow more complex and it becomes increasingly difficult for individuals to perform the kind of role that citizens played in the political system Aristotle describes, workplaces become the arenas in which modern men and women devote most of their energies and in which they have the most influence. Today, the terms of our employment contracts tend to be greater determinants of our lifestyles than are provisions in the social contracts we have with our city, state, and national communities. From this perspective, modern businesses have the greatest power to create conditions under which individuals can realize their potentials.

If Aristotle is right that the good life entails developing one's human potential, then providing conditions in which employees can do so is a clear moral responsibility of leaders of work organizations. The logic is inescapable:

Organizations that deny employees the chance to develop their potential deny them the opportunity to realize their humanity. And that is unjust. Hence, business leaders have inherited the ethical roles, tasks, and responsibilities of Aristotle's virtuous political leaders. In this view, virtuous business leaders serve not to make themselves rich, famous, adored, or powerful but to provide society with the goods and services it needs in an economically efficient manner *while at the same time providing the environment for the intellectual and moral development of employees*. Like Aristotle's political leaders, their task is to make "the good" of the company commensurate with the good of its employees; in fact, to make the two mutually reinforcing.

This task is easier today for business than for political leaders because people in work organizations self-select into systems in which there is general agreement about ultimate goals, whereas people in political systems have widely divergent values and views. In addition, research on group behavior reveals that size counts when it comes to decision-making: Aristotle's face-to-face model works when the number of people involved is small, *very* small, in fact. In small groups, most people will behave rationally and cooperatively, as he posits. However, when the number of participants approaches 20 or so, the group starts to break into factions, participants stop listening to each other, and the strongest individuals come to dominate, much as Madison said. The good news for managers is that, unlike political leaders, they have the ability to break down large numbers of employees into groups small enough to be effective.

But few modern workplaces are Aristotelian in this or any other regard. For example, Aristotle believes that the ability to reason is the main qualification for participation in political decision-making, but the criteria typically used in modern organizations to decide who gets to decide—status, titles, salary, power, ego, and the like—would be unjust and irrelevant in an Aristotelian workplace. And because the goal of governance is to determine the good and the best means to achieve it (in business terms, the right strategy, structure, policies, and products), what should matter in work organizations is tapping into all sources of practical wisdom, wherever those might be found. Hence, if good ideas come from middle managers or even front-line workers, they should be as welcome as if they had been developed in the executive suite. Exactly where good ideas come from will obviously vary by situation, but in an Aristotelian organization, decisions will no more be made by one or a small number of executives than by democratic vote. Hence, the first challenges of virtuous business leadership are to create (a) processes for eliciting and evaluating ideas from across the organization, and (b) systems of governance in which all employees find themselves in groups small enough for all to have a meaningful say in decisions directly affecting their own work.

There is a significant difference between modern work and the labor of Aristotle's day. In ancient Greece, slaves were a necessary part of the economic equation. Someone had to do the menial and dirty work, and by necessity, that meant most workers could not free themselves from drudgery in order to learn and grow. But looking forward to a distant future, Aristotle posits that "one day slaves and servants will not be necessary" in an automated world in which machines do the necessary heavy and grimy labor. Aristotle's pie-in-the-sky forecast has come true, if only recently, for the vast majority of workers in advanced societies. Most dirty, routine, and heavy tasks can now be done by machines. As organizational theorist Edward E. Lawler has shown, there is less practical reason today to have two classes of workers, one thinking, the other doing, and no reason why the vast majority can't be engaged in learning and growing on the job. Thus, the Aristotelian organization promotes the good of all, and not just a class of privileged individuals. It allows all its members "to deliberate well about what is good and advantageous . . . with a view to living well overall." Such an organization is not paternalistic; it does not force its members to participate or to fulfill their potential. But it does provide the context in which they can do so if they wish and in which each is encouraged to do so. If Aristotle is right about the conditions most men and women need in order to pursue happiness, odds are that the vast majority of workers will choose to do what is both good for them and for their organizations.

Extrapolating from my reading of Aristotle on politics, I conclude that a modern Aristotelian workplace will have four primary characteristics:

- A real opportunity for all workers to learn and to develop their talent and potential
- All employees participate in the decisions that affect their own work
- All employees participate in the financial gains resulting from their own ideas and efforts
- Virtuous leaders

The second and third points are inextricably linked: Participation in decision making without participation in financial gains is unjust because the fruits of employee contributions are reaped by others (executives and shareholders). And participation in a company's financial gains without participating in decision making also is unjust because workers are powerless to influence the conditions that determine the size of their paychecks. Importantly, the first three characteristics derive from the existence of the fourth, virtuous leadership.

231

WORKPLACE APPLICATIONS OF ARISTOTELIAN PRINCIPLES

Let me give an example of these principles in action. In the early 1970s, an era of unusual ferment in industrial workplaces, a corporate executive wrote the following Aristotelian words:

> The employer's obligations to society, stockholders and workers [are] intricately interrelated. One cannot, in effect, serve society at all if he does not serve its people. One cannot serve shareholders effectively if he does not act to make business itself an agent for human growth and fulfillment.

About the time the above was published, its author, Sidney Harman, was cooperating with the United Auto Workers in a widely publicized workplace experiment in an old, unproductive facility in the American South, where auto mirrors were manufactured. There, some 60 workers were given the opportunity to be self-managing, even though most of the workers were relatively uneducated and came from disadvantaged backgrounds. The average production of those workers was x mirrors per day. After negotiations between the workers, the union, and management, it was agreed that, whenever during the day the workers had produced $x + n$ mirrors, they would be free to (a) go home, (b) continue working and earn a bonus, or (c) attend a company-sponsored school where the courses offered ranged from work-related subject matter to basic ed to playing the piano. Fully a third of the workers chose to attend the company school in their found time.

To increase their productivity and get off work earlier, workers were allowed to find ways to organize their tasks in almost any way they wished and to redesign plant conditions to make their tasks less tedious and more interesting. The work itself became a learning experience, and once the workers got the hang of self-management, they began making changes, experimenting here and there with better, faster, more efficient ways to make mirrors. Ultimately, they improved their productivity to the point where they were reaching their stretch quota around midday. Moreover, as the workers gained confidence and experience, they began to suggest ways to redesign other jobs in the plant, and they invented imaginative ways to share in cost savings resulting from the changes they either initiated or supported. This was an Aristotelian workplace, designed not only to be successful economically but, equally, to allow for worker self-fulfillment, learning, and growth. Also present was worker participation in decision making and in the financial gains that resulted from their efforts and ideas.

In the 1970s, many similarly Aristotelian efforts were implemented to make work into learning experiences and, in particular, to permit blue-collar and other front-line workers to find the kind of intellectual rewards in their jobs that professionals and managers often find in theirs as a matter of course:

❧ At Chaparral Steel, manual workers were eligible for short sabbaticals in which they were funded to take time off work to learn a new skill or to do work-related research at a university or another innovative workplace.

❧ At office furniture manufacturer Herman Miller, all employees had the right to pursue self-fulfillment on the job, and their work was designed to have both developmental and economic functions.

❧ At Shell Canada, a union-negotiated contract contained the following provision: "Employees should be permitted to contribute and grow to their fullest capability . . . with compensation based on their demonstrated knowledge and skills rather than on tasks being performed at any specific time."

❧ At the Olga Company, lingerie sewers and seamstresses were periodically relieved from their duties in production and given the chance to work with managers in the creative process of new product design.

❧ At Polaroid, CEO Edwin Land put assembly line workers into the company's labs as full members of R&D teams alongside trained scientists and engineers.

❧ Xerox offered domestic "Fulbrights" for employees who wanted to take a year or two away from their regular jobs to engage in public service.

❧ In Topeka, Kansas, workers at a General Foods dog food plant had the goal of learning every job in their plant and were compensated for learning each new task.

❧ In many U.S. companies, the practice of job rotation was introduced in order to alleviate boredom by allowing workers to continually learn new skills.

❧ In Norway, front-line workers were encouraged to design their own training, with an eye to learning how to enlarge their jobs through adding tasks and dimensions previously done by managers.

❧ In the early 1980s, Jack Stack, CEO of the rust-belt Springfield Re-Manufacturing Company, taught all of his employees, mostly blue-collar workers with no more than high school educations, the financial

233

skills he learned when he had earned his MBA. When they were as adept as he was at reading the company's cash-flow statements and balance sheet and had been taught how to interpret and apply the information found in those financial reports, he gave them full authority to act on their knowledge. He then cut his new "partners" into the action by sharing with them the gains resulting from their ideas and efforts.

❦ In Japan, countless blue-collar employees participated in "Deming's Way," an approach to worker-led quality improvement based on teaching statistics to all workers, even those with little formal education. In Japan was also a system of continuous learning in which employees at all levels attended weekly training sessions designed to foster individual growth and a sense of community (and not to learn a particular skill). For instance, the president of a Japanese company might attend a lesson in welding taught by a worker. In 1976, Peter Drucker wrote that the purpose of this "Zen approach" to learning was self-improvement:

> It qualifies a man to do his present task with continually wider vision, continually increasing competence, and continually rising demands on himself. While there is a learning curve, there is no fixed and final plateau. Continued learning leads to a breakout, that is, to a new learning curve, which peaks at a new and higher plateau, and then to a new break out.

Drucker contrasted this to the typical Western approach in which "the purpose of learning is to qualify oneself for a new, different, and bigger job. The nature of learning is expressed in a [fixed and finite] learning curve. Within a certain period of time [the] student reaches a plateau of proficiency where he then stays forever."

The Japanese Zen approach was, of course, Aristotelian in nature; and the year before Drucker wrote the words above, it was advanced by Thomas

Green, a philosopher of education who encouraged American employers to design jobs as "mastery learning experiences." He urged employers to

> attend to the hidden curriculum of the job structure itself in an effort to see that there are no jobs that . . . lead to no subsequent lesson. . . . The structure of employment situations would then have to be examined in light of their *educational* potential as a setting for human learning and development.

In such workplaces, employees might learn the theory behind the work they were doing, studying chemistry, physics, engineering, economics, or whatever subjects were related to their jobs. Unfortunately, Green noted, few jobs offer subsequent lessons after the initial, short period in which the skills needed to do the task at hand are learned. Within a few weeks, the front-line workers in a General Electric plant learn most of what they need to know about making lightbulbs, including how to repair the machines that, in fact, do the work. In such cases, the opportunity for human growth is severely limited by the lack of complexity of the job and the degree of automation.

In contrast, in a system of continuous learning workers who make lightbulbs would be encouraged to learn what is going on behind the process: the physics of light and electricity; the sources and chemistry of tungsten, manganese, neon, or whatever raw materials were used in the making of the bulbs; the engineering principles on which the machinery that makes the bulbs is based; the management principles on which the plant is organized; and the economic theories involved in corporate management. In short, there is no limit to how deeply or how broadly workers might pursue knowledge about their work.

As Drucker recognized, such a system differs from traditional notions of worker training, the two main purposes of which are acquiring specific skills and promotion. That's why today, if workers learn anything on the job that amounts to an intellectual stretch, it is to do their bosses' jobs so they can one day replace them. As a result, typical on-the-job training does not develop the whole person; instead, it channels the individual to meet the requirements of a specific task.

Alas, most of the heady experimentation with workplace learning in the 1970s and early 1980s evaporated during the lengthy Reagan-era recession. By the 1990s, almost all the experiments had been killed or allowed to die on the grounds that they didn't contribute to the bottom line. To the extent the approach continues today, it is in the form of competence-based pay, but the intent and practice of this system has little to do with advancing human development. Indeed, one of the most important Aristotelian lessons learned from the 1970s' experiments was that workers desire the intrinsic benefit of learning and don't have to be paid extra to do something that meets a natural need. In fact, when employers have tried to base increases in pay on the number of skills learned, it has spoiled the natural pleasure of learning and done little but escalate labor costs.

236

WORKER DEVELOPMENT
AS OPPOSED TO TRAINING

Almost all employers today train their workers, but they do so for practical reasons, ranging from the need to reduce errors and improve quality to the belief that investment in training has an economic payoff similar to capital investment in automation and new plants. Economist Gary Becker theorizes that profit-motivated employers will invest in human capital by way of specific job-related training, but they are foolish to invest in the broader, or general, education of workers who would simply take their enhanced skills and sell them to another employer. Becker's theory is borne out in practice: American industry invests something like $57 billion in on-the-job training, and it makes good financial sense for it to do so. But the purpose of such expenditures is not human growth or fulfillment. Even employers who offer courses in basic education do so in order to upgrade the quality of their services or products and not to benefit their workers. In Aristotle's terms, the purpose of such training is useful but not noble.

Nonetheless, the prospects for true workplace learning were given a brief boost in the 1990s, when many corporations introduced the so-called "new employment contract." This contract made it clear that the company wasn't responsible for the job security of its workers; instead, it would give them marketable skills. The implicit promise, often made explicit in technology firms, was that workers need not worry about job security because, if layoffs were to occur, their skills would be in such demand that they could quickly find employment elsewhere. The supposed means to such mobility were continuous learning on the job and company-reimbursed tuition for courses attended in educational institutions. However, as the 2001–2003 recession showed, having all the skills in the world is of little use in a general, or industry-wide, economic turndown. Worse, at the first sign of recession, training was on the initial list of expenditures most employers cut. Worse yet, instead of investing in the training of even skilled and professional American employees, some companies replaced them with cheaper ones in India.

In hindsight, it appears the 1990s' talk about continuous learning was overblown. Although work is inherently a learning experience in settings where professionals and other highly skilled workers are involved in new product creation, that's true without help from management. And when the nature of most jobs is analyzed, even in high-tech settings, it is more akin to making lightbulbs than to creating the next new thing. Even under the new employment contract, there was little corporate interest in developing capabilities not directly tied to employees' tasks. Though most high-tech firms had tuition remission programs on their books, in practice, workers frequently were discouraged from taking time out from their often 6-day, 60-hour workweeks to attend even technical classes and faced rejection if they requested reimbursement for, say, a language class. So the history of the 1970s repeated itself at the turn of the millennium: For a brief moment, it appeared that the Aristotelian workplace might become a reality, but that moment faded and has now passed.

As with most complex issues, there is a contrary view: Some workplace authorities claim we are at the dawn of the era of "the learning organization." Such an organization is said to have processes, systems, incentives, and cultures that discourage workers from making the same mistakes twice and that encourage them to learn from the best practices of outsiders and across internal boundaries. These are sensible, probably necessary, goals in a fast-changing, competitive global economy. But they are not the goals of an Aristotelian organization (although the means might coincidentally be the same). To the extent the learning organization movement is more than a slogan, its subject is the development of the institution and *not* the individuals in it.

238   The following example from Hewlett-Packard (HP) illustrates how the goals of Aristotelian leaders, and what they do to achieve them, differ from today's so-called learning organizations. For some 40 years, HP was divided into numerous small divisions. This structure was designed to encourage innovation and self-management and was coupled with a supporting system of performance evaluation that assessed managers both on how effectively they produced products and how effectively they developed their subordinates. In 1996, the head of one of those divisions was falling down in terms of the first measure. His group was taking 26 days to deliver a product that HP's competitors were delivering in roughly half the time. He approached the problem in the "HP Way": He appointed two managers to lead an "action-learning" task force. The two women chosen were experienced managers, but they didn't have impressive titles. What they had was an understanding of HP's longstanding approach to leadership and learning.

These two women recruited an interdisciplinary, cross-functional, multi-level team of about a dozen individuals and began their task by clearly communicating the goal of delivering their product in 8 days, and to do so before 9 months had passed. Then they outlined the way the team would operate: no structure, hierarchy, rules, titles, or plans. What the team would do and how they would do it was up to them. There was only one condition: Every day, the team would meet to discuss and reflect on what they were learning.

The problem they sought to solve was incredibly complex, involving some 70 different computer systems and affecting the operations of dozens of different departments. So they started experimenting and, predictably, failing. Yet they found that their daily lessons began to add up, their mid-course corrections started to work, and lo, before their allotted deadline, they had met their goal. As a bonus, inventories were down and service levels up. Clearly, the process HP used is sound management and consistent with the utilitarian notion of a learning organization. What makes it *Aristotelian* is that the leaders' goals were concerned with both the good of the organization and the good of the employees. As proof of HP's commitment to the latter, its employees were constantly rotated on and off such task forces as part of their career development, even when there was no discernible return to the company or pressing business problem to solve.

Such experiences demonstrate that it's possible to make a workplace into an Aristotelian delivery vehicle of the good life, yet, in reality, it is the rare business leader who is committed to making it so and, particularly, to continue doing so when times are rough. Sadly, HP seldom operates that way today under top-down leadership more interested in generating short-term profits through cutting R&D and engaging in acquisitions than creating internal growth in the way that had made HP a model company in the past.

To be fair, it is extremely difficult to make workplaces into true venues for the pursuit of happiness, which is why Aristotle stresses the importance of individuals making virtuous use of their leisure time. Nonetheless, a few business leaders in the not too distant past—for example, the Watsons at IBM, four generations of the Haas family at Levi-Strauss, David Kearns at Xerox, Edwin Land and Tom Wyman at Polaroid, Robert Galvin at Motorola, Max

De Pree at Herman Miller, and William Hewlett and David Packard at HP—were committed to the development of their people through thick and thin. As this list implies, at least one of three factors appears to be present in the few companies with a deep commitment to the continuing development of employees: (1) founder (or family) ownership, (2) the presence of a strong and enlightened union, and (3) virtuous leadership. Such business leadership is as rare today in America as Periclean political leadership was in Aristotle's Athens.

DEVELOPING MANAGERS AND LEADERS

Although such leadership may be rare, many current CEOs claim the mantle of virtue based on their apparent commitment to the development of their top management teams. The problem in many cases is that the CEOs' own egos, and the related misuse of their power, get in the way of their effectively creating other leaders. According to contemporary philosopher Richard Kraut, Aristotle believes great leaders observe "decent limits" in order to allow opportunities for others to lead and to develop: "No virtuous person wants to be best if this turns his equals into people who are predominantly passive recipients of his moral feats." But, in practice, such celebrity CEOs as CitiGroup's Sandy Weill and Sun's Scott McNeely have behaved as if there were only one leader in each of their respective organizations—themselves—and not only have garnered credit for all good decisions made in their companies but have amassed for themselves the best opportunities to learn through leading. Worse, they dismissed executives who challenged their authority, particularly upcoming stars who shined too brightly and thus threatened the CEOs' status as the sole source of organizational enlightenment.

Larry Ellison offers a quintessential example of such anti-Aristotelianism. After 8 years as Oracle's president and COO, Ray Lane resigned abruptly in 2000. At the time, Lane participated in several candid press interviews on the subject of Ellison's increasing and, by then, near-total domination of the corporation, which Lane said made it impossible to develop a strong leadership team: "It's just like kids," he told the *New York Times,* "If you make all their decisions for them, they will go out as adults not knowing how to make decisions themselves." Lane said the managers reporting to Ellison "are not decision makers. They aren't leaders. They just do what Larry says. They wouldn't know how to make a decision without Larry making it for them." In contrast, Lane said he tried to "make himself expendable by recruiting and training other skilled managers."

Here we might recall Aristotle's assertion that political leaders, even effective ones, who amass too much power for the good of their community should be exiled because they limit the opportunity for others to participate in decision making and, thus, to develop fully. By analogy, if Larry Ellison centralizes all decision-making power in his office, the development of other leaders in Oracle is reduced if not stymied. As Lane implies, such a concentration of power isn't good for the organization, either, because it precludes innovative contributions from other qualified individuals, and the organization's ability to grow is thus limited to the brainpower of one person.

ANOTHER ARISTOTELIAN TEST

Of course, one need not be the CEO, COO, or head of a corporate division to be concerned with the issue of employee development. By the time we reach mid-career, and whatever our level in an organization, public or private, a great many of us have the standing and authority needed to affect positively the quality of life of those who work for us or with us, even if that is only a few people. If we choose to continue to make our workplace, as opposed to our community, the focus of our social contribution, and if we choose to do so virtuously, here are some questions Aristotle might say we need to ask ourselves:

❧ To what extent do I consciously make an effort to provide learning opportunities for everyone who works for me?

✢ To what extent do I encourage full participation by all my people in the decisions affecting their work? To what extent do I allow them to lead in order to grow?

✢ To what extent do I measure my own performance as a manager/leader both in terms of my effectiveness in realizing economic goals and, equally, in terms of using my practical wisdom to create conditions under which my people can seek to fulfill their potential in the workplace?

Based on 30 years of consulting experience, I reluctantly conclude that few CEOs I have met would be able to respond to those questions with positive self-assessments, although I have worked with dozens of general and midlevel managers who could do so. Indeed, many successful and admired corporate leaders consciously reject such Aristotelian measures of performance as inappropriate, impractical, and irrelevant to the task their boards hired them to do: create wealth. They say their responsibility is to their shareholders, not their employees; and if the "social responsibility" of employee development interferes with profit making, then trade-offs must be made. Aristotle would answer that virtuous leaders have responsibilities to both their owners and their workers, and if there is a conflict between the two, it is their duty to create conditions in which their interests can be made the same. He would remind us that although most political leaders measure themselves solely in terms of their effectiveness at obtaining and maintaining power, virtuous ones also measure themselves by ethical standards of justice. By extension, in a modern business context, it is appropriate that executives are evaluated in terms of their effectiveness at generating wealth for shareholders; in addition, virtuous ones also provide the opportunity for their followers to find meaning and the opportunity for development in the workplace.

Hence, what may be virtuous leadership behavior by narrow economic standards may not be so by the broader and more ethically inclusive measures Aristotle encourages us to use. Again, what matters ethically is how the motivations and desires of leaders influence the way they make tough choices and trade-offs. The measure of virtue is "the difference between the objects which they value and seek to achieve." For example, the most prominent business leader of our time, GE's Jack Welch, was considered a paragon of virtue by those who measure CEOs by the sole standard of wealth creation. Welch was willing to go to enormous lengths to create wealth for his shareholders. In doing so, if he needed to spend hours at the company's Crotonville training facility, then he was a more-than-willing teacher. But he was clear about the purpose of those efforts: He needed to build a cadre of managers who could effectively execute his plans and strategies. No sensible person would question him on that score. But it is clear that Welch would not have made the effort to train his top managers if the purpose had been their personal development, nor would he have wasted his time on people farther down the line as, for example, at the old Hewlett-Packard, where human development was valued as a good in itself. Welch would have found risible the suggestion that he should teach chemistry to those who made lightbulbs, and his reasoning is smack in the mainstream of contemporary business thought: He was willing to make the investment in training people only when the expenditure of his resources could be justified by the effect on the bottom line.

243

Doubtless, Welch's behavior was effective, and even Aristotle would say Welch did the right thing in teaching his famous "workout" courses at Crotonville to GE's top managers. But the Ancient also would note the countless examples of leaders like Welch who do the right thing accidentally, who do the right thing for the wrong reason, and who are successful at achieving their own instrumental ends while ignoring the good of their followers. He reminds us not to make the mistake of calling such leaders virtuous, even if they and the investing community choose to do so. The Aristotelian distinction of virtue is reserved for those rare leaders who measure their performance both in terms of their intellectual excellence (their effectiveness in realizing business goals) and in terms of their moral excellence (the extent to which they create conditions in which others can pursue the good *for their own sake*). And, yes, those are very high standards.

CONTEMPORARY ARISTOTELIANS

Although doing good for the sake of others became unfashionable in much of American business in the 1990s, it remained a focus of attention among the Crown Fellows I previously mentioned. Recently, I interviewed four of these successful young leaders by e-mail, asking them the question, *What do you do to encourage the personal growth and development of the people who work for you?* Peter Reiling, the CEO of TechnoServe introduced earlier, replied:

> I've tried to create a true learning organization with ample opportunity for staff to attend seminars, workshops, and, most important, to travel to our various field offices in the developing world. These span 10 countries on three continents. When I attend a great seminar or workshop, I do my best to repeat it internally. The same for when I read a great book or article—it circulates.

Jay Marshall, Principal in Alix Partners, answered:

> I try to engage them on stuff outside their jobs as much as possible. I'm probably projecting, but I'm a lot more interested in hearing what people's outside passions are rather than having one more job-related conversation. Knowing these, I try to talk to them about those interests and encourage them to pursue them (including kicking them out the door sometimes, if need be). For development that's more related to their professional skills or careers, I really enjoy the whole mentoring process. It's amazing to me how little I learned in school (undergrad or MBA) that was relevant to performance. Since so little can be picked up there, I really stress the apprenticeship aspect of what we're doing and try to make every transaction a learning opportunity. I

learn and develop this way myself, and people seem to respond well to it.

Michael Powell, Chairman of the Federal Communications Commission, added:

> I work very hard on this. I meet every 6 months with my staff to conduct not only performance reviews but to review personal development plans that include an attention to balance. I run a networking and mentoring group in the Commission and we discuss leadership topics, often challenging one of the members to develop the curriculum. I pass on articles, quotes, and books that I think offer insight into leading a successful and balanced life.

Crown Fellow Donna Auguste, CEO and cofounder of Freshwater Software, is a computer science engineer who has succeeded in developing cutting-edge hardware and software, with three patents to her name. At Freshwater, employee development is a driving element of its values-based culture. Auguste encourages employees to alter their work environment in ways to allow them to develop their unique talents. Instead of organizing employees hierarchically or functionally, they are intentionally seated near others who have different skills and experiences, so everyone is both a teacher and a learner, and all can be involved in working to solve customer problems. A central part of the Freshwater culture is "Employees are expected to be responsible to themselves as well as to the company and its customers." Auguste insists, "Family and personal responsibilities come before business responsibilities."

The Aristotelian behavior of these Crown Fellows reminds me that, in the 1980s, I had encouraged my business students and clients to accept the moral and ethical responsibilities of leadership. But in the 1990s, I had succumbed to what was fashionable during those go-go years, and to win approval from students, consulting clients, and colleagues, I had stressed the strategic and analytical aspects of corporate leadership to the near exclusion of the moral dimensions that were the focus of Aristotle's writings on the subject. I now see that I erred seriously, and I have vowed again to teach that leaders who fail to accept the development of their people as a prime responsibility are not virtuous, no matter how unpopular that message makes me. Moreover, as the sorry aftermath of the 1990s demonstrates, even fulfilling that difficult responsibility is an insufficient test of leadership virtue. An Aristotelian workplace is also one in which everyone participates fairly in the distribution of wealth created by the enterprise, so I must continue to remind myself to teach business leaders that they are responsible for creating the conditions under which such justice can occur.

246

DISTRIBUTIVE JUSTICE IN BUSINESS

THE QUESTION YOU WOULD HAVE ME CONSIDER IS NOT ONLY
HOW A STATE, BUT HOW A LUXURIOUS STATE IS CREATED; AND POSSIBLY
THERE IS NO HARM IN THIS, FOR IN SUCH A STATE WE SHALL
BE MORE LIKELY TO SEE HOW JUSTICE AND INJUSTICE ORIGINATE.
IN MY OPINION THE TRUE AND HEALTHY STATE IS ONE
[IN WHICH PEOPLE LIVE SIMPLY AND VIRTUOUSLY WITH
FAMILY AND FRIENDS]. BUT IF YOU WISH TO SEE A STATE
AT FEVER-HEAT, I HAVE NO OBJECTION.

—*PLATO,* THE REPUBLIC

As the fever heat of the 1990s came to a frigid end, corporate employees and shareholders awoke with a terrible case of the chills, wondering what on earth had happened to their investments, savings, and jobs. But not everyone suffered equally; in fact, a few prominent boomers made out all right:

- Gary Winnick, ex-chairman of Global Crossing, made $500 million while his shareholders lost $30 billion.

- Henry Silverman, CEO of Cendant, received a 41 percent increase in salary while the value of the company's stock was falling 47 percent.

- Gary Wendt, former Conseco CEO, earned some $30 million plus a $17 million pension while the value of the company's stock plunged by some $25 billion.

- Linda Wachner, ex-CEO of Warnaco, made over $70 million while her shareholders lost $2 billion from the stock's market high.

- Larry Ellison received $100 million in stocks and options while shareholders watched the value of Oracle drop by some $150 billion.

And yours truly got sucked up in all the hype and legerdemain, embarrassing myself by writing a 2000 article praising Enron's enlightened leadership! If only I had paid attention to Aristotle, who, it turns out, has useful things to say about the justice of the distribution of wealth among entrepreneurs, investors, managers, and employees that a business produces. As I now better appreciate, that issue isn't just the concern of executives and financiers. In our society, most of us are capitalists to one extent or another: If we have private retirement benefits—that would include most full-time teachers, professors, union members, and those who work for Starbucks and Wal-Mart—we are indirect owners of corporations. And even some of us who don't think of ourselves as capitalists occasionally play the role directly. For example, I have been on the board of directors of a small company since it began trading its shares on the NASDQ exchange in the mid-1990s, and that has given me object lessons in the ethical issues Aristotle explores with regard to distributive justice.

DIVIDING THE PIE BETWEEN
ENTREPRENEURS AND INVESTORS

When our little company went public, the first question we faced was the degree to which the various participants—those whose contributions were, variously, financial, entrepreneurial, and managerial—should benefit from the initial sale of our stock. We tried to answer the question without the help of Aristotle, but, in hindsight, I wish we had had the benefit of his guidance. For example, in deciding what is a just distribution of stock among investors and entrepreneurs, Aristotle's golden mean is a useful albeit limited tool. It is limited, he says, because, "Justice is a kind of mean, but not in the same way as the other virtues: it relates to an intermediate amount, while injustice relates to the extremes." Graphically, here is what he seems to be saying:

DEFECT	VIRTUE	EXCESS
INJUSTICE	JUSTICE	INJUSTICE

Though we can understand how there is injustice (excess) involved in taking too much of something, it is less clear what Aristotle has in mind by the moral defect of taking too little. Aristotle doesn't elaborate on the point, so "it's a puzzlement," as Yul Brynner used to say. But we can try to make sense out of it by relating it to the ethics of the distribution of wealth created by a successful start-up company. After all, injustice most often arises in the distribution of goods after a windfall, as Plato observes.

Many entrepreneurs argue that it is unfair when venture capitalists (VCs) make off with the lion's share of stock in an Initial Public Offering (IPO). They believe it is more just for the person who creates the idea for a business, and those who execute the idea, to be the primary beneficiaries of the wealth created by a start-up. VCs retort that, in fact, they deserve more shares because they take most of the financial risk, while the entrepreneur doesn't have as much "skin in the game." Although this debate feels like a modern one, in his *Ethics,* the protocapitalist Aristotle addresses the relationship between merit, contribution, and money in business transactions and the relative degrees to which ideas, performance, effort, and capital should be rewarded. The bad news is that he concludes there is no universal principle we can apply to determine who deserves how much. Still, he believes fair-minded people can reason together to derive a set of general, flexible guidelines that are useful in practice and rigorous enough to withstand logical and ethical challenge.

To begin such an analysis, Aristotle posits that a just share of rewards—a fair share of shares in an IPO—falls near the middle between too much and too little, but he says there is no formula for identifying exactly where that point is found. In essence, there is no rule concerning how many shares of stock should go to investors, how many to entrepreneurs, and how many to managers and employees. So where is distributive justice to be found on the ethical continuum? Like all questions relating to the exercise of virtue, businesspeople must discover, at least in its details and particulars, the golden mean for their own organizations. But Aristotle offers a few hints to aid in such deliberations. First, he says justice is related to equality, hence an unjust act results from an unequal sharing of some good. However, although equality before the law means sameness, equality in the distribution of material and psychic rewards means something else.

We can understand this by analogy to his comments on the distribution of political power. Aristotle disagrees with Athenian democrats who believe all free men in the polis are entitled to be equal participants in the city's governance. Instead, he argues that those who haven't bothered to educate themselves aren't entitled to be leaders of their community. On the other side, Athens's oligarchs argue that, because the rich contribute more to society in taxes and wealth creation, they should have an unequal share of power. Although Aristotle agrees with them that equality among unequals is unjust, he nonetheless insists that citizens can make important contributions to society besides and in addition to the creation of wealth. Some virtuous, yet relatively poor, citizens contribute time, effort, ideas, and even their lives in battle; so

Aristotle reasons that they are entitled to a fair share of respect and honor; in particular, they earn the right to participate in politics every bit as much as those who contribute large sums for the construction of public buildings. Aristotle thus differs with both egalitarians and aristocrats: He believes everyone must earn the privilege of participation through virtuous behavior.

He applies similar reasoning to the allocation of business profits. When it comes to dividing the wealth produced by partnerships, Aristotle observes that each partner typically claims he deserves the bigger portion. In trying to figure out which party actually deserves the lion's share, he says when fraud, violence, and other legal or moral malfeasance is involved, the scales of justice should be tipped in favor of the injured party to rectify the wrong. But that's an easy call. Justice is much harder to determine when there is a binding contract. For example, suppose you and I agree to divide, fifty/fifty, both the work effort involved in, and then the spoils produced by, a new enterprise, but I subsequently end up doing 90 percent of the work. Isn't it then fair to allow me to renegotiate a higher percentage of the returns? Anticipating Milton Friedman, Aristotle argues that all business transactions should be voluntary and informed. Under such circumstances, no one enters into a contract that gives him an unfair division of returns; only a fool freely trades a pound of gold for a pound of straw. Yet sometimes we are fools, or we are fooled. After the fact, when I realize I have freely made a bad bargain, Aristotle seems to say I am stuck with it. Yet, he adds that you, realizing I have made an error, act virtuously if you rectify my mistake.

In particular, he says there is inherent injustice in any exchange of desperation, as when a thirsty person on a desert willingly contracts himself into slavery for a jug of water. And because motivation is what counts to the Ancient, even people who simply try to get the better of others by outbargaining them, as opposed to providing them value for money, commit acts of injustice. He concludes: *A virtuous person tries to make sure every party to a transaction receives a fair share.*

Nonetheless, it is prudent to negotiate a good contract up front. When an entrepreneur strikes a deal with VCs, the first issue to be resolved is the relative shares of the action to be allocated among capital, entrepreneurs, management, and labor. In determining those amounts, Aristotle is a capitalist: He believes markets set the right value for most resources. And when capital is in demand, it is more costly than when it is not, so the entrepreneur is going to have to pay the going rate for the capital she raises. Yet, although there is a capital market, there is no idea market, per se. So how does one equate the market-determined value of money (the input of the VCs) with the subjective value of an idea (the input of the entrepreneur)? Aristotle answers that the return to each should be "in accordance with proportion and not equality." All parties are entitled to a return proportionate to their contributions, which must be determined by an understanding of the true value of those contributions, but, in every circumstance, "injustice lies at the extremes."

In assessing the value of those relative contributions, Aristotle recognizes not all activities are of equal worth. He believes food (the product of the farmer) is "nobler" than money (the product of the banker) because food is "necessary, natural, limited, and the means to a higher end." In contrast, making money is "unnecessary, unnatural, unlimited, and an end to itself" and, consequently, less virtuous. Aristotle's out-of-date thinking is at least more sophisticated than Marx's and Adam Smith's "labor theory of value" because he sees a product's worth as a combination of its labor input, market demand, quality, and especially its social utility. In sum, Aristotle agrees with the entrepreneur: Her ideas have greater social utility than the money of bankers because ideas can *directly* create wealth, solve problems, and lead to the happiness of the community. Investors of money are not as meritorious as inventors of ideas because money is merely an instrument and not a good in itself; money supports the brainwork of entrepreneurs, not vice versa. Needless to say, investors disagree, especially with Aristotle's barter-era notion that money is unnecessary; but the issue here is measuring relative contribution, not demeaning the role of capital. VCs might also argue that they add value in other ways besides money, for example, counseling the entrepreneur, recruiting seasoned management, and providing governance advice.

Taking all the above into account, Aristotle might well call it unfair when VCs take the lion's share of an IPO, leaving relatively little for the founder and those who were involved in helping her start the company. But before coming to that conclusion, he, as usual, asks a series of tough questions, including:

- To what extent was the original idea the founder's?
- To what extent did the founder organize the company and contribute seed-money and sweat equity?
- To what extent was the work of leadership, management, and especially technical and professional problem-solving done by the entrepreneur or others? What share of equity are those others receiving, and how was that determined?

Aristotle has no preconceived ideas about answers to such questions. His point in raising them is to ensure that rewards are divvied up legitimately based on deliberations about justice and proportionate contribution. Recent experience in American business indicates that such ethical deliberation is rare. Typically, founding parties to a start-up use distributive principles designed to reward themselves alone. Not all stakeholders (employees, for example) in a start-up have a voice in establishing those principles, and those who do have a voice often employ the unfair leverage involved in exchanges of desperation, such as when VCs enter the picture at a time when a young company faces threats to its survival and they are, thus, able to exact returns far in excess of market rates. Therefore, it is appropriate to ask if justice plays a role in such calculations. If the distributive criteria used are simply power and leverage, Aristotle concludes the process is unfair.

Applying Aristotle's ethical tests in hindsight to the way we distributed shares in the 1990s' IPO of our own little company, I am relieved to say we did rough justice by our various stakeholders. However, I would be a lot more comfortable with the outcome had we conducted an ethical analysis in a more rigorous and conscious manner. We did the right thing but almost unconsciously, so it would be hard to claim we acted virtuously.

JUST DISTRIBUTION OF REWARDS WITHIN ORGANIZATIONS

In light of recent corporate scandals, it is dismaying to find many executives still concerned that they might be getting less than *their* fair share of the wealth produced by the companies they manage. To them, the measure of what they are entitled to is the amount other executives in comparable companies earn. As often noted, this has little to do with performance or with relative contribution within the organization. Instead, it has everything to do with power and leverage.

The data on executive compensation have become depressingly familiar. In 1970, average total compensation (in 1998 dollars) for the CEO of a *Fortune* 100 corporation was $1.3 million, which was 39 times that of the average worker's salary ($32,522) at the time. In 1999, average compensation for top-tier CEOs was $37.5 million, almost a thousand times that of ordinary workers ($35,864). If we look at the entire *Fortune* list, CEOs currently take home over $10.8 million per year, on average, in real terms some 20 times more than in 1981 and some 400 times what their front-line workers earn. During the 1990s, the pay of those CEOs increased by 571 percent, while the average worker's salary grew by 37 percent (in unadjusted dollars). No matter how one cuts the figures, even moderately well paid CEOs of large corporations make about as much in a day as their workers make in a year. Even if the point of reference is the more modest salaries of CEOs of midsized American companies, the average for them was some 34 times that of industrial workers (the comparable ratios were 13:1 in Germany and 11:1 in Japan). In evaluating this data, keep in mind the $35,864 earned by the average American worker is exactly that, *an average,* which includes the astronomical salaries of CEOs, sports figures, and Hollywood celebs on the high end and the take-home of $5.15 per hour minimum-wage earners on the low end, who, if employed full time, make about $9,888 per year, before taxes.

Averages also conceal extreme behavior, such as Kmart's Charles Conway drawing down some $23 million during his 2-year reign as CEO, during which time some 22,000 of his employees were terminated with zero severance pay. In 2001, while Wal-Mart's CEO, H. Lee Scott, was receiving something like $17 million in compensation, many of his lowest-paid hourly employees were suing the company because they claimed they were forced to punch out at the end of their 8-hour day, then made to continue working overtime without additional compensation. These are egregious examples; nonetheless, few American executives appear to apply the same standards of justice they demand and expect for themselves to compensation issues relating to their subordinates. In 2002, employees of Hershey Foods went on strike after the share of health insurance premiums they bore was raised at a time when the company's sales and profits were up. The workers thought this hefty increase was particularly unfair because it occurred the year after the company's new CEO earned $4.7 million in salary and was awarded stock options that might be worth more than $10 million in the near future. Assuming Hershey's CEO was entitled to what he earned, the Aristotelian question is, *Was he virtuous in reducing the benefits of those who earned far less?*

The Ancient says it's a sign of fairness and virtue when a person is willing to take less than the share a contract permits her to take. By definition, one never takes less than one's fair share *when one does so voluntarily*. Thus, there would be no question of Hershey's CEO receiving less than his fair share if he were to voluntarily choose to absorb some of the costs of the increase in his employees' insurance premiums. Likewise, top executives in general would suffer no injustice if they were to choose to grant some of their stock options to others in their organizations who have none. On the other hand, by Aristotelian reckoning, if executives arbitrarily take away the options of less-powerful and lower-compensated employees, the possibility of injustice arises because they are doing something to weaker parties that may not be for their sake or good. In any event, there seems to be inherent injustice across the board in corporate America in the distribution of stock options, 75 percent of which go to CEOs, 15 percent to the next 50 highest-compensated executives, and only 10 percent to all other employees in the typical company.

Harder to reckon is what is just and fair. But it is not impossible to do so. For example, Disney's board compensated its CEO, Michael Eisner, with $285 million between 1996 and 2004. We can't pretend to have all the data required to decide how much Eisner deserves, but, thanks to Aristotle, we have a question that a virtuous member of the Disney board's compensation committee might ask in making that decision: *Is the CEO's proportionate contribution to the organization 10 (100, 1,000) times greater than that of a cartoon animator at our Burbank studios or the operator of the Space Mountain ride at Disneyland?* Although asking such a question is practically unheard of in the boardrooms of giant companies, a few small- and medium-sized companies have done so and gone on to establish ratios as low as 20:1 between the compensation of their highest-paid executive and average worker. That may sound unrealistic, but when you run the numbers it makes some sense. If the average worker makes $20 an hour, the CEO in even a "low-paying" company can make a million dollars. This ratio is "unrealistic" only because the current ratio in *Fortune* 500 companies approaches 500:1.

Deliberation about the just ratio between the highest- and lowest-paid person in an organization is a good way for corporate boards and executives to begin including ethical analysis in their compensation discussions. Alas, I sincerely doubt the Disney board has ever examined the ethics of its pay policies in this way. They certainly were logically inconsistent in applying the policies they had: During good times, they had accepted Eisner's argument that he was entitled to a fat paycheck based on the enormous amount of wealth he had created for shareholders; however, during the recent lean years, they didn't then ask Eisner to pay the shareholders back for the wealth they lost. Disney is probably not much different from most large

American corporations in using distributive compensation processes reflective more of employees' relative power than on objective and ethical analyses of their relative contributions. And it is hard to do such a just and objective analysis. I sit on the compensation committee of our small company's board, and we spend considerable effort trying to define relative justice, much as Aristotle would have us do. Nonetheless, I regret we too often let *realpolitik* drive out principle: We are far more responsive to the need to create equity for the company's top executives than we are to questions of fairness for people down the line.

As Aristotle would be the first to recognize, employees must be paid market wages. However, it is untrue that markets determine the compensation of executives. In many cases, this particular market is rigged: The widespread use of compensation surveys allows executives to continually ratchet up their salaries. At the other end of the salary scale, board members understand that a company would price itself out of business if it paid its clerks as much as it pays its managers, so they tend to skip over the issue of relative justice for lower-level workers, leaving the market to determine that. But the market doesn't work in quite the same way for workers as it does for top managers and skilled professionals. Because jobs are offered to lower-level workers on a take-it-or-leave-it basis, their conditions of employment often amount to exchanges of desperation. In contrast, professionals and managers may have other employment opportunities and, as a result, some bargaining power. Granted, that's the way of the world, and corporate executives and board members can't be expected to repeal the laws of economics. However, they are not without power to increase opportunities for even first-line employees to raise their own standards of living. For example, boards can distribute stock and stock options more broadly. Although the late Sam Walton couldn't pay his Wal-Mart service workers much more than the minimum wage, he had the moral imagination to cut them into the upside by making them equity owners. CEOs and boards tend to forget there are a number of well-tested methods for objectively and fairly linking rewards to relative con-

257

tribution: profit sharing, gain sharing, ESOPs, and the like, all of which are consistent with the rules of the market.

Especially when times are bad and hard choices have to be made, top executives often protect their fair share while cutting training budgets, decreasing employee benefits, and reneging on obligations to pension funds. During the 2001–2003 recession, many American executives dealt with the problem of declining revenues by terminating large numbers of employees, then giving themselves big raises as rewards for their skill in reducing labor costs. As Aristotle notes, leaders will not pay attention to these injustices until and unless they are as concerned with what is good for others as they are with what is good for themselves. Sadly, in most corporate boardrooms, it is considered uncivil to raise issues of distributive justice, especially when these issues are unrelated to what is fair for *investors, executives, and directors themselves.* It is hard to imagine the board of a *Fortune* 500 company engaging in the Aristotelian exercise of imagining themselves in the place of those in their company, in some cases the majority, who work for $35,000 a year and less. Yet it might be useful for board members and executives, some of whom spend multiples more on their second cars than their average employee makes in a year, to ask themselves what it would be like to live on the salary of an entry-level worker: What little luxuries would they have to forgo if they were making do on $35,000, before taxes? If that exercise is asking too much, they might ask if it is indeed true that their CEO is the only qualified person in the world willing to do the job for $X million and options?

By beginning their deliberations about compensation from the perspective of trying to create a nonarbitrary relationship between contributions and rewards, not only would directors serve the cause of relative justice, they might even begin to create a more virtuous and productive sense of community among workers, managers, and owners. Here are three examples of contemporary Aristotelian business leadership to illustrate how this can happen:

❧ In 2000, Massachusetts businessman Charlie Butcher shared the proceeds of the sale of his company, to the tune of $18 million, with all 325 of his employees. He cut them into the deal proportionate to the length of their employment, giving a $55,000 check, on average, to each worker. (In contrast, and at about the same time, when Chrysler was acquired by Daimler Benz, Chrysler shareholders and executives got fat checks, but hourly workers got nothing except reduced job security.) Over the length of his long stewardship of the company, it appears Butcher had aimed to create a model work environment for employees, offering them high starting salaries, flexible workweeks, and the opportunity to switch jobs to find a personally fulfilling one. Finally, Butcher sold the company to S.C. Johnson & Co., even though he had higher offers from other companies, because the family-owned Johnson organization promised to continue the employee-friendly culture and job security he had created.

❧ In late 1996, two Taiwan-born, high-tech entrepreneurs, David Sun and John Tu, sold the Silicon Valley business they founded, Kingston Technology, to a Japanese bank for $1.5 billion. Part of the deal was that Sun and Tu would continue to run the business and reinvest a half-billion from the sale in the company to fund future growth. That was unusual, but what truly was surprising about the deal was that Sun and Tu divided $100 million of the remaining windfall, 10 percent of the sale, among their 523 employees. Significantly, Sun and Tu had been sharing 10 percent of the company's profits with employees all along. They also practiced a highly egalitarian and participative form of management in which all employees had a chance to contribute their full talents to the company. Why did they behave in such an unusually virtuous manner? "The issue is really not money," Tu told the *New York Times*, "it's how you respect people and how you treat them. It's all about trust, isn't it?" The story didn't end there. In 1998, just when the Japanese bank was due to make its last $333 million payment to Sun and Tu, there was more surprising news: The two asked the bank to forgo the payment because Kingston Technology had underperformed during the previous year. The deal was then restructured, and the postponed final payment was linked to performance measures. Why this Aristotelian display of fairness toward all stakeholders? Tu explained that profits follow in the long term when a company behaves ethically toward its partners, vendors, customers, and employees. Besides, he added, "How much money do you need?"

❧ Hourly workers spend nearly every cent they earn to pay for food and clothing, to cover their rent or mortgage, and to send their kids to college. Those needs are unremitting and constant. That's why Aaron Feuerstein, CEO of Malden Mills, kept paying weekly checks to his workers, out of his pocket, when his factory burned down in 1995 and there was no work to do for months while it was being rebuilt. Feuerstein saw the ethical difference between meeting needs and wants and between the wealth he had in excess of what he needed and the much smaller margin between his employees' savings and their bankruptcy. So Feuerstein paid until it hurt, transferring most of his accumulated wealth to his employees until they could start to earn their own keep again. Sadly, for unrelated reasons, the company ultimately filed for bankruptcy in 2001. As Aristotle said, even virtuous people need good luck.

ANOTHER EXAM

Aristotle doesn't provide a single, clear principle for the just distribution of enterprise-created wealth, nor would it be possible for anyone to formulate such a monolithic rule. He admits it's harder to distribute wealth than it is to make it. Nonetheless, here are some Aristotelian guidelines in the form of questions virtuous leaders need to ask themselves:

❧ Am I taking more in my share of rewards than my contributions warrant?

❧ Does the distribution of goods in the organization preserve the happiness of the community, or does it have a negative effect on morale or the ability of others to achieve the good?

+ Would everyone in the organization enter into the employment contract under the current terms if they truly had other choices?

+ Would we come to a different principle of allocation if all of the parties concerned were represented at the table?

Again, the only hard and fast principle of distributive justice is that fairness is most likely to arise out of a process of rational and moral deliberation among friends and equals. Prescriptively, all Aristotle says is that virtue and wisdom will certainly elude leaders who fail to engage in rigorous ethical analysis of their actions. In my own case, I have resolved to raise these ethical questions in the many business roles I play as writer, teacher, consultant, investor, and board member, no matter how weak my standing may be to do so, and no matter how unpopular it makes me.

CODA: WHY ETHICS MATTER

Unlike many contemporary Americans, Aristotle is comfortable with the language of ethics: He speaks clearly about right and wrong, virtue and vice, should and shouldn't. He advocates the virtues of duty, responsibility, accountability, prudence, and magnanimous action. He salutes the character traits of moral courage and excellence. He makes no bones about the requirement for leaders to put the interests of their followers above their own and for all of us to contribute unselfishly to the welfare of our communities. In recent times, those on the left have shied away from such language, preferring the less judgmental guise of moral relativism. And those on the right have claimed that questions of morality, while appropriate in religious and family life, have no place in the pragmatic worlds of business and politics (instead, markets should be the ultimate judge of our public actions). To both, one can only reply *Enron, WorldCom, Tyco, Global Crossing, and Arthur Andersen.*

Aristotle understands what we in America conveniently chose to forget in the heady 1990s: Free societies cannot function effectively without a strong ethical foundation. Ancient Athens was no welfare state. There was no social security, no public assistance, and no free schooling. But there were many poor and needy citizens. Thus, if an old person fell on hard times, and a poor but promising child needed schooling, it was expected they would be taken care of by "friends." Such friendship was not based on dependency or utility; instead, it was predicated on the value of respect for others and the concomitant virtue of generosity. Or so it should be, according to Aristotle. If the state did not provide for the needy, then it stood to reason the wealthy had to—and, in return, they would neither get, nor deserve, special praise for fulfilling their responsibility to their community. Aristotle could not imagine a society with a market economy that did not also have an inherent commitment to social ethics and philanthropy.

In contrast, "communist ethics" is an oxymoron (as is "fascist ethics"). In authoritarian societies, there is no charity and no need for personal or social responsibility. A virtuous citizen in an authoritarian Marxist state is simply one who obeys the law. Those who visited the former Soviet Union (or China before Deng's reforms) will recall never having to count their change at the market. Shop clerks in communist countries could be depended upon to follow the rules and do what the state said was right. In fact, there were rules for everything and severe punishment for those who broke them. There also was no social expectation that anyone would ever go beyond what was required by the law. Making an "extra effort" by helping a stranger or making a donation to a worthy social cause was viewed as crazy as making an extra effort on the job.

Since the fall of communism and the subsequent rise of market economies in formerly Stalinist and Maoist countries, the once unheard of behavioral problems of corruption, cheating, stealing, price gouging, and tax evasion have become common if not chronic. That's because there is no social expectation of, nor enculturation to, ethical norms of behavior. New laws have helped, but they have been insufficient. The conclusion to be drawn is that people have to be taught the professional, personal, and social merits of virtue. That's why new business schools in formerly communist countries spend so much time dealing with ethics, a subject that had been totally foreign to the curriculum of communist universities. And as state welfare and guaranteed employment systems have crumbled, people in formerly Marxist societies are now being forced, for the first time, to consider a role for philanthropy. (Things are even worse in the developing world, where private enterprise exists side by side with poverty and human degradation. Ethics and social responsibility simply are not on the agenda in Chad, Cambodia, and Colombia.)

Curiously, in the 1990s, ethics and social responsibility disappeared from the agenda of many American corporations, business schools, and society in general. Too many influential Americans during that era came to understand freedom to mean they owed nothing to society, as we noted with regard to community leadership. They called for drastic reductions in federal, state, and local taxes and for cutting back government programs and regulations. What they didn't do was to increase their support of charity or take responsibility for ethical and moral self-regulation of their economic enterprises. But we cannot have it both ways, as the numerous corporate scandals in the early part of the new millennium demonstrated.

Over 2,000 years ago, Aristotle argued that a strong ethical foundation was a requirement for an open society. In fact, history has shown that no advanced society can avoid trade-offs between these two alternatives: private enterprise/ethics/philanthropy/individual responsibility on the one hand, and socialism/regulation/state welfare/social entitlements on the other. The first leads to freedom and progress, the latter to tyranny and a low standard of living. Something close to that trade-off was first described in 1900 by the Social Darwinist Yale professor, William Graham Sumner, but his philosophical heirs today act as if society needs neither regulation nor self-imposed ethical discipline. Aristotle understood otherwise. His teacher, Plato, had opted for a controlled society in which paternalistic guardians would make all the political and moral decisions for a dependent populace, who would then be free to spend all their time making and spending money. In contrast, Aristotle advocated a freer society, but he warned that such a society would function only for as long as, and to the extent that, its citizens engaged in moral deliberation and then chose to pursue the path to virtue. The Athenians did not heed Aristotle's advice, and, as Edith Hamilton explains, the consequences were dire.

> In the end, more than they wanted freedom, they wanted security. They wanted a comfortable life and they lost it all— security, comfort and freedom. When the Athenians finally wanted not to give to society, but for society to give to them, when the freedom they wished for most was the freedom from responsibility, then Athenians ceased to be free.

For the sake of our cherished freedoms, we should not make the same mistake as the Athenians.

11

PHILANTHROPY

To give away money is an easy matter and in any man's power.
But to decide virtuously who to give it to, the amount to give,
when, how, and for what purpose is neither in every man's
power, nor an easy matter.

—*Aristotle*

Shortly after writing the paragraph (in chapter 9) describing Crown Fellow Donna Auguste's virtuous leadership of Freshwater Software, I discovered that Donna and her partners had sold the company. Donna has since used her portion of the proceeds to fund the Leave a Little Room Foundation, at which she carries on a variety of domestic and global philanthropic activities. For instance, in Tanzania, she is funding a source of solar electricity to provide power for lights, a vaccine refrigerator, and satellite-based e-mail for a remote hospital adjacent to the Serengeti. Her philanthropic commitment is unusual for someone still in her forties.

More typical is Michael Zaleski who, at age 55, "retired" from his investment partnership in order to start a family foundation with his wife, Caroline, an architectural historian. In a *New York Times* interview, Michael Zaleski offered three motivations for starting the $5 million foundation: to get a tax break, to support favorite charities like his alma mater, and to become involved personally in philanthropic activities. The Zaleskis are hardly alone among their generation in choosing to become philanthropists. According to the Foundation Center, there was nearly a 20 percent increase between 1999 and 2000 in the total number of family foundations in America. Not counting those affiliated with family-owned businesses, there were over 24,000 such foundations, controlling some $200 billion in assets and annually giving away $11 billion. Nor are the Zaleskis' motivations unique. The question we explore in this chapter is: *To what extent are those motivations virtuous?* In particular, we examine how Aristotelian ethical analysis can help each of us to make more virtuous charitable contributions, no matter how large or small the sums involved.

Like almost everyone I know, I wish I had more money to donate to worthy causes (to be honest, I wish I actually donated more of what I have, which is a paltry percentage of my net worth). Because an analysis of the small amounts I give would trivialize the subject, it is useful to apply Aristotle's analytical method of exploring the philanthropic behavior of bigger-than-life characters. But remember, we do so only to gain perspective on the virtue of our own behavior, to help us assess if we give enough and if we give to the most worthy causes.

Of the many traits of excellence Aristotle cites, one of the most difficult to exercise is generosity. A generous person, by definition, is giving. This virtue, Aristotle says, lies between the defect of miserliness and the excess of extravagance. Although charitable giving is a common manifestation of generosity, Aristotle says it is not necessary to engage in such acts to live virtuously, nor does giving, no matter how generous, guarantee virtue. Indeed, when Aristotle left a sum of money for charitable purposes in his will, he regarded doing so as a duty not a virtue. He took it for granted that rich people and the relatively well off like himself would be generous. In his era, Greeks who could afford to do so were expected to contribute to religious and athletic events, support drama and music festivals, and pay for public monuments and statues. Meeting those civic responsibilities was simply a duty and not a virtue that expiated one's sins or compensated for one's failure to participate in politics and philosophy. To Aristotle, it would be as absurd to say one could make up for not living a good life by acts of charity, as it would be to suggest a bank robber can compensate for villainy with a good sense of humor.

VIRTUE BEGINS WITH ASKING
THE RIGHT QUESTIONS

Aristotle would agree with the contemporary view that it's nobody's business but our own what we do with our money. After we have serviced our debts and paid our bills and taxes, we are free to invest, spend, save, or give away the remainder as we each see fit. Although not compelled to do so, many people today, as in Aristotle's era, choose to donate some of their disposable assets to charitable causes. In doing so, Aristotle says the ethical man or woman carefully considers a set of interrelated questions: *To whom, how much, when, why, how, and for what purpose should I give my money?* Before giving, the virtuous person engages in moral deliberation, attempting to answer such questions as:

- ❧ Is the recipient worthy?
- ❧ Is this the best among many worthy causes?
- ❧ How much is needed?
- ❧ Will the money really help the recipient?
- ❧ Does the recipient need more than just my money (what about my help, advice, or knowledge)?

As with all questions requiring the exercise of practical wisdom, what matters to Aristotle is our philanthropic motivation: Am I giving this money away for my good or for the good of others?

Though it is difficult to answer any of these questions, identifying motivation is the trickiest. Some people are clearly and simply generous. But for most of us, our motivations are many and mixed, and one needn't be a cynic to conclude that the following are among the reasons we make donations:

- ❧ To achieve social status and a reputation for generosity
- ❧ As displays of conspicuous consumption
- ❧ To attempt to achieve immortality
- ❧ For purposes of atonement and contrition
- ❧ It is not painful to give because we get tax breaks

At the turn of the millennium, Jean-Marie Messier, then CEO of Vivendi Universal, moved to New York from France, and he and his wife found the fastest way to gain acceptance in Manhattan society was by making large contributions to the Whitney Museum, the New York Philharmonic, and a handful of other "A-list" causes. Don't get me wrong; we all should be thankful for such useful donations. Visiting some of the institutions the Messiers supported is high among my reasons for vacationing in the Big Apple. But would Aristotle consider the Messiers' useful gifts noble in light of the social benefits they received?

In similar acts of public benefaction over the last decade, many wealthy individuals donated large sums to endow business schools and, in particular, to support the construction of business school facilities. In the development trade, these are called "naming opportunities." In fact, professional schools are among the easiest university programs to fund, and more rich people give more money to business schools, which are already the largest campus moneymakers in terms of tuition revenue, than to resource-starved undergraduate liberal arts programs. Being an indirect beneficiary of such largesse, I feel entitled to question the motives of the hand that fed me: In the case of the individual whose name graces the business school where I am employed, the gift was useful, the decision to give was freely made, and there were many resulting benefits enjoyed by students, faculty, the dean (who won praise for fund-raising prowess), and the donor himself, in whose honor the school is now named. Yet one wonders if the donor first inquired if the university had a more pressing, nobler, or harder-to-fund cause?

Consider a similar, considerably larger gift recently given by the heirs of Sam Walton's Wal-Mart fortune that was not, as far as I am aware, a naming opportunity. After considerable deliberation, the Walton family gave its money to the woefully underfunded University of Arkansas largely for the purpose of providing access to higher education for thousands of young students the university otherwise would not have been able to accommodate. How can one tell if this philanthropic act was more or less virtuous than the gift to erect a new building for my business school?

Aristotle helps us to think about the earmarks of virtuous giving by offering a few commonsense observations. First, he says the amount given is, in all regards except one, irrelevant to the question of virtue. In fact, "It is quite possible that one who gives less is more generous if his gift comes from smaller resources." That's encouraging to the vast majority of us who are neither self-made billionaires nor heirs to great fortunes. Then, he adds, people who have been virtuous throughout their lives probably would never accumulate great sums in the first place because they have a strong tendency to give and not to horde what they earn. But he is realistic. Given the behavior of the young, it isn't surprising that most people accumulate throughout middle age and don't start to think seriously about philanthropy until they are in their fifties. But no matter when we begin to give, Aristotle says the amount we give must be adequate by one measure: Rich people who give away a fortune are not virtuous if they still have a fortune left.

Those conditions noted, he says a "generous act does not depend on the amount given, but on the characteristics of the giver." Virtuous donors "give to the right people, the right amount, and do everything else that is implied in correct giving." Everything else is measured in terms of *right desire:* The only motive in virtuous giving is the good of others. Not only must the cause be noble, there can be no gain for the giver except the pleasure to give.

According to Aristotle, gifts rendered to buy honor and respect are not virtuous. He says there is no excellence in philanthropic acts that "follow the appetite for honor and self-aggrandizement" because such self-indulgence is a childlike characteristic. He warns us not to mistake the excess of magnificence for the virtue of generosity. People building monuments to themselves, even when endowing such worthy causes as concert halls, hospitals, and museums, are doing so for their own good and, thus, are engaged in what he calls "vulgar" displays of wealth. In Aristotle's day, kings and conquerors built palaces and pyramids to create a sense of awe among contemporaries and in hopes of establishing their immortality throughout generations to come. He says virtuous people do not engage in such conspicuous consumption. After your death, if others decide to honor your generosity by putting your name on the opera house you funded, that's fine and fitting; just don't claim virtue when you fund it as a naming opportunity.

Because Aristotle feels that achieving immortality is out of our hands and dependent on the judgment of future generations, he would ask, on seeing a name on my business school, *For what noble deed is that person being honored?* Would the faculty, students, or business community have nominated the donor for such an honor based on his contributions to business, to the local community, or whatever? Or did he simply decide to pony-up to honor himself?

Of course, it is almost always better to give than not to give. Aristotle believes it is even worse to be a miser than it is to build monuments to one's self. Dying rich and leaving it all to the kids and the government is the least-generous act because it evidences both miserliness and extravagance, but wasting money while we are alive on unworthy expenditures is not much better. That's why Aristotle has little respect for rich people who spend fortunes on their daughters' weddings while giving pennies to charity (damn, there's another low grade on my ethical report card).

Even giving appropriate amounts to worthy causes isn't noble in Aristotle's eyes if the donor hasn't applied practical wisdom to the choice. He would ask if potential donors to museums have inquired if there is a decent community hospital before they choose to support arts institutions, which, in the main, serve people who can afford to support them themselves. This doesn't mean cultural contributions can't be virtuous; instead, Aristotle says potential donors should learn to make distinctions between those that are and those that aren't.

Consider three comparable acts of giving to museums, all in Southern California: (1) Oil magnate Armand Hammer funded a museum on Wilshire Boulevard near UCLA for which there was no demand or apparent need (there was no substantial art collection to house). Moreover, he used Occidental Petroleum's shareholders' money to erect the imposing edifice, which he named in honor of himself. (2) Ten miles or so east on the same boulevard, oil magnate Robert O. Anderson funded a wing for the Los Angeles County Museum of Art, at the request of the museum trustees, in order to house the institution's collection of modern art. He used Atlantic Richfield's shareholders' money to erect this monumental building, which he allowed to be named for himself. (3) In nearby Pasadena, packaged-foods magnate Norton Simon used his own money to buy an existing museum that he renovated to house the first-rate art collection he had assembled and paid for himself. He left the Norton Simon museum and its collection as a public bequest.

The ethical distinctions between these three examples are subtle but not obscure. The issues involved in a CEO using corporate money to build a monument to himself were clear enough to the boards of Occidental and

Atlantic Richfield to precipitate the dismissals of Hammer and Anderson from the employ of those corporations. But that's obvious stuff. More difficult, but not impossible, at least for Hammer, Anderson, and Simon themselves to have assessed, was the degree to which they weighed alternative ways, means, conditions, and stipulations in making their gifts. For all charitable contributions, Aristotle says donors must first assess their own motivations, "For whose ultimate benefit am I doing this?" and then ask, "Is what I am creating 'suitable' (not showy), is it 'worthy of the expense' (necessary), and 'a proper object' (useful)?" And "Am I just giving money, or am I also giving of myself?" Surely there was more than a small degree of vanity involved in Norton Simon's gift; nonetheless, it seems more worthy of praise on Aristotle's scoreboard than the other two bequests.

DIVINE LOVE

The Greek root of the word philanthropy, *philia*, means, as noted in the context of friendship, the "love of others." Because there are numerous ways one can demonstrate the love of others besides doing charitable acts, Aristotle says philanthropy is not a necessary virtue. Obviously, a poor person who has little to give nonetheless can lead a virtuous life. But if we choose to give, the act requires "divine love" in order to be altruistic. Divine love involves acting for the good of others and giving of oneself.

Aristotle noted that most of what passed for philanthropy in his era lacked the element of divine love. Although things have changed over the passing millennia, it still is easy for those who donate their names and time to fool themselves into thinking they are acting for others. Recently, I witnessed such an act of self-delusion: A trustee of a sizable bequest decided to divert a substantial sum from the educational program it was supporting into an annual prize she had the honor of personally bestowing on famous individuals. In so doing, she starved the worthy educational program in order to gain the pleasure of hobnobbing with notables, individuals who, not incidentally, did not need the prize or the money.

The *New York Times* notes there are now nearly 100 such annual international prizes, most of fairly recent origin, offering awards of $100,000 or more. For example, the annual million-dollar Dan David Prize is awarded to an individual "for contributions to the improvement of the world." It turns out Mr. David is an entrepreneur who can easily afford this route to name recognition. The first recipient of his prize was another wealthy but more famous entrepreneur, which raises a series of ethical issues related to such high-profile awards: Are they merely marketing gimmicks? Is their purpose to enable the donor to bask in the reflected glory of the recipient? Do they go to people who don't need either the money or the recognition? Do they siphon funds away from more worthy causes? For instance, if prize money goes to an individual, it may be taxed and a large part end up in government coffers; instead, if the money goes to a nonprofit organization as a grant, the entire, nontaxed sum might be put to a worthy cause. Aristotelian moral deliberation is valuable because it helps us make distinctions between the good and the bad or, more practically, the better and the worse among such awards. The Nobel Prize, regardless of the motivation of its original donor, seems noble because the worthiness of its recipients is the subject of serious deliberation. But one might question the motivation of the donor of the Templeton Prize because, in order to garner maximum publicity, the amount given is recalculated annually to exceed the dollar value of the Noble Prize. (The donor says the reason he keeps ratcheting up the prize money is to show that the spiritual accomplishments he rewards are more valuable than the materialistic ones rewarded by the Nobel committees.)

LAST REFUGE OF THE SCOUNDREL?

Aristotle tells us charity is always good, but it may not be virtuous if a donor acts charitably for the wrong reasons. In the early part of the 20th century, aging business moguls often engaged in philanthropy to atone for abuses of corporate power committed in their names when they were younger. Alfred Nobel, who made his fortune as a dynamite manufacturer, sought public "rebranding" through the establishment of a peace prize in his name. Doubtless, it was better for him to put his money to good ends rather than to spend it in acts of conspicuous consumption (like William Randolph Hearst's anachronistic castle). But is such atonement-seeking virtuous?

When used to buy a good name, philanthropy may be the last refuge of the scoundrel. In the era of the robber barons, Andrew Carnegie, J. D. Rockefeller, Andrew Mellon, and J. P. Morgan famously sought to expiate real, observed, supposed, and imputed sins by giving money away. Not only did they seek respectability in the eyes of the public through philanthropy, they established foundations for the express or implicit purpose of winning back their souls. Two of the greatest philanthropists of the 20th century, Carnegie and Rockefeller, gave away fortunes as acts of atonement and to win honor after lengthy business careers in which they had earned the enmity of their employees, competitors, and business associates.

Rockefeller, a deeply religious man, sought to atone for decades of intemperate business practices that had made him both rich and reviled. In the 1880s, his Standard Oil trust had gained a virtual monopoly in the domestic market, and he had been repeatedly warned about the potential consequences of the growing hostility toward himself and the trust. Even so warned, Rockefeller did not halt the practices that made him the object of scorn among his employees, customers, competitors, suppliers, and dealers. J. D.'s moral defense of his actions was more creative than contrite. Years later he wrote, "I did not choose or seek to be the recipient of such wealth. It has not been the greatest happiness." Clearly the first sentence was disingenuous; did the Devil force the money on Rockefeller? But photos of Rockefeller as an old man cause us to believe he was telling the truth in the second sentence. And much has been written about him since to confirm he wasn't greatly happy. Nor, apparently, was the philanthropist son who followed closely in his footsteps and whose life ended in a sanitarium.

Not until long after the Supreme Court ruled his trust illegal in 1911 did Rockefeller begin the philanthropic activities through which he sought to scour his blemished reputation. His charitable acts were driven by concern for his reputation and his soul; as far as we know, his giving involved no Aristotelian ethical deliberations. Although his money was put to good use, his motivations were not virtuous, and thus, as Aristotle would have predicted, his philanthropy did not make him happy. Indeed, Aristotle admits it is devilishly difficult to make charity virtuous until and unless a philanthropist has developed the habit of giving based on the exercise of practical wisdom. To Rockefeller's credit, he and his son raised the Rockefeller grandchildren to behave not as the old man did but as he preached, and many of them grew up to become virtuous donors. Even so, it took several generations for the Rockefellers to learn how to engage in effective moral deliberation about philanthropy. In the late 1960s, one of John D.'s grandchildren hired a young lawyer to ghostwrite a book on the subject of his philosophy of giving. In their first session together, the lawyer asked the obvious question: "Sir, can you give me a general view of your beliefs about philanthropy?" The Rockefeller answered: "Young man, if I knew the answer to that question, I would not have needed to hire you."

In contrast, Andrew Carnegie thought deeply about the issue and developed a logical and morally defensible theory of philanthropy. Convinced of the Aristotelian precept that "it is a sin to die rich," the Scottish-born steel baron believed one should spend the first half of one's life amassing a fortune, the second half giving it all away. Unlike the intemperate J. D. Rockefeller, Carnegie's moral weakness was a lack of self-discipline. Throughout his business career, he acted in ways he knew were morally wrong. At age 33, Carnegie had written in his diary "$50,000 per annum . . . Beyond this never earn . . . but spend the surplus each year for benevolent purposes . . . the amassing of great wealth is the worst species of idolatry." For the next 3 decades, the great Scot dedicated his every moment to the pursuit of "the worst species of idolatry." In the process, he let nothing stand in the way of amassing great wealth. In 1892, he even ordered the use of violence against his own striking workers.

Aristotle would have questioned Carnegie's virtue. To the Ancient, the source of a donor's wealth must be virtuous in order for his gifts to be virtuous. A drug dealer can't become virtuous by giving away his ill-gotten gains. While Aristotle doesn't address issues of business misconduct or whether dirty money can be "scrubbed" in subsequent generations by virtuous children (like the Rockefellers) or by virtuous administrators (like those who run today's Carnegie foundations), he does consider the issue of late-in-life atonement. He says it is highly unlikely that past evil can be expiated by subsequent, albeit noble, philanthropy.

Nonetheless, Carnegie's claim to philanthropic virtue was stronger than Rockefeller's. The Scot's atonement seems to have been genuine, and, second, the charitable causes he supported involved moral analysis based on the needs of recipients. His overarching, near-Aristotelian principle was to support causes from which "the masses" reap the principal benefit. Indeed, he educated himself in order to develop his practical wisdom, which he then applied to what were arguably the most creative and effective philanthropic acts of his era. Carnegie gave away his money both wisely (he donated $55 million to build public libraries around the world in an era when a dollar would buy several quality hardback books) and thoughtfully (he gave seed money to start the first pension fund for university professors). The latter act illustrates the ethically creative way Carnegie worked as a philanthropist. While serving as a trustee of Cornell University, Carnegie observed professors meeting classes until their dying day. When he inquired why profs, many in their eighties, some infirm and dotty, were still on the job, he was told they had not been able to save enough on their meager salaries to afford to retire. Since even the few well-endowed colleges in the early 1900s could not pay their faculties well or offer them pensions, Carnegie developed the solution of giving seed money to create a private, nonprofit retirement fund for professors. Eventually, this fund would become self-financing as the result of

276

subsequent contributions by educational institutions and professors themselves. In creating Teacher's Insurance (today's TIAA-CREF), he made it possible for the thinking class to retire in relative comfort.

Because of his unusually imaginative giving, Carnegie came the closest among the robber barons to being a virtuous philanthropist. Unlike Rockefeller, Carnegie practiced what he preached. In Aristotelian terms, he warned his fellow millionaires "the man who dies rich thus dies disgraced" and, by his own terms, went on to die full of grace, having dispensed with his entire fortune well before his death in 1919. Unlike today's philanthropists, Carnegie received no tax breaks from his giving. However, he did buy a share of immortality thanks to the ongoing Carnegie foundations; and, to the extent such honor was his motivation, his gifts lacked Aristotelian virtue. The Ancient's admonition that donors are not virtuous when they dangle the possibility of gifts to encourage fawning and flattering may have disqualified Carnegie, as well. Nonetheless, today's philanthropists could do worse than study the good works of Andrew Carnegie.

277

Why didn't the public at the time embrace the efforts of Carnegie, Rockefeller, and others who, in old age, showered society with munificence? As Aristotle might have told Carnegie, he and his peers failed to buy forgiveness because dying poor is only one, small aspect of virtue. The real test is *How did you live?* That's the test the public seems to use. Carnegie et al., unfortunately, waited until the ends of their lives before seeking virtue, thus recalling the prayer of a man facing temptation in the form of a voluptuous woman who was, alas, not his wife: "Lord, make me virtuous, but not just yet." The public could neither forget nor forgive Carnegie and Rockefeller for getting rich at the expense of weaker business partners, using ethically questionable business tactics, and, worse, mistreating workers. Indeed, throughout history, there are few examples of formerly bad people who successfully bought respectability through philanthropy, but that hasn't stopped people from trying.

Financier and convicted felon Michael Milken is following in the great tradition of the robber barons. The Milken family foundations' Web site displays photos of the philanthropist in the company of Jimmy Carter, Colin Powell, Kofi Anan, and other notables to advance the impression that Milken is a virtuous man who bestows largesse on worthy people. In fact, many Milken donations do go to worthy causes; unfortunately, other gifts appear to be made for the purpose of presenting himself in a positive light. His motivation is often transparent: He wants to buy back his good name. Unlike Carnegie, Milken's attempts to buy respectability through philanthropy show little sign of being informed by practical wisdom. His gifts to educational institutions often come with the expectation that Milken will be invited to speak before students or at public events where he may subtly plead the case for his innocence. He thus uses the prospect of a gift as a means to making recipients subservient to his agenda. Aristotle would ask if his choice of causes to fund is influenced by that motive, and, if so, does he then choose the less over the more worthy?

Worse, from an Aristotelian perspective, Milken has demonstrated no public contrition for the acts of financial manipulation that led to his conviction. He and some of his supporters continue to argue he "did no wrong" legally, while the prosecutor in the case, Rudolph Giuliani, argues otherwise. Whichever way one comes down on the legal questions involved, there is little doubt Milken's acts were ethically wrong. As *New York Times* writer Floyd Norris noted when Milken was being considered for a pardon in 2002, subsequently denied by President Clinton, he "has never faced up to the reality of the way he abused power."

Aristotle says we are incapable of doing just acts without being just ourselves, and to do just acts, we must choose to do them consciously, habitually, and with true charitable intent: "We can say that some people who do just acts are not, for all that, just—one must do them as a result of choice, and for the sake of the acts themselves." So when Aristotle asks us to consider "What is the point of being virtuous?" he expects we will reply, "because virtue is splendid, fine, and noble." If we have that disposition to do noble things, we ennoble our acts of charity.

In contrast, morally unreflective people tend to do good things "because virtue pays." Colin Powell told *Time* that business leaders should give because it is in their self-interest to do so: "If you want to keep making a profit, then you've got to keep growing the society, so that you have people out there who are workers and consumers." That's a riff on Henry Ford's 1907 justification for paying his workers the unheard of sum of $5 a day: so they could afford to buy a Ford. That didn't make old Henry virtuous; it made him shrewd. So when the likes of Michael Milken engage in an act of charity in order to meet their business or personal ends, their base motives cheapen the good deed and turn it into a less-than-noble, albeit useful, act. As a postscript, we should note that Powell, during the years when he was out of public service, failed to heed his own mistaken advice: His own charitable acts were, in fact, virtuous by Aristotelian standards.

The Aristotelian is made particularly uneasy when the lately virtuous justify their reformed behavior using arguments inconsistent with their life-long principles and beliefs. There is the faint odor of hypocrisy when former sinners tie themselves up in theological knots trying to offer moral justification for newly adopted charitable roles. Throughout his long life, Rockefeller wore his Baptist faith on his sleeve, yet, in the end, sought redemption through good works, a practice not necessarily in keeping with the tenets of fundamental Protestantism, which, to oversimplify, state that redemption comes through accepting Jesus as God. Similarly, Michael Milken, who often explains his philanthropy with reference to Jewish tradition, at the same time ignores a basic principle of that tradition: Virtuous charity is anonymous.

Like the ancient Hebrews, Aristotle says donor anonymity is a sign of virtue. This may raise some questions about the motivations of high-profile celebrity philanthropists who advocate causes directly related to their personal agendas and personal medical problems, while enjoying the limelight that falls on them as the result of their "good works." This is a complex issue, as Paul Newman, who has raised some $150 million for charity over the last 2 decades by selling Newman's Own salad dressing and other food products, explains.

One thing that really bothers me is what I call "noisy philan-thropy." Philanthropy ought to be anonymous, but in order for this to be successful, you have to be noisy. Because when a shopper walks up to the shelf and says, "Should I take this one or that one?" you've got to let her know that the money goes to a good purpose. So there goes all your anonymity and the whole thing you really cherish.

One can see how celebrities like Newman might be virtuous in lending their names to raise public awareness of worthy causes, but the question for each of us to examine is our own personal motivation for associating ourselves with any cause, no matter how worthy. According to Aristotle, we must each ask: *Who is the real beneficiary of my act?*

EASY VIRTUE?

Aristotle's standards for virtuous giving are extremely high. Short of con-sciously developing a theory of philanthropy based on the needs of recipients in which the sole motivation to give is the good of others, it is hard to imagine a philanthropic act that would qualify. Alternatively, a donor would have to turn over her money, anonymously and without strings, to philanthropic trustees or administrators who were themselves virtuous. By setting such high standards, Aristotelians run the risk of discouraging people from giving. That wasn't the Ancient's intent. Instead, as with all attempts to achieve the com-plete good, he is warning us that we won't reach our goal if we don't subject our assumptions to rigorous moral testing.

When assessing virtue of any kind, a key metric for Aristotle is complete-ness. He is not interested in a little bit of virtue, partial justice, or an almost good life. So when people engage in worthy acts of charity to advance a selfish agenda—to buy atonement, social status, celebrity, or whatever—he doesn't say it is wrong; he simply warns that the act is not completely virtuous. Similarly, donors who exploit loopholes in the tax code lack complete virtue. One well-meaning group, called New Tithing, offers advice to the wealthy on how to make charity almost costless. The organization shows how a married couple with $18 million in investments could give up to $1 million per year and not experience erosion of their asset base (albeit, they would have a reduced amount of disposable income). Couples who could afford to give away $1 million might only be parting with $120,000 per annum, after taxes are factored in.

In light of this, one wonders why the rich don't give more, because, with a little tax consulting, the act can be virtually painless. An article in a glossy magazine sent gratis to American Express Platinum Card holders outlines how one can create a Charitable Lead Trust (CLUT) that offers a dandy inducement to giving. If a sum of approximately $1 million is well invested in a CLUT, it can throw off about 5 percent per year to charity and—here's the incentive—more than $2 million eventually can come back to the donor's family. CLUTs bestow benefits on many, but Aristotle would award no points for virtue to those who establish them.

Similarly, Aristotle might question the motives of latter-day Fords and Rockefellers who create charitable foundations in their own names that are designed to last forever, or as long as tax laws remain unchanged. He would particularly question the virtue of such foundations when they accumulate assets faster than they pay them out. But he would look favorably on the current philanthropic practice of quick distribution of assets with the intent of solving pressing social problems, instead of creating high-overhead institutions.

At last count, there were nearly 2.5 million millionaires and 267 billionaires in the United States, many freshly minted during the 1990s. According to a *Time* cover story, almost all of the newly rich among those ranks are starting to think about philanthropy. Tax advisors have counseled many of them to give their money away, "otherwise the government will take it." Yet choosing to direct the expenditure of their own money, instead of leaving that choice up to Uncle Sam, seems more an act of good sense than of virtue. While Aristotle never heard of a tax break, little harm is done in extending his reasoning to this issue: Taking advantage of a tax break does not disqualify a donor from being virtuous, but, by Aristotelian ethical standards, tax avoidance cannot be the purpose of giving. Since Aristotle's key metric of virtue is motivation, he might find the uses of tax breaks self-serving rather than altruistic.

Nonetheless, we now have tax laws, and as a result, the ethics of giving are more complicated today than in the Ancient's era. Here's an example of a complex contemporary moral issue related to taxes, which Aristotle could never have anticipated. In 2002, the United States Senate acted to repeal inheritance taxes in the future. Arguably, the vote of Senator Dianne Feinstein of California allowed the bill to pass by the narrowest of margins. Apparently, Feinstein had received considerable pressure from her Silicon Valley constituents, who argued it was unfair they couldn't leave their hard-earned fortunes to their heirs. About the same time, Bard College president Leon Botstein wrote that many of the largest gifts made to colleges and other nonprofits are motivated by the existence of the inheritance tax, because many wealthy people would rather leave a large part of their estates to charity than to pay taxes to the government (if they don't have the third option of leaving it to their heirs tax free). Hence, when the new tax law eventually comes into full force, loyal Stanford grads who petitioned Feinstein to ax the inheritance tax will have succeeded in abolishing the incentive to leave bequests to their beloved university. If one advocates the value of philanthropic donations to private higher education, is it consistent to work at the same time to abolish the prime incentive for taxpayers to give to the same? 'Tis a puzzlement.

Of course, as Andrew Carnegie demonstrated, some wealthy individuals will donate their money absent tax incentives. Moreover, from what Carnegie wrote, one is encouraged to believe his philanthropic decisions would not have been influenced by the existence of inheritance tax laws. Carnegie believed rich parents did their children no favor by making them rich. He held to an Aristotelian belief in the value of individual merit and concluded that children are better off morally if they have to earn their own livelihoods. Carnegie believed the duty of parents is to educate children so they have the moral

282

foundation and parental role models to act virtuously themselves. Hence, the current phasing out of inheritance taxes raises fascinating questions: How many wealthy people will be like Carnegie and continue to give; how many will be like the Rockefellers and teach their children to be responsible philanthropists; and how many will leave their fortunes to ne'er-do-well offspring to fritter away money that might have gone to good purposes?

Aristotle says painless giving is not likely to be as virtuous as when the act involves sacrifice. Although big sums may be involved in the gifts of the fabulously rich, to Aristotle it is less virtuous for a billionaire to give $100 million than it is for a working stiff to give $100 if the latter sum represents a larger share of the working person's disposable income or savings. Though facts show that rich Americans give a higher percentage of their incomes than people with average incomes, the relative difference is smaller than one might expect. Boston College's Social Welfare Institute reports those with fortunes in excess of $10 million give away 9 percent of their annual income, those worth $5 to $10 million give 4.8 percent, those in the $1 to $5 million range give 3.8 percent, and the national average is 2.2 percent. Now, is 2 percent of $25,000 ($500) more virtuous than 4 percent of $5 million ($200,000)? Which hurts more? That's a subjective call; but, according to Aristotle, proportionality is a valid measure of the virtue involved in an act of charity, as it is with all ethical acts.

VENTURE PHILANTHROPY: AN OXYMORON?

Issues of philanthropic motivation and right desire are being raised today in ethically puzzling ways. In an interview with *Fortune,* the head of the Community Foundation of Silicon Valley, Peter de Courcy Hero, claims the argument "Giving is a moral obligation—you're rich, they're poor; you have to give your money away"—"doesn't fly" in the high-tech community. Thus, Hero says he has had to invent other arguments to encourage charitable contributions in the Valley, home to some 75,000 millionaires, but where a full quarter of households with incomes over $100,000 give less than $500 per year. His approach has been to repackage philanthropy with slick marketing in which the language and principles of venture capitalists are applied to social problems. Fundable projects are presented in terms of risk assessment, and cost effectiveness is offered as the measure of relative worthiness. Similarly, *Time*'s special section on "The New Philanthropy" concludes:

> This new breed of philanthropist scrutinizes each charitable cause like a potential business investment, seeking maximum return in terms of social impact—for example by counting the number of children taught to read or the number inoculated against malaria.

Modern Aristotelians are realists and appreciate that it may take a little hype to market even the noblest ideas, and Aristotle himself says it is both prudent and virtuous to make sure the money one gives is used wisely and for the intended purpose. So the New Philanthropy's measures of efficiency and effectiveness are relevant in moral deliberations about alternative uses of charitable dollars. But surely there is also danger that marketing, economic, and engineering concepts will drive out ethical principles. At best, the New Philanthropy seems based more on practicality than morality. According to *Time*, venture capitalist John Doerr makes philanthropic decisions the same way he makes investment decisions in start-ups, stressing such issues as "pricing, revenue assumptions, and sustainability." Though bringing some efficiency to the nonprofit world is a plus, from an Aristotelian perspective, the rationale for charitable giving is nonetheless different from investing in a business. If the two activities were identical, solutions to all social problems could be turned into self-sustaining businesses, and there would be no need for charities.

This isn't to say Doerr doesn't do considerable good as a philanthropist and isn't a positive influence on potential donors. For example, a middle-class professional friend tells me he has changed the way he gives in order to get more bang for his buck: "I used to give a lot of small donations, twenty-five here, a hundred there, which got lost in the administrative noise of receiving organizations. Now, I have shifted my strategy to concentrate my giving on one or two organizations where I can make a difference." This makes sense for relatively small givers, and I am considering following suit myself. But in Aristotle's view, doing so will increase the effectiveness of my giving, not its virtue.

Moreover, thinking about philanthropy as a form of venture capitalism obscures the fact that the neediest causes almost always are the least efficient in market terms. When basketball star Dikembe Mutumbo was interviewed in 2000 by CBS's Ed Bradley, he described himself as a businessman; when Bradley asked him how he justified building a hospital in Zaire in terms of business efficiency and return, Mutumbo shook his head and explained there's "a difference between a business proposition and a gift." That difference is enormous and fundamental, and it is blurred by the New Philanthropists to the point where the act of "venture giving" may not be virtuous.

Clearly, there is no virtue in throwing money away, but should charity be based on measures of cost effectiveness? The Gates Foundation's boast that it had only 25 employees compared with 525 at the Ford Foundation could be irrelevant. For example, charity A's efforts to distribute free movie tickets to the poor may be more cost effective than charity B's soup kitchen, but should we therefore choose to fund the former over the latter? Although economic measures may be appropriate in evaluating charitable activities, in many instances they are neither the relevant nor the primary metrics that should be used. Investments in medical research are particularly difficult to justify using conventional metrics. Billions have been spent, so far without great results, on finding cures for cancer. Though these investments have not been particularly effective, few would argue they were wasted or shouldn't continue to be made.

Using conventional methods and measures, it's also difficult to demonstrate justifiable returns on most investments in education. It is hard to imagine a more inefficient institution than Stanford University if one uses

285

common cost-effectiveness measures such as weighing the vast amounts of capital invested and the large number of faculty employed against such outputs as useful knowledge created and imparted. Because my own university would fare no better against those criteria, the example is offered only to show that some important activities are inherently inefficient, like opera companies and systems of mass transportation, and some are inherently ineffective, such as university research and teaching. But the inefficiency and ineffectiveness of such institutions doesn't automatically equate with moral unworthiness.

In 2002, then U.S. Treasury Secretary Paul O'Neill inadvertently demonstrated the shortcomings of applying business metrics to the evaluation of social programs. O'Neill, who had demonstrated intellectual excellence as CEO of Alcoa, revealed himself to be morally tone deaf on a fact-finding trip in Africa with rock star Bono. According to the *New York Times*' Bill Keller, "Mr. O'Neill talks about 'productivity growth' as the litmus test of whether aid is effective . . . [while] James Wolfensen, president of the World Bank, notes that Mr. O'Neill seems to be setting a standard of effectiveness we don't even apply to our own government." By insisting on applying inappropriate metrics to programs designed to help poor people in the underdeveloped world, O'Neill was blinded to the demonstrably positive results of such aid programs as education for girls, rural roads, birth control, clean drinking water, vaccination, and financial credit for farmers and small businesspeople. O'Neill was right, the United States has thrown billions away in aid to prop up corrupt dictators like Zaire's Mobuto Sese Seko, but it doesn't follow that smaller amounts given to NGOs and democratic governments for the activities cited above aren't effective or efficient *if* the measure is improvement in quality of life of the poorest of the poor.

Ironically, efforts to market social programs in business terms are probably less efficient than old-fashioned moral suasion. As impulsive as Ted Turner's $1 billion cash contribution to the United Nations may have been, it was efficient in that it involved no administrative overhead, it was big enough to make a difference, and it went directly to programmatic activities (instead of creating a monument to the donor). Most significant, the gift was effective in achieving Turner's goal of "leverage." It shamed other billionaires into giving big bucks to unpopular but worthy causes. One might also add that it was courageous for a business leader to support a cause as reviled by most of his peers as is the United Nations.

Moreover, Bono and Turner may be more effective than venture philanthropy's marketing sorts in clarifying for potential donors the difference between a useful and a noble gift. Prior to 2000, Bill Gates, like many other high-tech multimillionaires, had not been deeply involved in philanthropy; to the extent he was, his charitable acts were limited to donating computers, and cynics say the funding of the Bill and Melinda Gates foundation coincided rather too neatly with the bad press he was receiving during the Microsoft anti-trust case. Doubtless, Gates had been a prisoner of his own background, believing the biggest problem in the developing world was "bridging the digital divide." Now, thanks to educational efforts by Bono, Turner, and others, he sees the world through the eyes of those on the receiving end of his generosity and, in the process, has come to understand that the wretched of the earth need food, clothing, shelter, and, above all, health care before they need laptops. He now says he was "naïve—very naïve"—for having believed computers were the answer to the world's most pressing social problems. Gates explains:

> That's why my wife, Melinda, and I decided to make polio eradication one of the primary goals of [our] Foundation. And once polio has been wiped out, just as smallpox was eradicated in 1977, we want to reduce or eliminate other diseases. . . . Toward this goal, we have made a $750 million commitment to the Global Fund for Children's Vaccines and have joined with UNICEF, the World Health Organization, the United Nations, Ted Turner and many other organizations, individuals and governments who have made remarkable strides in this direction.

And Gates echoed Turner's courage when, in 2002, he chose to address the World Economic Forum on the subject of "AIDS in Africa," a topic not on the radar screens of the assembled business leaders, and not one likely to win him social approbation among those who had come to hear him pontificate on the miracles of the computer age. Moreover, Gates now publicly dares to ask executives the Aristotelian question: "Do people have a clear idea what it is like to live on $1 a day?"

GOOD FOR ME, NOT SO GOOD FOR THEM

It is obviously much easier to raise money for popular causes, for causes that benefit "people like us," and for causes that are close to home than it is for causes that involve dreadful suffering and disease among exotic peoples in distant lands. When I lived in Aspen, I recall attending a successful fund-raiser in support of a local community arts center. At the end of the event, in which hundreds of thousands were raised, the donors (most of whom had first homes in such metropolitan locales as Dallas, Chicago, and Los Angeles) congratulated each other on their public-spirited generosity in support of the art classes they took during their summer sojourns in the Rockies. Aristotle would ask whether those donors were as generous to arts programs in the depressed inner cities of their hometowns?

The Community Foundation of Silicon Valley now gives about $1 million a week to worthy groups in neighboring communities in Santa Clara and San Mateo counties. Although many of those recipients are quite needy, Aristotle would ask if they are needier than people who live a few miles farther north in depressed Richmond and central Oakland, let alone people in Africa, Latin America, and Asia? To address this difficult question in a disciplined way requires more than metrics of efficiency and effectiveness; it requires the very moral deliberation Mr. Hero says "doesn't fly" in Silicon Valley.

The New Philanthropists' metric of "risk assessment" may be a good measure misapplied. By adopting this measure, donors are looking to invest in charitable activities they think are likely to work, much as they would seek to invest only in new business ventures for which there is a reasonable likelihood of a return. Yet if one applies Aristotelian analysis to the activities of, say, the Ford Foundation, the most ethically sound projects it funds are ones that governments and other risk-averse organizations can't or won't fund precisely because they have a seemingly low probability of success. Often, the perceived undesirability of such programs is because they are controversial, unorthodox, or innovative approaches that are "wrong" only in that they haven't been tried. Thus, the ability to engage in truly creative funding may be the strongest rationale for the tax-exempt status enjoyed by private charities.

Philanthropy becomes truly noble when donors put aside preconceived notions of what recipients need in order to help beneficiaries invent new ways to help themselves. Over a century ago, Jane Addams argued that noble philanthropists involve recipients in the definition of their needs. In *The Metaphysical Club,* Louis Menand describes how Addams formed her philanthropic philosophy while inventing the field of social work on Chicago's mean streets:

> She found that the people she was trying to help had better ideas about how their lives might be improved than she and her colleagues did. She came to believe that any method of philanthropy or reform premised on top-down assumptions— or more simply, that philanthropy is a unilateral act of giving by the person who has to the person who has not—is inefficient and inherently false.

To put this in perspective, we might note that practical activities like philanthropy rank below engaging in the life of the mind on Aristotle's hierarchy of virtues. Why? Because he believes first things come first; in particular, one must have a clear understanding of a problem and a clear sense of what one should do to solve it before acting. The first order for philanthropists is to understand that the purpose of their actions is to create conditions under which others can realize their own potential. Aristotle argues that we cannot realize the potential of others for them; all we can do is remove the obstacles preventing them from doing virtuous things for themselves. Hence, the question a philanthropist must ask is the same one a virtuous politician or business leader must ask: "What can I do to provide conditions in which others can pursue happiness?" The philanthropist begins by asking what others need, indeed, by asking *them* what they need.

Asking such questions, Bill Gates discovered basic needs must be met before people can begin to achieve their potential. However, among many wealthy donors, there is little interest in the unglamorous charities that provide the basic food, clothing, and shelter poor people need before they can help themselves. Of the $212 billion that individuals, foundations, and corporations donated in 2001, I calculate that less than 20 percent went directly to programs addressing the basic needs of the poor. Instead, many wealthy techies gave computers to schools, an activity, which, if not self-serving, is morally unimaginative. And if the real problem is that kids can't read, write, or do math, such gifts aren't even particularly effective when compared with such alternatives as David Guggenhime's tutoring program.

On the subject of charity, Larry Ellison suffers the confusion common to others in his neighborhood. For years, his pet project was giving schools inexpensive "network computers" he had been trying to sell to the world, unsuccessfully, as a business venture. Abandoning that, Ellison later told *Time* he could do more good investing in for-profit start-ups than he could through philanthropy. He asked rhetorically: "Which did more good for the world, the Ford Motor Company or the Ford Foundation? That's an interesting question."

It is also the wrong one because, although both Ford organizations have done great good, their purposes and methods cannot be equated. The act and consequence of giving (I do this for you, for your benefit, at my expense, and without expectation of thanks or reward) is completely different from the act and consequence of investing (I do this for me to make a profit, understanding that you, too, may benefit as an unintended consequence of my self-interested action). Thus, the good done by the Ford Motor Company, in terms of job and wealth creation and contributions to community tax rolls, is a consequence of its business activity, not its purpose.

For the record, Ellison heads *Business Week*'s list of "cheapskates," having given only 0.4 percent of his total wealth thru 2002, compared with Bill Gates's 60 percent and growing. *Business Week* asked Ellison, "Do you ever think about competing with Bill Gates in philanthropy?" He replied:

> I've got very strong feelings about philanthropy. For one thing, it's measured entirely the wrong way. Let me posit the following question: Mr. A, sitting over there, has given $10 billion to cure cancer. Mr. B, sitting over here, has given $10,000 to cure cancer. Mr. B cures cancer. Mr. A does not. Who is the biggest philanthropist? We measure philanthropy by how much money you waste. We measure the size of your donation, not results.

Ellison's "strong feelings" on the subject are, apparently, neither channeled nor consistent. When asked by *Time* to explain his motivations for engaging in philanthropy, he answered, "Why do I do this? It's a strategy for happiness. If you're on the road to self-esteem, it's not about accumulating as much money as possible. The best way is to help someone else." According to *Time,* he thinks the best way to do that "is by making virtue profitable." So he is now onto a new "philanthropic" venture, a large investment in a for-profit Israeli corporation searching for a cancer cure. When asked about his motivation, he answered, "What do you think is cooler, being the richest guy on earth or helping find a cure for cancer?" In contrast, one can't help but think of Oracle's late cofounder, Bob Miner, who created a foundation to give his money away anonymously.

ANOTHER TEST

It is time for us to go back to Aristotle's ethical tests of philanthropy found at the beginning of this chapter. I leave it to the readers' consciences to test the ethics of their own giving. Having done so myself caused me to rethink the motivations for my own small effort in support of the Fine Arts Museums of San Francisco and reluctantly to conclude that there is little virtue in the act. I give because I enjoy going to the museums and because, when I was young, I had spent many hours in rapt study of the Rembrandts then hanging in the old De Young Museum a few blocks from where I grew up. Over some 20 years, I never paid for the pleasure of entering the museum. So my donations are, in fact, payback and a self-serving investment to ensure that my daughters will have the same opportunity I enjoyed. Besides, I get a tax write-off, free admission, catalogues, opening night social galas, discounts at the museum store, and my name etched in the wall when the new De Young opens in 2005! So, after asking myself some of Aristotle's probing ethical questions, my meager giving no longer feels so altruistic.

BUT IT CAN BE DONE AND DONE WELL

Negative examples not withstanding, there are numerous examples of virtuous philanthropists who satisfy Aristotelian criteria for virtue. I am particularly taken with Ann Bowers's leadership of the Noyce Foundation. Bowers, a former human resources executive at Intel and Apple, created the foundation in honor of her late husband, Intel cofounder Robert Noyce. After considerable research and deliberation, she decided to focus the foundation's efforts on the problems of public primary and secondary schools. Before she could become an effective donor, she realized she would have to make herself an expert in the educational field. Hence, for many years, she has devoted herself to understanding the underlying issues facing public schools; as a result, she now gives not only generously but wisely. Moreover, she gives more than money; she gives her time and herself.

Grants made by the Noyce Foundation are hardheaded; they go to support initiatives designed to improve academic achievement, and the programs supported are rigorously evaluated. The goals of the foundation reflect the scientific spirit and entrepreneurial risk-taking of Robert Noyce, the inventor of the integrated circuit. Noyce's personal beliefs were Aristotelian: His ideal society was a democratic meritocracy, and he concluded that those who had the means to do so had a responsibility to provide the educational tools needed for economic opportunity, social mobility, and political participation in such a system. Noyce believed that having high expectations about the performance of people caused them to rise to the challenge. In educational circles, the Noyce Foundation is known for challenging conventional wisdom about public education and for supporting creative approaches to deep-seated problems. That few Americans have ever heard of Ann and the relatively large Noyce Foundation, with over $200 million in assets, indicates that she gives not for her sake but for the sake of others.

Finally, there is John Wood, a modern-day Carnegie of relatively modest means. Former head of business development in China for Microsoft, Wood took "early retirement" from the company in his late thirties and cashed out his stock options to the tune of some $2 million. In 1998, he created the Room to Read organization with the intent of creating libraries in some of the poorest parts of southern Asia, from India to Vietnam. By greatly leveraging his stock, Wood has raised enough money to date from fellow techies to start a thousand libraries, donate 500,000 books, and provide scholarships to over 900 poor girls. He also has enlisted others to join him in the effort, including his chief operating officer, Erin Keown Ganju, who says, "I fell in love with the work, and now I'm doing it full time for half my old salary."

12

NONRETIREMENT

READING A CLASSIC IS LIKE PSYCHOANALYZING OUR OWN CULTURE. WE
FIND TRACES, MEMORIES, PATTERNS, PRIMARY SCENES. . . . THERE! WE
EXCLAIM, NOW I UNDERSTAND WHY I AM LIKE THAT—OR WHY SOMEONE
WANTS ME TO BE LIKE THAT: IT ALL BEGAN RIGHT HERE ON THIS PAGE.
AND TO OUR AMAZEMENT, WE DISCOVER WE ARE STILL ARISTOTELIAN
OR PLATONIC . . . IN THE WAY WE ORGANIZE OUR EXISTENCE—EVEN
DOWN TO THE MISTAKES WE MAKE IN THE PROCESS.

—*UMBERTO ECO*

As the oldest boomers approach their 60th year, one hears increasing use of the "R word." Many of us are saying things like, "I just have to slog it out on the job for 5 or 6 more years, then I'll really start to live." Odds are that when you sketched out the "map of your life" at the beginning of this book, you penciled in some form of retirement in your own future. I know I did. But before we make those plans concrete, let's consider the Aristotelian alternative: virtuous nonretirement.

It is admittedly a bit of a stretch to talk about Aristotle's views on retirement. Most men and women in ancient Greece died in what we today consider the prime of life, so for them the question of what to do in old age was moot. In fact, most people died young in the Classical era. Women often succumbed in childbirth (Aristotle buried his beloved Pythias when she was in her early twenties), and men often died while at war (Alexander in a battlefield tent at age 33, albeit more likely from the ravages of hard living than hard fighting). Philosophers seemed to be the exception: Aristotle was a vigorous 62 or 63 when he died of some form of stomach ailment, Socrates was in good health when forced to drink the hemlock at age 70, and, remarkably, Plato made it to 80 before dying, some say, while partying at a wedding feast! And it's good to be a philosopher in the modern era: My teacher, Mortimer Adler, passed away at 98. Had he ever exercised—and not smoked cigars, drank martinis, and subsisted on a diet of chocolate during most of his adult life—there is no telling how long he might have lived! When we asked Mortimer the secret to his longevity, he would answer, "Work." He would then quote his hero, Aristotle, on the positive health effects of mental exercise: "Learning is the one activity in which we can engage as fully in old age as when we are young." Mortimer, like his role model, never retired and was busy planning his next book and next seminar almost to the end of his days. In fact, he hated the word *retirement,* pointing out that because Aristotle never had used it, ergo, it couldn't be a good idea!

Of course, in Aristotle's day, the only people who ever "retired" were

Olympic athletes who had grown too old to compete, so it stands to reason the Ancient didn't have much to say about the subject. Still, it seems safe to conclude he would have been against it. As Mortimer reminded us, Aristotle advocates "leisure work" as the key to a good life. As far as Aristotle is concerned, being engaged in leisure work is as close to the gods as one can get and still be alive. He feels the more leisure work one does, the happier one will be; retirement couldn't be nearly as good for us.

As I thought about the contemporary Aristotelians I know, it became clear that, in their late forties or early fifties, almost all of them made the decision not to retire. Instead, they chose to change the way they lived in order to pursue happiness as Aristotle and Adler did: by making a lifelong commitment to engage in leisure work, choosing to pursue the highest good of individual excellence and the complete good of community service. As illustrated by the lives of the men and women introduced in these chapters, the forms that leisure work can take are as different as there are people with diverse interests, talents, and opportunities. Grace Gabe, Norton and Jane Tennille, Bill Mayer, Buie Sewall, Stephen Carter, Catherine Dain, Tom Peters, Dave Guggenhime, David and Lucy Eisenberg, Sheena Berwick, Skip Battle, Ben Dunlap, Charles and Geraldine Van Doren, Ron Gottesman, Ann Bowers, and the other exemplars I have cited come from different backgrounds, experiences, and professions, have different goals, and have chosen to follow his or her unique path to happiness. Their examples reinforce the essential point that the good life is available to everyone willing to seek it, and underscore that there are countless ways by which it can be created.

I know these men and women just well enough to assert that none was "born" Aristotelian. In their own ways, each had to struggle in midlife to identify the good and to develop the discipline needed to lead a virtuous life. They had to ask themselves tough questions along their various routes to self-discovery. Most important, they would say that one shouldn't wait until age 65 to start the journey.

ARISTOTELIAN NONRETIREMENT

Peter Thigpen is one of the few business executives I know who, at midlife, consciously chose to change the trajectory of his life as the direct result of taking the Ancient's self-examinations. Things were going well for Pete in his forties when he was appointed president of Levi Strauss's domestic operations. At first, Pete had the time of his life implementing the Aristotelian business philosophy of the Haas family, the company's owners. He was involved in creating opportunities for his employees to grow on the job through participation in decision making and sharing in the financial fruits of their efforts. For example, at each of Levi Strauss's manufacturing plants, the stitchers and sewers who made the company's famous jeans were responsible for deciding which charities in their communities would receive donations from the company. After hours, workers met to assess the needs of various community groups, then decided where to volunteer their own time to reinforce the impact of the donations of company money. Imagine the loyalty hourly workers had to a company that turned them into philanthropists! But Pete's immediate boss was committed to moving the company's manufacturing operations offshore, so, after undergoing the painful experience of overseeing the closing of plants he had earlier made into productive workplaces, good for both Levi's owners and workers, he vowed never to go through that again.

At about the same time, Pete turned 50, and he and his wife, Shelley, had a new baby. Pete says this confluence of events caused him to realize "how much I had been wrapped up in my career and myself for 20 years. I was about chest high in business and shoe-top level in everything else." After mulling it over (and reading Aristotle), he says, "I came to understand I was living, but not living well. So I decided to give up the title, the car, and the big bucks." Then he got lucky: The company went through a successful leveraged buyout, and Pete calculated that if he cashed out and invested his accumulated wealth wisely, he could live the rest of his life in comfort, although not in luxury. But not retire.

So about 10 years ago, Pete chose to engage in leisure work. He began by studying subjects he hadn't been taught at the Stanford Business School: literature, philosophy, ethics, history, politics, science, and the arts. Pete is a man of action and no pointy-headed intellectual, but I've been observing him closely over the last decade, and I've yet to see him without a book in or near at hand. Taking Aristotle to heart, he has embarked and stayed on a challenging program of continuous learning, pushing himself to develop his mind in ways he had never even considered while he was a business executive. And he has used his learning to serve his community: as a volunteer in San Francisco's public schools, a teacher of business ethics at U.C. Berkeley, a member of the board of the Josephson Institute of Ethics, a trustee of Mills College, and, most recently, an elected member of two school boards. For 5 years, he tutored in Dave Guggenhime's program. Over this same period, Pete committed to being an equal partner with Shelly in raising their son, Zach.

I speak with some confidence about Pete's beliefs and behavior because, over the years, I've had long, serious discussions with him about how to create a good company and a good society. However, Pete is not a perfect Aristotelian: Ignoring the Ancient's warnings about excessive physical exercise, Pete and Shelly are fitness fanatics who, among other excruciating endeavors, seem actually to enjoy long-distance bike trips at home and abroad! In the last decade, Pete also built himself up from a "C" to a "B" tennis player, much to my chagrin; trust me, it's no fun being on the receiving end of his serve. He is now working on lowering his golf handicap. In his spare time, Pete keeps his hand in the world of business, serving as board member and consultant to several corporations. Paradoxically, as he has broadened his outlook, he has become more in demand to consult on and to speak about business matters than when he was a successful executive. And thanks to the nonbusiness things he now has learned, he is convinced he would be a far-better executive today than he was at Levi's, when he was narrowly focused on applying his marketing skills.

RETIREMENT AS DEATH

As noted, Pete is the exception. Most successful executives wait until they are retired before engaging in leisure work, and many wait until they are in their mid-sixties before they even begin to draw up a plan for the rest of their lives. In this regard, I recall a story told by a friend in 2001. It seems she had been to dinner at a home in suburban Connecticut, where she found herself seated next to the fabled CEO of the General Electric Corporation, Jack Welch. When postprandial conversation turned to Welch's much-publicized decision to retire and turn the company over to a younger executive, my friend asked her famous tablemate what he planned to do next. The 66-year-old executive—whose unfailing self-confidence and assertiveness is often noted in the press—uncharacteristically hesitated before quietly confiding, "I guess I'll have to find another big company to run. . . . I don't know how to do anything else."

A month or two later, General Electric announced plans to acquire the giant Honeywell Corporation—along with reassurance to investors that Welch reluctantly had agreed to extend his tenure as CEO for another year to oversee the integration of the two companies! He finally did retire, of course, and now occasionally appears on television sounding, for the first time in his once-busy life, like a lost soul. Out of work, his life doubtless seems to have lost much of its meaning and purpose. Welch's problem is common among busy executives, and he is not the most extreme example of withdrawal from "the action": Recall Kodak's George Eastman's suicide note, "My work is done, why wait?"

To address this problem effectively, the process of planning a life probably has to start in one's fifties if not sooner. To this end, as a society, we need to celebrate as role models those executives who continually seek to develop their minds even while they actively lead their organizations. For whatever else one may fault them, AOL TimeWarner's Gerald Levin, Intel's Andy

Grove, and CitiCorp's John Reed are examples of recently retired CEOs who pursued the highest good of self-development while still running their companies. And Levin, along with the retired CEOs of Merck, Roy Vagelos, and Johnson &Johnson, Jim Burke, did so while also putting their impressive capabilities to the service of society, the latter two pursuing the highest and complete goods while making great profits for their respective companies. Let's not kid ourselves, that hat trick isn't easy to pull off.

The executive most fully engaged in Aristotelian philosophy and politics who also enjoyed a hugely successful business career was the late Thornton Bradshaw, former CEO of RCA. Bradshaw read widely; frequently engaged in thoughtful discussions with labor leaders, environmentalists, government officials, and educators; wrote good books and articles on serious subjects; developed his employees; and served the community by heading several nonprofit organizations. While still in the prime of his life and with a full plate of other activities, he didn't hesitate for a moment to walk away from the executive suite when he sold RCA to GE's Jack Welch. He even read Aristotle.

It might be argued that no business leader as successful as Welch could be as prepared for leisure work as Bradshaw, but there is evidence they can. As he completed his fifties, and when about to retire from IBM, CEO Lou Gerstner announced plans for how he intended to spend the next decade. Like the aforementioned Bill Mayer, Gerstner planned to divide the time of his life into three parts: personal (more time with his family and formal study at Cambridge University, where he has enrolled to learn Chinese history and archaeology); public service (he's establishing a commission focused on improving the quality of teaching in America's schools); and professional (he has been appointed chairman of the Carlyle Group, a private investment firm). That sounds nothing like traditional retirement.

The alternative, of course, is to stay on the treadmill. But the problem with waiting even until one is 65 to start pursuing happiness is (a) by then one will have devoted the majority of one's life to activities that don't bring happiness, and (b) one might die rather inconveniently at say, age 66, and thus have wasted the one opportunity for happiness we get (in his early sixties and in perfect health, Thornton Bradshaw died during oral surgery). Although it is the standard operating mode, waiting until one is old and rich in order to retire and pursue happiness entails high investment costs and considerable risks on the return. Aristotle reminds us that happiness is *a full life* well led.

AN ANTI-ARISTOTELIAN

To many driven individuals, Aristotelian thinking, learning, discussing ideas, and engaging in family, community, and philanthropic activities may all be well and good, but such things distract from the real reward in life: the thrill of career success. In this view, there is nothing more satisfying than being at the top of one's chosen game, whether that be politics, business, art, science, a sport, or profession. Everything else is, well, boring. It has been said that Alexander the Great would have chosen to live his life exactly as he did even if he had had foreknowledge of his untimely death. No one ever subscribed more fully to the Homeric ideal of *Better a short and exciting life than a long and dull one* (or, as that boomer philosopher, Neil Young, put it: *Better to burn out than fade away*). It might be argued Alexander would have been a nobody, would never have conquered the world, had he been burdened by a family, reading, sports, introspection, and all those other nice-to-have but ultimately distracting pastimes. My colleague and mentor, Warren Bennis, quotes former American Airlines' CEO Robert Crandall on that very point:

301

> For all the years I was working, I was trying to achieve a particular goal. So I wasn't interested in balance. I didn't sail very much. I didn't play any golf. I didn't take much time off. I ran American Airlines and it pretty much took up my entire life. Which suited me fine. I was having a great time. . . . Now you read a lot about balance. In today's world

people say, "I have to have a more balanced life. I have to have time for my kids and my job and my hobbies." That's all well and good. But people who worry about balance have no overriding passion to achieve leadership.

At the peak of his career, Crandall was widely portrayed as the paradigmatic forceful, no-nonsense business leader. Briefly in the late 1980s, his company was a financial winner in an industry characterized by losers, and he credited his single-minded focus on profitability and unabashed toughness as reasons for his record. He was called "the bully of the skies." *New York Times'* Robert Solomon reported, "Crandall retains a volcanic temper and frequently erupts with a range of expletives that would stand out on the docks of New York." Admirers and critics alike called Crandall autocratic, hard on people, and even abusive. Virtuously providing American's employees with the opportunity to pursue happiness on the job was not on his leadership agenda.

302   Crandall believed he had no choice but to act as he did if he were ever to realize his passion for success. But Aristotle begs to differ: The choice isn't between either career success or a balanced life. Alexander was just a kid when he assumed he had no choice but to be single-minded, but Crandall was in his sixties when he said his overriding passion for leadership left him with no choice but megalomania. Aristotle argues that we have to begin at an early age to develop our moral imaginations to the point where we see the alternative to conquest and mayhem isn't a life of knitting and tatting. To him, Crandall's giving in to his passions for success and power is not the same as engaging in rational choice. Indeed, in Crandall's interview with Bennis, there is little evidence of moral deliberation; instead, he simply assumes and asserts. He sounds like the executive on the phone in Charles Barsotti's cartoon: "Introspection, J. B., is for losers."

There is at least anecdotal evidence that successful business leaders can live balanced, examined lives: George Soros's several decades of balancing of career, family, and community activities presents an interesting counterexample to Crandall's. Now in his seventies, Soros is a powerful, wealthy businessman and philanthropist who consciously chose to pursue both the highest good and the complete good beginning as early as in his fifties. Soros has predicated most of what he believes and does on the work of the philosopher Karl Popper. Not coincidentally, Popper's major work on moral and political philosophy, *The Open Society and Its Enemies,* begins its defense of economic and political freedom where Aristotle began his *Politics:* with a refutation of Plato's belief that, for the sake of efficiency, all groups need a single, all-powerful, all-knowing leader. Soros, following Popper, is a foe of totalitarianism in all forms, even the relatively benign form of corporate autocracy.

Soros is a business success par excellence, yet he has chosen to measure his life by the extent to which the political and philanthropic activities he supports make the world more just, saying his "goal is to become the conscience of society." Though that sounds grandiose, those who have had a serious discussion with Soros, as I have had, come away impressed with his humility and selflessness. My impression was confirmed by Anthony Gottlieb, editor of *The Economist,* who writes that Soros "has cheerfully described himself as a failed philosopher." Gottlieb defends Soros against the charge that he is "messianic" because

> . . . there is no trace of self-aggrandizement in Soros's actions. Although far from secretive and no recluse, he has done little to trumpet his good works, which outweigh those of powerful saints. When one thinks of the noise made by other tycoons on smaller philanthropic sprees, his modesty is striking.

Although Soros has given away hundreds of millions with relatively little fanfare, what is Aristotelian about his actions is not the large amounts he gives but the thoughtful process he uses to choose the causes he supports. That is not to claim Soros is a heavyweight intellectual. In fact, his writings and speeches explaining his philosophy are often less than logically compelling. Still, he is not your typical do-gooder. His philanthropic activities are informed not only by Popper's libertarian philosophy, he also brings his own considerable moral imagination to bear on the process of choosing which activities to fund. One of his most creative acts was to donate photocopiers in then-Communist Hungary in order to undermine censorship. In general, he has tried to the best of his ability to think through some of the most difficult social questions, then asked what contribution he could make to the ends he has identified as worthy and noble. Though one may disagree with the ends he seeks or the means he chooses (like his efforts to decriminalize drug use in America), even his critics concede he is a serious and moral man. And that didn't just happen: He had to consciously commit himself to a life of leisure work.

Soros has been a role model for younger, wealthy men and women, most notably Bill and Melinda Gates, who, as we have seen, have been adopting Soros's model of philanthropy. As he approaches 50, Gates has shown signs of Aristotelian maturation in other aspects of his life, as well. Maybe it's because he and Melinda are now parents, but Gates has toned down the hardball, public-be-damned stance of his initial, and in my view immature, reaction to the Justice Department's anti-trust investigation of Microsoft. What distinguishes Gates from his techie peers is not a lack of traditional ambition—Gates also loves money and power—but that he is, at base, a thoughtful man and a learner (one of Gates's Microsoft associates told me he never saw his boss without a large canvas bag full of the latest serious books).

In his forties, Gates began to undergo what his friend Warren Buffet calls a "renaissance." *Fortune* writer Brent Schlender claims Gates "also seems more serene and contemplative—and just plain funnier—than at any time in the 18 years I've known him." Buffet adds, "There was a time he was not enjoying life. Now he is very happy." Buffet credits three Aristotelian instrumental goods for the observed change in Gates: his family, friends, and foundation. Gates seems now to have a close, confiding relationship with the thoughtful fellow billionaire, Buffet, with whom he plays bridge and shares family vacations. Gates also appears to have a soul mate in Melinda, about whom Buffet says, "There couldn't be anybody better for Bill. He thinks of her in every way as an equal. If she expresses an opinion, that carries as much weight as his own." In sum, Buffet offers this Aristotelian assessment of Gates:

> If you end up with a business you've created that's had incredible impact on the world, a foundation that is probably going to have more impact than any foundation in history, and a happy family life, then you're batting pretty damn good.

Perhaps the clearest sign of Gates's maturation has been his willingness to hand over to Steve Ballmer operating authority at Microsoft. Gates candidly admitted to *Business Week* that it was hard for him initially to surrender the exercise of power, but he has disciplined himself to appreciate that wielding authority isn't what gives him satisfaction. Instead, he now understands he is happiest when creating solutions to advanced technical problems. And he has gone a step further, creating opportunities for Microsoft employees to learn and to grow. To the end of developing his people, Gates has changed his organizational role from being a czar and commander to that of a mentor and coach. The mature Gates now says, "If we look ahead to the next century, leaders will be those who empower others." According to Schlender, Gates spends half of his time at Microsoft in brainstorming sessions with new-product developers, "usually in very small groups, and sometimes even one-on-one." Gates thus seems to be working toward a mature melding of both the highest and complete goods. Clearly, this process of maturation isn't easy for him; the lesson for all of us is that it requires hard work on the part of everyone who has the courage to try it. He wins Aristotelian kudos for not waiting until he was ready to retire before opting for leisure work.

It takes courage to unlock our potential, and the older we get, the more courage it takes. John McCarter is one who almost didn't take the risk, and the entire city of Chicago would have been the worse for it if he hadn't had the courage to change. In 1996, McCarter, then 58, was sailing in smooth seas, heading toward conventional retirement as a partner at the management

305

consultancy Booz • Allen & Hamilton. Then, out of nowhere came an offer he was at first inclined to refuse. The Field Museum of Natural History, which had grown seedy since its heyday in the 1920s, was looking for a director who could resuscitate the institution. Because the museum was basically broke, many experienced people turned down the job as a hopeless cause; and McCarter, whose technical background was in the field of agriculture, confided to me at the time that he wasn't sure he was the right person to do it, and, anyway, who needed the headache? But the more he thought about it, the more he became convinced he wasn't ready to vegetate. He wanted to continue to grow and take intellectual risks. And career risks, too. On the job at the museum for less than a year, McCarter masterminded the purchase of Sue, a 42-foot-long *Tyrannosaurus rex* skeleton recently unearthed in South Dakota. Using a mix of business skill, creativity, and Barnum-like salesmanship, McCarter bet the store that Sue could provide the key to turning around the museum's fortunes. So he begged, borrowed, and connived $8.3 million to buy the old girl, and sure enough, within a year, over two million visitors had come to see her; the most to pay to enter the museum since King Tut had displayed his wares there in 1977.

Within a year of acquiring Sue, McCarter announced he had bagged the Dead Sea Scrolls. He had been on a busman's holiday in Europe, scouting museums to steal good ideas, when he saw the scrolls were drawing large crowds in Edinburgh. He dropped in, said, "We've got to have 'em," and signed them up for the next season in Chicago. McCarter's current crusade is to make the institution the world leader in the conservation field. So the days of milk and honey have returned to the Field, and now McCarter even has a bit of spare time to mentor young Chicago business leaders about their social responsibilities. And, yes, McCarter had read Aristotle the year before he made his momentous decision to pursue the Ancient's highest and complete good.

In making his decision to take on the Field Museum challenge, did John McCarter (a) retire from a well-paid career to take what was for him, essentially, a volunteer position, (b) postpone his retirement, (c) create a second act for his life, or (d) re-pot himself? A case can be made for each of the above explanations; but, whichever it is, McCarter's decision led to his rejuvenation and active participation with a community at exactly the age when many people are considering a more sedentary and solitary form of retirement.

THE REST OF US

Today, a question on the minds of the oldest boomers is *What's next for me?* The most financially secure among us answer: *retirement.* Many of us believe we will at last get our just reward of happiness at Leisure World. But that may not be true, at least not for everyone. For men and women who have been actively engaged in careers and professions, particularly ones with a high level of social interaction, the experience of retirement can feel like the pain of withdrawal to a drug addict. Witness Jack Welch. Of course, one option is to stay on the job. Perhaps in the future, when brainpower has completely replaced the need for muscle in the workplace, employers will see the value of hiring and retaining older workers. But that isn't where employment has been headed over the last decade. Continuing to work is less an option for many older people today than it was even 5 years ago, as corporations have downsized, outsourced, and introduced de facto policies to substitute lower-paid younger workers for higher-paid older ones. This is good for productivity (younger workers check you out at the cash register faster than older ones) but bad for customer service (older workers are more likely than self-absorbed younger ones to put themselves in the shoes of the customer).

And it can be deadly for those who are used to working. Indeed, there is some evidence of a statistical spike in the death rate among men at age 65. More common is to find older people who simply can't adjust to retirement and who age visibly when no longer part of the action. Ronald Reagan's biographer, Edmund Morris, observes that the late-president had lacked curiosity and had stopped being open to new ideas decades before he became ill with Alzheimer's. Had Reagan continued to learn into his sixties and seventies the way in did in midlife, one wonders if this mental stimulation might at least have postponed the onset of the dread disease that destroyed the quality of his last decade of life.

Yet, for generations, the approved, canonical, life plan has been to work like hell for as long as it takes to fill a larder with enough eggs to support you in kicked-back comfort, 'til death parts you from the need of a nest egg. But retirement is changing. An ever-larger percentage of the working population is retiring early, people are living longer than ever before, and those who retire are no longer old because what was once "ancient" is "midlife" today. Those who retire at age 65 now have a good shot at 2 decades of good health and full activity. That's a lot of time to fill playing golf and watching TV, particularly when it is incontrovertibly the case that older men and women who continue to use their minds and who stay actively engaged in communities are healthier and happier than those who vegetate and isolate themselves.

Here's how some recently "retired" people have used and are using that once placid time of their lives to actively pursue happiness: Former President Jimmy Carter "retired" at age 56 to become the "greatest former U.S. president," devoting himself to the cause of human rights. He and his wife, Roslyn, pitched in to help build houses for Habitat for Humanity at an age when many people, as recently as a generation earlier, had been considered infirm. The late political commentator I. F. Stone learned to read ancient Greek in his late seventies, then penned the best book ever written about Socrates. Common Cause founder, John Gardner, became a professor of business at Stanford in his eighties. And healthy people in their nineties are proving capable of learning new things; nonagenarian Peter Drucker is positively gaga over the Internet. At age 93, Columbia's renowned former provost, Jacques Barzun, wrote an acclaimed history of the last 4 centuries. Recently deceased philanthropist Brooke Astor was actively involved in community affairs in New York well past her hundredth birthday. Finally, in

2003, the oldest person "still working" in America died at age 104: William Sunderland, M.D., was a man of infinite curiosity, inventor of a famous tool for treating diabetes, participant in the Manhattan Project, author of 40 books (he was working on another when he died), and also a regular performer in a string quartet. His favorite quotation came from Voltaire: "How infinitesimal is the importance of anything I do, but how infinitely important it is that I should do it."

Morley Safer's recent *60 Minutes* report on people in their eighties and nineties who are still working reveals several mistaken notions about the benefits of employment in old age. Safer interviewed a sociologist who claimed the problem with retirement is the "loss of identity." But if Aristotle's notion is correct that the purpose of life is development, then the real problem with retiring is the loss of one's humanity. Safer implied that the reason the people he profiled kept working was because they found retirement a vast wasteland of TV viewing that "bored them stiff." However, most of the jobs done by the people he featured were also boring and repetitive, and the people doing them seemed dour. They were satisfied with their tasks only to the extent they didn't have a clue how to use their time in a more rewarding or meaningful way. The implication was that the choice older people face is between routine work and the boredom of doing nothing.

That may be the case for the people Safer interviewed who clearly had never experienced the joys of development in the first 65 years of their lives, and now it was too late for them to learn. But Safer also interviewed older workers who had been committed to self-development since midlife, and they were the most engaged, lively, and "youthful" workers in his report, including a centurian scientific researcher who asked the Aristotelian question, "How can this be work when it is so interesting?" and 99-year-old cartoonist Al Hirschfield, who was merrily involved in the act of creation up to the time he died (shortly after the program was filmed). These older workers were happy because they appreciated that their capacity for acquiring knowledge and wisdom was limitless. Like the contemporary Aristotelians cited in these

309

pages, the cartoonist and scientist had learned the Aristotelian difference between work/work and leisure/work. Hence, the real lesson of the *60 Minutes* segment was that older people shouldn't wait until retirement to prepare for the rest of their lives.

Without meaningful work to do, there are signs of increasing boredom among those too young to retire: growing numbers of divorces among older couples and the fact that over half of the buyers of Harley motorcycles now are 45 or over. Aristotle offers a more positive alternative: keeping your brain alive. There are numerous ways that can be done at any age, some quite simple. A 2004 National Endowment for the Arts report demonstrated that people who read regularly are many times more likely than nonreaders to attend museums, plays, concerts, and sports events, and to participate in charity and volunteer activities. In sum, nonreaders tend to lead passive lives in front of televisions, while readers—regardless of age, gender, race, or income—are more likely to be actively engaged in their communities and in pursuit of the good life. As Aristotle points out, people who make healthy choices in one part of their lives tend to do so in other parts. Virtue is a contagion that spreads to all aspects of our being.

In sum, Aristotle's ancient ideas seem to have become ever-more relevant in recent years; his emphasis on the need for continual renewal is almost trendy. His beliefs that no humans ever reach their full capacity to learn, and that they all should be engaged in learning up to the moment of their passing, are now tenets of conventional wisdom. There is even some science to back his observations: We may be able to postpone the effects of aging. Gerontologists say that older people continue to learn throughout the course of their lives, and those who remain actively engaged in continual development of their many capabilities, feel and act younger than those who abandon the pleasure of seeking self-actualization. Because people today who are in their sixties and seventies have many good innings ahead of them, what better use is there for their time than to follow Aristotle's advice and learn and do the things they missed in their youth?

PLANNING THE GOOD LIFE

Although it is human nature to spend one's twenties, thirties, and even forties accumulating and aspiring to accomplish great things, most mature men and women arrive at a time when they wish to reassess the trajectory of their lives, to see where they have been, and then identify paths to deeper sources of fulfillment. As we have seen in these pages, this is not an easy task because it requires sacrifice: the letting go of comforting but unhealthy notions that have clogged our mental arteries. Though some older people continue to hold the view that the examined life is not worth living, many eventually come to see the need to ask tough questions of themselves. Because it is best not to wait until retirement to do so, each of us needs to develop a life plan as soon as possible. Not the kind of career development plan that corporations use to identify the skills executives need to get ahead in their organizations, but a plan that identifies the experience and knowledge we personally need in order to lead the good life. This plan identifies the bull's-eye we eventually want to hit in old age, and the questions we need to keep asking ourselves along the way if we are to have any hope of hitting it. As we have seen in these chapters, creating a meaningful plan and learning to stick to it requires exercises to build our self-discipline, along with a course of reading, studying, traveling, and serious discussion with "virtuous friends" to create the foundation of experience and wisdom needed to carry it out. In its advanced drafts, such a plan identifies how we will allocate our time and pinpoints things we need to stop doing because they distract us from achieving our goals.

Aristotle observes that virtue requires balance in most endeavors. He notes that people who are thoughtful, ethical, and happy in the long term seek to create moral symmetry in the economic, social, creative, contemplative, familial, political, and recreational aspects of their lives. But how do they strike such equilibrium? He believes there is no universal formula for finding balance in life, no prescription guaranteed to lead all men and women to the desired golden mean. Instead, he says it takes great personal effort for each of us to find the good for ourselves, a process of discovery greatly enhanced when undertaken in the company of other thoughtful men and women who are on the same journey in search of understanding.

A key to developing a robust plan is to keep an eye on the long-term. Aristotle says a great difference between those who choose to lead good lives and those who don't is that the latter are prisoners of short-term thinking. In his view, those who choose the goals of voluptuaries and sultans are not bad; they are myopic and immature. Indeed, almost everyone suffers disappointing years of trying to achieve instant gratification before they are ready to admit their lingering and increasingly age-inappropriate desires won't make them happy. But as we grow older and come to realize we have a dwindling amount of time before us, we paradoxically start to learn the value of deferred gratification. As we begin to see we have a finite number of days ahead, we come to appreciate we must make the best use of those diminishing assets in activities that will lead to our continuing development. By the time we reach midlife, we see we can no longer afford to waste time in misdirected pursuits.

What is magic about midlife? What is it that allows some people to seize the opportunity of a lifetime during their forties and fifties? By then, many men (and, increasingly today, women) will have recovered from midlife crises to find themselves stronger for having outgrown the vanities of youth. Many women (and, increasingly today, men) will have successfully carried out the heavy responsibilities of raising children to find themselves free to put their own needs before those of dependent others. In sum, a kind of liberation may occur, a freeing up from the psychological chains of self-delusion and the practical fetters of middle-age responsibilities.

But Aristotle also observes that age is an insufficient precondition for finding wisdom and happiness. By midlife, we may have acquired the necessary tools, but we still have the work to do. On this score he is optimistic, believing most lives can have second acts and the greatest opportunities come at the stage of life when people are often said to be "too set in their ways" to escape their behavioral ruts. In fact, Aristotle says some people defy stereotype as they grow older and begin to behave in the only way that will lead to happiness: *They change how they live.* To be precise, they change what they do, not who they are. Over 2,000 years of experience demonstrates the way people become truly happy is by abandoning their youthful fantasies and adopting plans for pursuing more appropriate ends. Therefore, in order to change course, we must reexamine our most fundamental assumptions about the goals that drive our behavior. Aristotle says that requires us to do three things: (1) define clearly our ultimate life goals, (2) plan consciously how to achieve those goals, and (3) commit to changing our behavior.

FINAL EXAMINATION

To help us with those tasks, Aristotle drew up the practical framework for analysis and action we have reviewed in these pages. He created tools to allow us to test the validity of our assumptions about what happiness really means and to help us create effective plans to realize the ends we seek. But he didn't say we can ever arrive at a perfect and final plan; instead, he believed the greatest benefit we will derive is from the process of *planning*, which is never complete. Indeed, it is when we are struggling with his moral exercises that we are engaged in that necessary and ultimately rewarding process.

313

As I near my sixtieth birthday, I find myself raising Aristotle's tough questions with greater frequency.

- On my deathbed, will I be able to look back and say I led a good life?
- What will make me truly happy at the end?
- What work puts me in "the zone"?
- What should I be doing now to get where I want to be in the long-term?
- What am I doing that I should stop doing—that is, what gives me gratification but will not contribute to my lasting happiness?
- What do I need to discipline myself to do and not do in order to stay focused on what is truly good for me in the long-term?

As I have confessed, answering those questions has not been easy. These last few years have been nothing so much as a process of alternating progress and retreat toward the goal of happiness. Nonetheless, repeatedly doing Aristotle's simple exercises finally has helped me to draw several personal conclusions about what I want in life and what I have to do to get it. Asking these questions has allowed me to outgrow my habituation to the Philosophy of the Few. It is now manifestly clear that I don't want fame or fortune, and even if I should win those by chance, there still would be a hollow spot in my life. I have asked myself what would happen if I were to win the lottery, and I am now certain I wouldn't kick back and play golf or buy a yacht as big as a battleship. Instead, I would seek to fill the hole remaining in my life through writing. And even if I were to write a bestseller, that alone wouldn't make me happy. I would still want to spend a large portion of every day writing, because that is how I make sense out of life and how I get into the zone. So I have concluded that, for me, writing is "good work." And because that is what I would do if I were rich and famous, I've concluded, *Why not just get on with the work?* Who needs to be rich and famous!

Immersing myself in Aristotle also has whetted my appetite to read more, and to read more broadly, particularly classical literature and philosophy. The more I read, the more I realize how much I haven't read and how much I don't know about so many important subjects. To die without that knowledge seems to me to miss out on one of life's greatest rewards. But gaining that knowledge comes at a cost; one must set priorities, and that entails ceasing to do things that seem important or pleasurable. To make room in the day to do serious developmental reading, I am now spending far less time reading newspapers and magazines, particularly business periodicals. There is no real sacrifice involved in this, because it has been years since I have read anything new about business that strikes me as profound. Nonetheless, not keeping up with business trends and personalities will make me a lot less marketable as a business writer and consultant. But that is fully consistent with my plan, because I have scaled down my financial expenditures to the point

314

where I don't need nearly as much income from those activities, activities that also distract me from my focus on the highest good. Ultimately, I am working toward clearing my calendar of all activities that keep me from doing "leisure work."

As I have confessed, over the years, I have been remiss in the pursuit of the complete good. I have been too much the social isolate; and to remedy that, I have started to become more involved in community and political affairs. I have started to get my feet wet in my community by ending the clever dodge that kept me out of jury duty for 3 decades and by volunteering to work on a political campaign for the first time since I was in my twenties. And I am revising my charitable giving to focus my modest resources on supporting programs that help the neediest members of society.

Because what I found most missing from my life is a community of friends, I have created a seminar with an Aristotelian circle of mature men and women with whom I can discuss the important issues Aristotle says should be the concern of all thoughtful people. And in the long term, I think the best way I can serve my community is through teaching in a program like Dave Guggenhime's. I also have disabused myself of the attraction of the Geographical Cure: I have come to see I won't find happiness "somewhere else" relaxing under swaying palms. And I now see that I would go nuts in conventional retirement, even in Maui. Those insights should help me to pay more attention to being a participating member of the community in which I live, and the communities of shared interests of which I am a part.

Although it is too soon to tell for sure, doing these new things seems to be giving me greater insight into my own weaknesses and greater sympathy with regard to the frailties of others. That would be a big step toward becoming less selfish, and I might become a better husband and father in the process, all of which would make me much happier with myself. As I finally was able to understand Plato's *Republic* as I grew older, I also have started to appreciate what poets say about the process of maturity, in particular, what T. S. Eliot means about the need for an old man to be "an explorer" and why

Dylan Thomas counsels older people, "Do not go gentle into that good night." Indeed, I have decided to go out raging, particularly on the subject of the ethics of corporate leaders. Because of my craving for approval, I had been far too reluctant to speak out on that and the related subject of the moral responsibility of leaders to provide developmental opportunities for their followers. I also have sworn to pay far more attention to that moral responsibility in my own roles as an employer and corporate board member. In sum, I now see what Aristotle means when he says we can't be happy ourselves if we don't make it possible for our friends, family, and followers to find happiness for themselves.

Finally, my evolving plan for finding the good life includes a few instrumental goods Aristotle says we need, even though they don't constitute happiness in and of themselves. So I am now exercising regularly, and recent tests at the doc's indicate the wisdom of cutbacks in the salami and chardonnay departments.

316   *Has all this made me any happier?* That's the key question, of course, and I must admit the answer isn't as clear as I would like it to be. In truth, I am a work in progress, and lest I become too impatient on that score, I must keep reminding myself that Aristotle says we can't really know the answer until the end of our days. But I will say that the initial signs are promising. As I have begun to get the upper hand in controlling my life-long need for approval, I think I am far less angry about my career disappointments than I was when I began writing this book. In and of itself, that gives me a few more minutes of happiness every day. And looking forward, as I focus more of what I do on achieving the highest and complete goods, I honestly believe those minutes will stretch into hours.

Thanks to Aristotle, that's how I plan to go on from here.

Now it's your turn.

NOTES AND REFERENCES

INTRODUCTION

pp. xxi–xxii. Will Smith, "What Are You Reading?" *Book,* September/
October 2002, p. 13.
  p. xxii. Alain de Botton, *The Consolations of Philosophy,* Vintage, 2001.
  p. xxiii. *David Oldfield, Private Paths, Common Ground.* p. 95–106.

CHAPTER ONE

pp. 3–4. Maureen Dowd, "Bye, Rudy, Yerts and All," *The New York
Times,* December 12, 2001, p. A31.
  p. 7. David Denby, "Heart of the Country," *The New Yorker,* September
29, 2003, p. 118.
  pp. 17–18. Jean Jacques Rousseau, *The Social Contract,* bk. I, selection 9.
  p. 23, Denby, *Great Books,* p. 124.

CHAPTER TWO

p. 29. John Lahr, *The New Yorker,* December 2, 2002, p. 54.
  pp. 32–33. Fromm, cited in Richard Ryan and Edward Deci, "On Happiness and Human Potentials," *Annu. Rev. Psychol.,* 2001. 52:141/66.
  p. 34. Seligman and Csikszentmihalyi, cited in Ryan and Deci, *ibid.*
  p. 35. Adam Smith, story from Heilbroner, *The Worldly Philosophers,*
Chapter 3, pp. 42–74.
  p. 35. "Subtract Rows, Add Sex," *The Economist,* July 27, 2002, p. 50.
  p. 36. James Surowiecki, "Boom and Gloom," *The New Yorker,* November
11, 2002.
  p. 36. Erica Goode, "A Conversation with Daniel Kahneman," *The New
York Times,* November 5, 2002, p. D1.
  p. 43. Frederick Herzberg, *Work and the Nature of Man.*
  p. 46. Tom Peters interview in *BizEd,* May/June 2002, pp. 17–18.
  pp. 49–50. Harriett Taylor Mill, "Enfranchisement of Women."

CHAPTER THREE

p. 59. Lewis, *The New New Thing,* p. 79, 128, 160, 259–261.
  p. 60. David Kaplan, "The Missed Fortune," *Worth,* October 2000, pp.
121–24.

p. 62. Joseph Menn and Alex Pham, "Ellison's Style May Be a Factor in Tech Industry Consolidation," *Los Angeles Times,* June 22, 2003, p. C1.

p. 62. "The Dark Side of Silicon Valley," *Business Week,* July 17, 2000.

p. 63. Karen Southwick, *Everyone Else Must Fail,* p. 3.

p. 64. D'Souza, *The Virtue of Prosperity,* p. 108.

p. 70. David McCullough, *John Adams,* p. 289.

p. 75. Denby, *Great Books,* p. 121.

p. 77. Bruce McCall, "The Most Successful Writer," *The New York Times Book Review,* September 29, 2002, p. 36.

CHAPTER FOUR

p. 84. John Underwood, "It's the Little Things That Made Ted Williams Special," *The New York Times,* Sports Sunday, July 7, 2002, p. 7.

p. 86. Frank Litsky, "Kim Gallagher, 38, Olympic Track Medalist," *The New York Times,* Obituary Section, November 21, 2002.

p. 93. Martin Miller, "In the Grip of an Obsession," *Los Angeles Times,* November 18, 2002, p. F5.

pp. 96–97. Susan Jacoby, "Money: America's Love-Hate Relationship with the Almighty Dollar," *Modern Maturity,* July–August 2000, pp. 35–41.

p. 97. Ray Lane, quoted in *The New York Times,* October 1, 2000.

pp. 102–103. Patricia Cohen, "In Defense of Our Wicked, Wicked Ways," *The New York Times,* Sunday Styles, July 7, 2002, p. 1.

p. 104. David Brooks, "Bitter at the Top," *The New York Times,* June 15, 2004, p. A23.

p. 106. For more on Bill Joy, see Jon Gertner, "Proceed with Caution," *The New York Times Sunday Magazine,* June 6, 2004, pp. 32–36

pp. 110–11. Carolyn Heilbrun, *The Last Gift of Time,* pp. 44–45

CHAPTER FIVE

p. 118. Bettelheim, p. 3.

p. 120. Bettelheim, p. 35.

p. 121. James Stewart, "Spend! Spend! Spend!" *The New Yorker,* February 17 & 24, 2003.

p. 124. Anthony Kenny, *Aristotle on the Perfect Life,* p. 10.

p. 127. Bettelheim, op. cit.

p. 128. Stephen J. Dubner, "Calculating the Irrational in Economics," *The New York Times,* June 28, 2003, p. 17.

CHAPTER SIX

p. 142. Denby, *Great Books*, p. 121.

p. 145. Randy Cohen, "Best Wishes," *The New York Times Sunday Magazine*, June 30, 2002, p. 12.

pp. 147–8. David Owen, "From Race to Chase," *The New Yorker*, June 3, 2003, p. 56.

p. 150. Keynes, quoted in E. F. Schumacher, *Small Is Beautiful*, Harper & Row, 1989, p. 24.

p. 150. Mimi Avens, "The New Ideal," *Los Angeles Times*, Calendar Section, June 13, 2004, p. 1.

p. 153. Albert O. Hirschman, *Exit, Voice and Loyalty*, Harvard University Press, 1970.

p. 158. Larry Stewart, "Hot Corner," *Los Angeles Times*, Sports Section, December 30, 2003, p. 2.

p. 161. David Heenan, *Double Lives*.

CHAPTER SEVEN

p. 174. Jennifer Warner, "Money Can't Buy Happiness, but Health and Family Can," *WebMD Medical News*, August 25, 2003.

pp. 175–77. James O'Toole, Jay Galbraith, and Edward Lawler, "When Two Heads Are Better than One," *California Management Review*, Vol. 44, No.4, 2002.

CHAPTER EIGHT

pp. 206–07. Elizabeth Kolbert, "The Mogul Mayor," *The New Yorker*, April 22–29, 2002, pp. 138–147.

pp. 206–07. Buzz Bissinger, "The Mogul of City Hall," *Vanity Fair*, December 2003, pp. 220–238.

p. 212. James Mann, "Close-up: The Young Rumsfeld," *The Atlantic*, November 2003, pp. 89–101.

p. 217. W. F. R. Hardie, *Aristotle's Ethical Theory*, Oxford, 1968.

p. 219. Bruce Adams, "Finding His True Calling," *San Francisco Chronicle*, May 13, 2001, p. D2.

p. 220. Richard Rothstein, "How to Solve the Teacher Shortage," *The New York Times*, December 6, 2000, p. A29.

p. 221. Natalia Mehlman, "My Brief Teaching Career," *The New York Times*, June 24, 2002, p. A23.

CHAPTER NINE

p. 229. Edward E. Lawler, *High Involvement Management,* Jossey-Bass, 1986.

p. 230. Edward E. Lawler, *Treat People Right,* Jossey-Bass, 2003.

p. 231. O'Toole, *Work in America,* p. 25.

pp. 233–35. O'Toole, *Making America Work,* Chapter 5.

pp. 236–37. David Finegold, George Benson, and Susan Mohrman, "Harvesting What They Grow: Can Firms Get a Return on Their Investment in General Skills?" *Organizational Dynamics,* 31,2, pp. 151–164.

pp. 238–39. Stratford Sherman, "Secrets of HP's 'Muddled' Teams," *Fortune,* March 16, 1996.

p. 239. Sy Corenson, "The End of the HP Way," letter to editor of *Fortune* commenting on January 12, 2004 article about Carly Fiorina.

p. 240. Kraut, *Aristotle on the Human Good,* p. 127.

CHAPTER TEN

p. 254. Gretchen Morgenson, "Explaining (or not) Why the Boss Is Paid So Much," *The New York Times,* January 25, 2004, section 3, p. 1.

p. 254. Kathy M. Kristof, "Working to Retire Overcompensation," *Los Angeles Times,* Business Section, p. 1.

p. 255. Nelson Schwartz, "Greed-mart," *Fortune,* October 14, 2002, pp. 139–148.

p. 255. Kristine Larsen, "Sweet Surrender," *Fortune,* October 14, 2002, pp. 224–234.

p. 256. John F. Dickerson and Adam Zagorin, "The Options Debate," *Time,* July 29, 2002, p. 21.

p. 263. Sumner, *The Challenge of Facts and Other Essays.*

p. 264. Edith Hamilton, *The Greek Way,* Norton, 1994.

CHAPTER ELEVEN

p. 266. Stephen Strom, "The Newly Rich Are Fueling a New Era in Philanthropy," *The New York Times,* April 25, 2002.

p. 266. "Helping Hands," *Business Week,* July 29, 2002, p. 14.

p. 269. "Walton Endowment Intrigue," *The New York Times,* August 11, 2002, section 3, p. 2.

p. 271. Joseph Weber, "Boardroom Charity," *Business Week,* June 10, 2002, p. 128.

p. 273. Warren St. John, "Cash Aside, Is That Prize Meaningful?" *The New York Times,* May 25, 2002, p. A17.

p. 273. David Alexander, "The Marco Polo of the Class of 1934: Sir John Templeton," *The American Oxonian,* Spring 2003, no. 2, pp. 186–191.

p. 278. James Stewart, "The Milken File," *The New Yorker,* January 22, 2001, pp. 47–61.

p. 279. Newman and Hotchner, *Shameless Exploitation,* pp. 199–200.

p. 279. Reed Abelson, "Now Appearing in Your Favorite Cause," *The New York Times,* Giving Special Section, November 20, 2000, p. F1.

p. 281. "The New Philanthropy," *Time,* July 24, 2000, pp. 48–59.

p. 283. Peter Elkind, "The Man Who Sold Silicon Valley on Giving," *Fortune,* pp. 182–184.

p. 284. *Time,* op. cit., p. 51.

p. 286. Bill Keller, "Pollyanna Meets Cassandra," *The New York Times,* June 1, 2002, p. A25.

p. 287. Bill Gates, "First Step: The Gift of Health," commentary issued by the Bill and Melinda Gates Foundation.

p. 287. Geoffrey Cowley, "Bill's Biggest Bet Yet," *Newsweek,* February 4, 2002, pp. 45–52.

p. 288. Elkind, op. cit.

p. 289. Menand, *The Metaphysical Club,* p. 311.

pp. 290–91. Brent Schlender, "The Playboy Philanthropist," *Fortune,* September 3, 2001, pp. 163–166.

p. 291. Ellison quoted in *Business Week,* February 26, 2001, p. 101.

p. 291. John A. Byrne, "The New Face of Philanthropy," *Business Week,* December 2, 2002, pp. 82–94.

p. 293. Bob Cooper, "Rich in Books," *San Francisco Chronicle Magazine,* September 26, 2004, pp. 7–9.

CHAPTER TWELVE

p. 300. Steve Lohr, "Gerstner to be Chairman of Carlyle Group," *The New York Times,* November 22, 2002, p. C3.

pp. 301–2. Warren Bennis and Robert J. Thomas, *Geeks and Geezers,* Harvard Business School Press, 2002, p. 45.

p. 302 Stephen D. Solomon, "The Bully of the Skies Cries Uncle," *The New York Times Magazine,* September 5, 1993, p. 12.

p. 303. Anthony Gottlieb, "Who Wants to Be a Billionaire?" *The New York Times,* Book Review, March 3, 2002, p. 11.

pp. 304–5. Brent Schlender, "All You Need Is Love," *Fortune,* July 8, 2002, pp. 59–67.

p. 305. Bill Gates, "Reorganization: A Necessary Art," *Executive Excellence,* December 2002, p. 3.

p. 306. Mike Conklin, "Building Momentum from the Bones Up," *Los Angeles Times,* December 4, 2000, p. F8.

p. 307. Penelope Wang, "Is This Retirement?" *Money,* November 2000, p. 101—102.

p. 309. "William Sunderman," *The Economist,* March 22, 2003, p. 79.

p. 310. Charles McGrath, "What Johnny Won't Read," *The New York Times,* July 11, 2004, p. WK3.

p. 310. Linda Bronte, "Is Retirement Dangerous to Your Health?" *Across The Board,* pp. 52—62.

☙ BIBLIOGRAPHY ☙

The works of Aristotle were translated into English under the editorship of W. D. Ross in 1925 and are now in the public domain. I have drawn on his Oxford University Press editions of Aristotle's *Nicomachean Ethics, Politics, Rhetoric,* and *On Poetics,* freely translating in order to clarify the meaning of the quotations used in this book.

Adler, Mortimer J. *Aristotle for Everybody.* Macmillan, 1978.

———. *Desires Right & Wrong.* Macmillan, 1991.

Bender, Sue. *Plain and Simple.* HarperSanFrancisco, 1991.

Bennis, Warren, and Robert J. Thomas. *Geeks and Geezers.* Harvard Business School Press, 2002.

Bettelheim, Bruno. *The Uses of Enchantment.* Vintage Books, 1977.

Broadie, Sarah. *Ethics with Aristotle,* Oxford, 1991.

Carter, Stephen L. *Integrity,* Basic Books, 1996.

D'Souza, Dinesh. *The Virtue of Prosperity,* Free Press, 2000.

Denby, David. *American Sucker,* Little, Brown and Company, 2004.

———. *Great Books,* Touchstone, 1996.

Erikson, Erik. *Gandhi's Truth on the Origins of Militant Nonviolence,* Norton, 1993.

Heilbroner, Robert. *The Worldly Philosophers,* Touchstone, 1986.

Heilbrun, Carolyn. *The Last Gift of Time,* Ballantine, 1997.

Heenan, David. *Double Lives,* Davies-Black, 2002.

Heenan, and Warren Bennis. *Co-Leaders,* Wiley, 1999.

Herzberg, Frederick. *Work and the Nature of Man,* World Publishing, 1966.

Hutchinson, D. S. "Ethics" in Jonathan Barnes (ed.) *The Cambridge Companion to Aristotle,* Cambridge, 1995.

Isaacson, Walter. *Benjamin Franklin,* Simon & Schuster, 2003.

Kraut, Richard. *Aristotle on the Human Good,* Princeton, 1989.

Kenny, Anthony. *Aristotle on the Perfect Life,* Clarendon Press, 1992.

Kenny, Anthony. *Aristotelian Ethics,* Clarendon Press, 1978.

Lear, Jonathan. *Happiness, Death, and the Remainder of Life,* Harvard, 2000.

Lewis, Michael. *The New New Thing,* Norton, 2000.

McCullough, David. *John Adams,* Simon & Schuster, 2001.

Maslow, Abraham. *Maslow on Management,* John Wiley and Sons, 1998.

Menand, Louis. *The Metaphysical Club,* Farrar, Straus and Giroux, 2001.

Mill, Harriett Taylor. "Enfranchisement of Women," in John Stuart Mill (ed.) *Dissertations and Discussions, vol. 2,* 1859–75.

Morris, Edmund. *The Rise of Theodore Roosevelt,* Coward, McCann & Geoghegan, 1979.

Newman, Paul, and A. E. Hotchner. *Shameless Exploitation,* Doubleday, 2003.

Oldfield, David. *Private Paths, Common Ground,* The Foundation for Contemporary Mental Health, 1991.

O'Neil, John. *The Paradox of Success,* Tarcher/Putnam, 1994.

O'Toole, James. *The Executive's Compass,* Oxford, 1993.

———. *Making America Work,* Continuum, 1981.

———. (principal author) *Work in America,* MIT Press, 1974.

Rousseau, Jean Jacques. *The Social Contract,* 1762.

Rubenstein, Richard. *Aristotle's Children,* Harcourt, 2003.

Sumner, William Graham. *The Challenge of Facts and Other Essays,* Albert Keller (ed.), 1914.

Symonds, Matthew. *Softwar,* Simon & Schuster, 2003.

Southwick, Karen. *Everyone Else Must Fail,* Crown Business, 2003.

Wilson, Mike. *The Difference Between God and Larry Ellison,* Quill, 1997.

INDEX